INFORMATION
MARKETS

INFORMATION MARKETS

*What Businesses
Can Learn from
Financial Innovation*

William J. Wilhelm Jr.
Joseph D. Downing

HARVARD BUSINESS SCHOOL PRESS
BOSTON, MASSACHUSETTS

Requests for permission to use or reproduce material from this book should be directed to permissions@hbsp.harvard.edu, or mailed to Permissions, Harvard Business School Publishing, 60 Harvard Way, Boston, Massachusetts 02163.

Library of Congress Cataloging-in-Publication Data

Wilhelm Jr., William J., 1959–
  Information markets: what businesses can learn from financial innovation / William J. Wilhelm Jr. and Joseph D. Downing.
    p. cm.
  Includes index.
  ISBN 1-57851-278-6 (alk. paper)
    1. Financial services industry—Information resources. I. Downing, Joseph D., 1956– II. Title.

HG151.5 .W55 2001
332.1—dc21

                                                    2001026392

The paper used in this publication meets the requirements of the American National Standard for Permanence of Paper for Publications and Documents in Libraries and Archives Z39.48-1992.

To Anna, Benjamin, and Caroline

To the memory of
Sanford Maurice Downing Jr.

CONTENTS

PREFACE

FINANCIAL MARKETS have always depended on complex information networks. Traditionally organized around personal relationships embodied in powerful men (rarely women) and institutions, these networks were an exclusive domain dominated by the likes of J.P. Morgan and the New York Stock Exchange. Exclusivity and dependence on human judgment checked the free flow of information, sometimes to good effect and other times not. The discretion exercised by financial intermediaries promoted exchange of information and innovation in areas where the rule of intellectual property law was weak. As substitutes for the rule of law, however, financial intermediaries sometimes wielded enormous political and economic influence.

Advances in information technology are democratizing financial markets by undermining the influence of key individuals and institutions. The primary force for change is the increased capacity for codifying and mechanizing intermediary practices that previously depended wholly on human relationships and judgment. But this transformation upsets the delicate balance of incentives embedded in existing relationship networks and institutions. Thus, advances in information technology drive reorganization and consolidation as market participants reestablish the incentive structure necessary for information exchange and financial innovation.

This book aims to provide the reader with a durable framework for understanding the tensions that arise in information-intensive markets and how organizations adapt to these tensions in the face of continuous technological change. Although the book is cast in the financial markets, we believe that the experience of financial intermediaries offers valuable lessons for nonfinancial managers struggling with the challenges posed by what many perceive as a "new economy" more nearly centered on information exchange. The book is aimed not only at finance professionals but more generally at managers, students, and policy-makers in need of an anchor in an increasingly turbulent market.

Our challenge in undertaking this project has been coping with the accelerating pace of events in the financial marketplace as we've written. We've sometimes felt like weather reporters stationed in the midst of a raging storm, on the one hand providing a timely report on the current state of events while on the other trying to track the storm's future path and consequences. We're pretty confident that it's raining, but we also hope that we've provided a more durable analysis than is typical of weather forecasting.

If we've achieved this goal, in large part it reflects the generosity of a number of professional contacts, students, and colleagues. Geoff Boisi, William Hambrecht, Tim Opler, Mike Millette, Stephen Pelletier, Steven Wallman, and Susan Woodward were particularly generous with their time, information, and contacts. Martin J. Grasso Jr., Christopher Knowlton, and John P. Tuke read and provided helpful comments on chapter drafts. Alec Petro and Vic Simone are due special thanks for regularly lending support for our efforts in addition to sharing their deep knowledge of the markets. Magruder H. Dent's enduring contributions ensured Downing's availability for the project.

Wilhelm's students at Boston College and the University of Oxford endured the special burden of having some of the ideas in this book formulated before their very eyes. It was not always pretty, and their patience and feedback are deeply appreciated. Several brave souls read and commented on early chapter drafts to great effect. Sarah Strasser deserves special thanks in this regard. We also thank Bharath Srikrishnan for his diligent background research on electronic communications networks and Zhaohui Chen for his considerable influence on our thinking at various points in the book.

Among our academic colleagues, Bharat Anand, Bruno Biais, Josh Lerner, Alexander Ljungqvist, Alan Marcus, Alan Morrison, and Jay

Ritter read and provided valuable comments on parts of the book. We also owe a substantial intellectual debt to Mel Jameson and Larry Benveniste and thank Don Chew for encouraging and publishing our early musings on the material.

Finally, Erin Korey and Jill Connor provided attention to detail in editorial and production, and Jennifer Nixon, Kirsten Sandberg (our editor), and Caroline Wilhelm took their red pens to our prose at key junctures. We cringe, as you should, at thoughts of what could have been.

PART I

AN ANALYTIC FRAMEWORK

I

INFORMATION MARKETS

> When it was evening, the disciples came to him and said, "This is a lonely place, and the day is now over; send the crowds away to go into the villages and buy food for themselves." Jesus said, "They need not go away: you give them something to eat." They said to him, "We have only five loaves here and two fish." And he said, "Bring them here to me."
>
> Matthew 14:15–18

JUST AS the simple act of sharing fed the multitude, so sharing amplifies the value of information. Information's capacity for simultaneous use means "that we can take all of the poor people in the world right now, let them use all of the knowledge, all of the discoveries that we already take advantage of—and we can raise their standard of living without reducing our own."[1] In the jargon of the economist, this means that information, like little else in this world, is *non-rival*. Little wonder that Stewart Brand, founder of The WELL, concluded that information wants to be free.

Feeding the multitude took a leap of faith, and so too does sharing information. In spite of information's non-rival nature, the rewards from its strategic use are a powerful temptation. For this reason, nations, business organizations, and individuals spend enormously on intelligence and security to ensure that they are among the well informed. Even when someone willingly shares information, as a reader might share her preferences with Amazon.com, it's difficult to prevent further dissemination. And yet an inability to control personal information might prove costly or embarrassing. Who among us would want her life to be an open book? The problem is that once free, or disembodied from its originator, information is virtually impossible to recapture. In short, although sharing information is the path to collective benefit, sharing information also makes one vulnerable.

3

This book is about the intermediaries who promote trade in financial markets by balancing the tension between self-interest and collective interests in information. Financial markets always have been dominated by information. For those who envision the world in the midst of transition to a "new economy," a world in which economic welfare depends heavily on trade in information, we believe there is much to be learned from the experience of bankers, traders, and other practitioners of high finance. Financial markets have witnessed a slow, steady shift in the balance of power between Wall Street and Main Street over the course of the twentieth century. The Internet has punctuated this shift, but its effect is different in degree, not in kind, from previous advances in information technology. Careful attention to the slower-paced democratization of financial markets offers perspective that few managers and entrepreneurs operating in Internet time have the luxury of gaining first-hand.

Financial intermediaries manage the tension created by self-interest in information among their clients, but they endure a similar tension in their dealings with one another. Competition among intermediaries, traditionally fueled by the human capital of key individuals, is now technology driven. Primitive information technology enabled early financial intermediaries to form information networks by scattering human repositories for information as widely as possible.[2] Fair dealing over time within the network led to strong relationships bound by trust through which information moved more freely than it would have otherwise. Reputations and relationships, the foundations for trust, are simply composites of information regarding a series of human interactions that are not easily disembodied from the originator—you can't buy a reputation.

Among information assets, those that remain embodied in their originators are the most easily protected because the originator simply can choose not to share. But the embodiment of information within key individuals, whether by design or the nature of the information, limits the scope of its application. J.P. Morgan and Michael Milken, perhaps Morgan's only near equal among modern bankers, were known for their direct involvement in virtually every deal that passed their way. This concentration of power diminished the threat of competition from underlings who might break off on their own with knowledge and reputation formed under Morgan or Milken. But concentration of these powerful intellectual assets in the hands of their originators limited their scope of application. Morgan, for example, was prone to long absences from 23 Wall Street, and Milken found it necessary to sleep for at least a few hours daily.

Sometimes the lure of exploitative use of information is too great for trust alone to support cooperation. An intermediary can still add value, but it must either acquire or be granted the power to act as a benevolent dictator. When all else failed, Morgan forced cooperation among railroad concerns at the turn of the twentieth century by (credibly) threatening to shut the pipeline for European capital. Modern society is rich with instances in which individuals voluntarily submit to coercive intermediation. We'd all like to drive at higher speed, but we also recognize the collective danger and voluntarily submit to speed restrictions enforced by traffic patrols or speed cameras.

Setting aside the threat that benevolence diminishes with power, this heavy-handed approach to intermediation is more vulnerable to competition than intermediation built on trust. When the rules defining the intermediary's value-added responsibilities are easily codified, there is little to distinguish one person's capacity for carrying them out from another's. The originator of codifiable human capital suffers diminished control, which undermines the incentive to invest in human capital in the first place. In the extreme, machines execute instructions previously carried out by people—with the advent of speed cameras, it's fortunate for traffic cops that their function extends beyond simply monitoring adherence to traffic regulations. But codification of human capital serves the public interest by expanding its scope of application.

When human capitalists dominated financial intermediation, innovation often flourished in the context of close relationships and powerful intermediaries that tempered competition but protected easily copied ideas and products. This protection encouraged financial innovation by more nearly ensuring a fair return on investment in intellectual property. Today, human networks are giving way to technology that vastly expands the speed and scope of information dissemination and storage media that provide rapid access to information and indefinitely preserve its integrity. Technological advances expand the possibilities for codifying human capital and thus weaken the grip of the human capitalists. Seen in this light, it is natural that financial intermediaries only recently have aggressively sought patents and other protections for intellectual property. But even with the large-scale substitution of information technology for human intermediaries, the subtle maneuvering of financial dealmakers that frees information to flow through the vastly expanded pipeline remains largely a black art. Can further advances in information technology provide for codification of even this element of human capital?

This tension between human capital and information technology has profound consequences for the organization and management of intermediary firms. The small family partnerships that dominated early financial markets provided an environment in which human capital was nurtured and passed from one generation to the next. By contrast, the modern financial firm depends far more on financial capital to support the large-scale but low-margin operations that remain when intermediary functions are codified. But, contrary to predictions of the demise of intermediaries by many early proponents of the Internet, subtleties in the institutional fabric suggest that intermediary functions, although being reshaped by information technology, will not soon be displaced. The two brief vignettes in Boxes 1-1 and 1-2 will help to fix these ideas as we pose several questions about the interplay between human capital and information technology in financial markets and its potential implications for the modern economy.

The diminished power of financial intermediaries in the aftermath of the 1933 Banking Act did not signal the demise of the functions they carried out. In fact, many economists argue that diminishing their power held back the economy for decades until institutional investor networks began to reform in the 1960s. But there is a fine line between intermediaries having sufficient market power to warrant investment in the intellectual property at their foundation and having so much power that they stifle innovation or extract undeserved profits from consumers.

If you've followed the U.S. Justice Department's prosecution of Microsoft for alleged anti-competitive behavior, this argument should sound familiar; it likely will reappear ever more frequently. Intellectual property is more difficult to protect than physical property, and so firms pursue market power to complement or substitute for institutionalized protections for intellectual property. At what point and how aggressively should we limit the market power of firms dealing in intellectual property? Where network effects arise, can policymakers do better than simply dismantling the network?

The lawsuit brought by the recording industry against Napster reflects the opposite side of the coin—the rising difficulty in controlling

---

Box 1-1   Turn-of-the-Century Investment Banking, Circa 1900

At the turn of the twentieth century, J.P. Morgan dominated U.S. and world capital markets. Although his organization comprised about ten partners, fewer than 150 other employees, and about $147 million in capital (in current dollars), Morgan and his men oversaw an immense web of relationships—the "money trusts" that controlled the bulk of the day's industrial activity. Morgan's visibility equaled that of heads of state and he simultaneously was feared and revered. For all of his well-known assertions of the centrality of character in financial dealings, Morgan wielded a heavy club when necessary to achieve his goals.

As Morgan's power grew to the point of influencing national and worldwide economic events, the public balked; ultimately, the House of Morgan was divided by the 1933 (Glass-Steagall) Banking Act. The resulting investment bank, Morgan Stanley, specialized in advising large corporations and assisting them in raising debt and equity financing. The commercial bank, J.P. Morgan & Co., served wealthy individuals and made loans to large corporations. The webs of influence that enabled Morgan and other prominent bankers to match and marry capital with investment opportunities were essentially destroyed.

---

software or codified intellectual property as the costs of storage and dissemination plummet. However, this struggle has also been experienced by financial intermediaries. As both information technology and economic theory advanced over the course of the twentieth century, intermediary functions carried out by people were codified and mechanized. Program trading, involving the coding of investment strategy for computer execution, is perhaps the extreme example.

Given the relative ease of reverse engineering financial products and strategies, the financial analogue to digital recording of copyrighted material, one might be concerned for investment bankers' incentives to develop clever new strategies. Investment bankers aren't starving artists, but the starving artists might learn something from how investment bankers protect intellectual property that rarely has been served by patent, copyright, and trademark law. In some instances, we'll see that sharing intellectual property in a controlled setting, exemplified by the partnership culture of The Goldman Sachs Group (see Box 1-2), sets off a virtuous cycle for its further development and preservation.

The mobility of key individuals like Geoff Boisi and the resulting pressure on firms to control investments in human capital seem the order of the day among law firms, accounting and management consulting organizations, and other professional service organizations. Simultaneously, professional firms are reexamining the partnership organization that made owners of key human capitalists, often turning to public incorporation and so placing human capitalists in control of outsiders' financial capital. With the exception of Goldman Sachs, this shift was complete among bulge-bracket investment banks by the mid-1980s. Might something be learned from the experience of these banks as well as the ones that chose to continue as relatively small partnerships?

Finally, the large-scale consolidation sweeping financial markets has strong parallels with reorganization movements in the media and other information-intensive markets in which advances in information technology are forcing a reexamination of the balance of power between content and distribution. We'll suggest again that while the shift in the balance between content and distribution—human capital and information technology if you will—has been abrupt, leading to the likes of the AOL/Time Warner merger, it has been more nearly a continuous process in financial markets. If so, might we learn something from the experience that will shed light on what appears to be a regime shift in some non-financial markets?

Financial Intermediaries

We're not claiming to have answers to all of these questions. If we did, it would take more than a book contract to persuade us to share them! But we do believe these questions lend themselves to analysis of the kind economists have long applied to financial intermediaries. Development of such an analytical framework is the focus of chapters 2, 3, and 4. Chapter 2 examines the functions carried out by financial intermediaries. Technology and regulation influence how these functions are carried out and bundled with one another, but the basic functions are quite stable.

If we see intermediaries as institutional responses to impediments to trade in the markets they serve, the relative stability in their functions is not surprising. The ideal market that brings all relevant

Box 1-2 Turn-of-the Century Investment Banking, Circa 2000

In November 1991, Geoffrey Boisi announced his retirement from partnership at Goldman Sachs. During twenty-two years with Goldman Sachs, Boisi had been the youngest-ever partner, had led the firm's investment banking operations, had founded the global finance department, and was widely regarded as a key "culture carrier" because of his mentoring of junior bankers. Boisi was well-known in Wall Street circles, but his commitment to Goldman Sachs's culture of teamwork kept him from the public eye. At his retirement, Boisi was a member of the firm's management committee and headed strategic planning for the firm, including periodic consideration of the costs of maintaining the partnership as profit margins in traditional banking functions narrowed. Upon his departure, Boisi perceived Goldman Sachs, now with 128 partners and about 6,400 other employees, as remaining a partnership in name only. Chief among his concerns was the trend toward non-partner traders, supported by information technology worthy of NASA, putting partners' capital at risk in exchange for huge bonuses and public visibility when they succeeded, but little personal cost when they failed.

Boisi resurfaced in 1993, along with three former Goldman Sachs partners, to form the Beacon Group, a small, private partnership specializing in corporate advisory services and private equity management. By 1999, Boisi concluded that investment banking was becoming a game of scale, and in May 2000 he sold the fourteen-partner firm to Chase Manhattan for an estimated $500 million and was appointed head of Chase's investment banking business. *The Economist* characterized the outcome for Boisi as perhaps "the largest signing bonus in Wall Street history."[3] In short order Chase acquired J.P. Morgan & Co. to complete a series of acquisitions predicated on the recent demise of the Glass-Steagall Act. The acquisition propelled J.P. Morgan Chase & Co., now with a capital base of $42 billion (equity capital) and almost 100,000 people worldwide, into a select group of full-service global banks.

Meanwhile, Goldman Sachs went public in June 1999, with one stated goal being to position the firm for the acquisitions necessary to compete with the new breed of full-service bank.

parties together at no cost, in one time and place, with equal access to all relevant information does not exist. In fact, if we ignore the institutional fabric that physically defines a market, all but academic economists might find it difficult to imagine the presence of a market. Institutions and people embody the rules and practices carried out by intermediaries.

To make the discussion concrete, throughout the book we use the investment bank, broadly interpreted, as a point of reference. By *investment bank* we mean organizations such as Goldman Sachs and Morgan Stanley that have long conducted the high finance of coordinating large-scale institutional investor networks and providing strategic advice to senior business and government officials. In chapter 3, we take Goldman Sachs as our representative of the traditional investment-banking platform and examine the range of its intermediary functions. We then introduce three pioneering "Internet investment banks," OffRoad Capital, Wit Capital (now Wit SoundView), and WR Hambrecht + Co., which appear throughout the book as representative challengers to the traditional intermediary platform.

OffRoad Capital uses the Internet to carry out several intermediary functions in the private debt and equity markets that previously were either technically or economically infeasible. In doing so, OffRoad is creating a market where one previously did not exist. In contrast, Wit SoundView and WR Hambrecht are pioneering innovative approaches to well-established and highly successful intermediary functions carried out in the primary equity markets. The vibrancy of the U.S. primary equity market—otherwise known as the initial public offering (IPO) market—is often cited as a key force underlying U.S. industrial innovation generally and the burgeoning information economy specifically. And yet the IPO market and its intermediaries, investment banks, are coming under increasing criticism for practices that are perceived as both inefficient and discriminatory.

Wit SoundView's efforts to open the IPO market to retail investors provide a case study in the democratizing power of modern information technology and the capacity for forming communities of interest among previously fragmented parties. WR Hambrecht's online electronic IPO auction mechanism goes a step further, illustrating the potential for realization of ivory tower visions of bringing all interested trading parties together in one (virtual) time and place. This and similar virtual marketplaces provide a laboratory for examining how advances in information technology in concert with advances in theoretical knowledge of the functions carried out by information intermediaries are driving the codification and mechanization of practices that previously demanded human judgment.

In addition to examining how these entrants are challenging the status quo in the marketplace, we consider why established firms have not been pioneers in this area. Where networks of customer relationships bind processes and products together, interdependence within the network substantially raises the costs of incremental innovation. Financial markets are an extreme case of a networked industry, and intermediaries are the glue that binds the network. Existing intermediaries find it difficult, or at least cannibalistic, to make incremental changes to their network structure. Entrants such as OffRoad, Wit SoundView, and WR Hambrecht essentially begin with a clean slate.

But while existing networks might impede innovation, they also provide the foundation for a powerful competitive response to innovators if they are complementary to the new technology. OffRoad, Wit SoundView, and WR Hambrecht may have ideas whose day has come, but can these ideas be protected from adoption by firms with established reputations and relationships? In fact, this form of expropriation already is occurring wholesale as established investment banks, most prominently Goldman Sachs, scramble to establish a presence on the Internet. By raising this point in chapter 3, we introduce questions related to the nature of competition in information-intensive markets between entrants and established firms that will surface repeatedly throughout the book.

The Economics of Information Intermediation

The second part of the book takes us more deeply into how information intermediaries (or *infomediaries*, to use the word coined by McKinsey & Co. consultant John Hagel) carry out their functions in the marketplace. Chapter 4 examines how intermediaries balance the competing interests of parties to a transaction. For example, a car dealer has an interest in squeezing as much as possible from a potential customer, and vice versa. But if either party or both are too aggressive in their pursuit of private interests, the transaction may fall through, leaving both worse off than had it not. The essence of the intermediary's role here is leading the counterparties away from the purely competitive strategy of grabbing as much as possible of a fixed economic pie and toward the cooperative strategy of accepting a smaller fraction of a substantially larger pie.

In many instances, the value in a network or community of interest derives from members' willingness to contribute to a common pool of resources. In financial markets, individuals contribute to market liquidity through their willingness to trade, thus setting off a virtuous cycle of increasing returns. In information networks, whether in financial markets at large, in individual firms, such as those being formed within many management consultancies, or in voluntary communities of interest, the pool of information is more valuable than the sum of its parts. Unfortunately, it is often difficult or simply not worth the effort to block those who contribute little from the benefits generated by more prolific or cooperative contributors. But failure to do so undermines incentives to contribute in the first place.

These are a few of the problems that arise in the brokering of strategic information. We've mentioned that one solution involves granting coercive power to a benevolent dictator. But for a variety of reasons it's useful to identify business models that promote voluntary cooperation among members of an information network—what economists refer to as *incentive-compatible* mechanisms. Simply put, incentive compatibility means that network participants find it in their own self-interest to cooperate in a manner stipulated by an intermediary. The intermediary's function is to identify and commit to upholding an incentive-compatible set of rules that best serves the interests of its network membership.

Chapter 4 offers a simple example to illustrate the concept of incentive compatibility and then develops it more fully in the context of the IPO market. Our purpose in this chapter is to convince you that an admittedly abstract concept has considerable power to explain traditional, human-capital-intensive practices in a market where human judgment is still considered by many as central to the market's success. But if we make a convincing case, then we've already gone well down the path toward codifying traditional practice. From there it's a short step to mechanization along the lines proposed by Wit Sound-View and WR Hambrecht. Thus, careful attention to the design principles for incentive-compatible mechanisms provides both the tools for designing new business platforms and a benchmark for judging the competition for new standards.

The Organization of Information Intermediaries

How do you build a business around products, services, and processes that are easily and cheaply replicated? Should advances in information technology change the way we think about managing such assets? How much competition can we expect in markets where firms struggle to preserve their claims over information, and should answers to this question have any bearing on the thinking of policymakers charged with promoting competition in the marketplace?

Chapter 5 lays the foundation for addressing these questions by examining how advances in information technology and our understanding of intermediary functions are shifting the boundaries between human judgment and codified knowledge. The goal of any system of intellectual property rights is to strike the right balance between the innovator's incentives for discovery and the interests of society at large. We contend that this delicate balance is being altered as advances in technology and theory provide for codification and therefore a greater threat of expropriation of what previously only a select few exercised as judgment or discretion. In the economy at large, this is forcing a reexamination of the foundations of intellectual property law. Given the historical weakness of legal protections for intellectual property in financial markets, we argue that the organizational structure of financial firms and markets responded to this tension. The industry's ongoing reorganization thus represents a parallel reexamination of the rules of engagement in the development of intellectual property.

This idea is fleshed out in chapter 6, where we outline recent developments in the theory of the firm that emphasize the link between organizational structure and the nature of a firm's assets. We then examine the rather unusual organizational structure of the underwriting syndicate and its contribution to the development and preservation of human capital by investment banks. The syndicate made its way into U.S. investment banking practices around the turn of the twentieth century as small-scale banking concerns collaborated with one another to meet the increasingly large-scale demands of the industrial economy. But the syndicate also represents an early and successful example of the virtual firm or strategic alliance that emphasizes modularity and that many see as the potentially dominant business platform for the new economy.[4] We offer some thoughts on why the syndicate for so long played such an important role in financial markets and how the

Internet and other technological advances are altering its role and shifting the balance of power between content providers and distributors.

Chapter 6 concludes with a synopsis of our thinking about the ongoing reorganization of financial markets. In most instances, intermediaries provide the foundation for trust in instances where the force of law cannot be counted on. In doing so, they create opportunities for trade that otherwise would not exist. This human-capital-intensive role is particularly important in jump-starting a new market because the foundations for cooperation are fragile. Intermediaries act as trusted arbiters exercising discretion or judgment to balance the interests of competing parties where widely accepted rules for engagement do not exist.

As community standards and trust evolve, human-capital-intensive functions diminish, particularly in instances where they can be partially codified. Codification supports large-scale application of previously monopolized human capital and permits redeployment of scarce human capital to new, higher value-added opportunities. And so we observe a cycle within market segments in which intermediaries initially earn large returns on human capital but eventually are forced to pursue financial-capital-intensive scale economies as their product or service becomes a commodity. This perspective sheds light on two prominent, and seemingly paradoxical, features of the changing landscape in financial markets: the apparent race for scale in the financial markets at large and the simultaneous existence of financial supermarkets and boutiques.

Chapters 7 and 8 offer two case studies that bring this perspective into greater focus. First we examine the relatively recent evolution in organizational structure among investment banks from the private partnership to the public corporation. This movement culminated with the 1999 Goldman Sachs IPO. Partnerships were a particularly effective organizational structure given the industry's traditional dependence on a human-capital-intensive business model. In recent years, advances in theoretical knowledge that support the codification of investment banking practices in conjunction with advances in information technology have forced banks to put more financial capital at risk to maintain their profit margins. Although the industry continues to depend heavily on human capital, the financial capital constraints imposed by the partnership increasingly outweigh its benefits. The public corporation provides greater capacity for raising financial capital but creates a host of new problems related to the development and preservation of human capital that investment banks continue to struggle with.

Just as firms reorganize in response to technological advances, so do the industries they form. Chapter 8, examines the ongoing restructuring of the secondary securities markets as electronic communication networks (ECNs) compete with traditional exchange floors. In many parts of the world, the competition is over and the electronic platform has prevailed. In the United States, however, where the public capital markets have historically played a more central role in the economy, the traditional platform survives, although perhaps not for long. A review of the tug of war between the established exchanges and those who would displace them, many of which include members of the establishment among their financial backers, provides an opportunity to consider whether the sterling reputations, if not the technology, of the establishment will be preserved. A reputation or brand is a valuable asset for any firm and especially so for an intermediary whose effectiveness is in large part dependent on the ability to make credible commitments.

Although the long-standing reputation of the New York Stock Exchange (NYSE), for example, is probably an impediment to technological innovation in the U.S. financial markets, perhaps we should not be quick to encourage its demise in the name of progress. Just as ECNs have something to offer the NYSE in the way of technology, so too the NYSE has a reputation to which ECNs can only aspire. As we recover from the dot-com mania, we might consider in the future whether our capital resources would be more effectively utilized if fewer were devoted to reinventing the wheel and more to integrating new technology with what remains valuable in existing organizations. Granted, large organizations are not the most receptive to innovation. But dot-coms spent billions to lock in large customer networks that already existed around the most visible "old economy" firms. As the dot-coms drop one by one, old-economy firms are rapidly moving down the path they cut into the new economy.

The battle for control of the stock markets also raises a number of important questions regarding competition policy generally. In financial markets, liquidity begets liquidity. In other words, like most information markets, they exhibit network effects. It is not surprising, and perhaps desirable, under such circumstances for one or a few dominant firms to emerge. Put simply, this may be the only way for innovative firms to capture a fair return on their investment. But should regulators cast a blind eye on concentrated markets? As one observer of Michael Milken's pioneering effort and decade-long domination of the junk bond market stated, "Mr. Milken's arrival was the greatest boon that the junk bond market ever received. His forced departure was the second-greatest."[5] We'll suggest some guidelines for when regulators should intervene and when they should let market forces take their course.

Lessons Learned from the Financial Markets

We conclude the book by reviewing the key lessons learned from the financial markets about the role of intermediaries in information markets. As the preceding outline suggests, we believe that financial markets are in the same state of upheaval as much of the rest of the economy, but that the sources of upheaval have been percolating within the financial markets throughout their history. So whereas the changes occurring within the economy at large are in many instances changes of kind, the changes in the financial markets are more nearly changes of degree. This suggests that managers struggling to understand how to reposition their firms relative to customers and suppliers in the information economy will gain considerable insight from the experience of intermediaries in the oldest of information markets.

We hope that we've shared enough ideas and engendered sufficient trust that you'll stay with us for the remainder of the book.

2

A Primer on
Financial Markets and
Intermediaries

Banking is not about money; it is about information.
Walter Wriston

MONEY IS a means of keeping score, a way of tallying the relative
purchasing power of individuals and organizations. It can be a
physical tally, such as a coin made from rare metals, or a paper claim
on a government or other reputable agent that is difficult to counter-
feit. But records of relative purchasing power also can be stored digi-
tally as strings of ones and zeros if the storage medium is secure. Money
is information.

Primitive money was local, but over time networks developed for
transmitting the information embodied in money over ever-greater
distances.[1] The physical infrastructure of early financial markets was
embodied in human intermediaries who represented the interests of
less reputable or less frequent market participants. These networks
evolved into today's modern financial markets. Today, human networks
are giving way to technology that vastly expands the scope and speed of
information dissemination and to storage media that provide rapid access to information and indefinitely preserve its integrity.

This chapter provides an overview of the financial markets, which
emphasizes their functioning as information networks. This perspective
sheds light on why trade in information demands so much attention
from intermediaries and why traditional economics sometimes fails us
in understanding their functions, and sets the stage for learning from
their experience.

Financial Markets: A Brief Taxonomy

Financial markets, like any other market, provide a means for exchange between buyers and sellers. Buyers and sellers in financial markets borrow and lend financial capital. Typically, sellers exchange a current cash surplus for claims on the buyers' future cash flows. Broadly speaking, these claims are one of two kinds. Fixed claims, or *debt*, involve periodic interest payments and repayment of principal. Residual claims, or *equity*, entitle the holder to cash flows that remain after fixed claims are satisfied. In a perfect world, competitive bidding within a price system would ensure that goods being exchanged, whether hammer and nails, physical labor, or financial capital were put to their most highly valued use. An efficient capital market directs scarce capital resources to investment opportunities in accordance with market perceptions of their relative future productivity.

The fabric of financial markets is a complex weave of individuals, institutions, and organizations, and its texture varies dramatically from country to country. One dimension along which variation can be described involves a distinction between public and private capital markets. *Public capital markets* include the highly visible stock exchanges, markets for trading both corporate and government debt claims, and an expanding class of less visible markets for derivative securities (such as options and futures) and securitized assets (which encompass the likes of home mortgages and credit card debt). This segment of the public markets is referred to as the *secondary market* to distinguish it from the *primary markets* through which traded securities are first issued. For example, when a privately owned company goes public, it raises capital through an initial public offering of equity. The IPO takes place in the primary market, whereas subsequent trading of the issuing firm's shares takes place in the secondary market. Investment banks are the dominant intermediaries in both the primary and secondary capital markets.

Private capital markets are characterized by the relative inability of lenders to trade their debt and equity claims. The private capital markets in the United States have long been dominated by commercial banks, and throughout the remainder of the world, by universal banks. *Universal banks* are characterized by their ability to arrange both debt and equity financing.

Until very recently in the United States, the 1933 Glass-Steagall Banking Act's prohibition on banks arranging equity financing for their customers left a void in the private equity markets. By mid-century this void was being filled in varying degrees by investment banks, venture capital partnerships, and a variety of professionals who used their personal contacts to raise equity financing from individuals and institutions willing to sacrifice liquidity for a higher expected return. Broadly speaking, the U.S. and U.K. financial markets more nearly evolved around the public capital markets whereas most other countries depended more heavily on private markets organized around universal banks. Although the relative balance is shifting in favor of public markets, U.S. and U.K. institutions such as the New York Stock Exchange and the London Stock Exchange still tower in importance over their counterparts in other countries.

The Functions of Financial Intermediaries

Bankers, brokers, market makers, and other financial intermediaries grease the wheels of exchange in financial markets. *How* financial intermediaries do this depends on the state of technology and regulatory constraints. In the midst of great upheaval in both the technology and regulation of financial markets, it is easy to lose sight of the fact that *what* financial intermediaries do is relatively stable. Robert Merton and Zvi Bodie propose a perspective that draws a sharp distinction between these stable functions of a financial system and their sometimes arbitrary execution that is particularly useful for understanding how financial intermediaries adapt to changes in technology and regulation.[2]

At the core of any financial system must lie a means of *clearing and settling payments*. In modern economies, this function is already highly mechanized. Electronic transfer systems such as FedWire and the Clearing House Interbank Payment System currently account for about 85 percent of payments by value, although 98 percent of transactions are carried out by check or credit card.[3]

A second function of any financial system is to provide means for *pooling savings*. Large-scale industrial production requires investment well beyond the means of most individuals. Banks, mutual funds, pension funds and the like, pool the resources of many individuals for investment in large-scale projects. Pooling resources also promotes more efficient *risk sharing* by providing investors who have relatively small savings a level of diversification that would be costly, if not impossible, to achieve otherwise. Once pooled, savings are generally *transferred across time and space.* A geographical correspondence between savings and investment opportunities would be purely happenstance. Likewise, individuals, organizations, and economies at large are net borrowers at some stages of their life cycle and net savers at others. Finally, a financial system must *provide liquidity* for financial claims to allow both borrowers and lenders to respond to changes in the economic environment.

Given a well-functioning legal system that protects contracts and individual property rights (a condition often taken for granted), these five functions are largely a matter of record keeping and therefore lend themselves to a high degree of mechanization.[4] Transferring and storing information is one thing, however. Promoting the exchange of information among many self-interested individuals is quite another. When information serves private interests but only at the expense of collective interests, individuals have little incentive to share their information. But failure to do so drives a wedge between potential parties to a financial transaction. Financial intermediaries create value by promoting the trust and cooperation necessary to increase the flow of information. Because the frictions introduced by informational differences take several forms and are mitigated through a variety of subtle maneuvers on the part of intermediaries, we examine this aspect of financial markets in greater detail.

Barriers to Trade in Information

The most insidious, and subtle, frictions in the financial marketplace are associated with differences in information among trading partners—what economists refer to as *asymmetric* or *private information* problems. For example, corporate borrowers often have a clearer understanding of their ability to repay loans than do potential lenders. This difference in understanding places the borrower at an advantage because it only accepts loan terms that are commensurate with or better than what its credit quality warrants. From the lender's perspective, borrowers *adversely select* transactions that favor them. Although individual borrowers have an interest in protecting this strategic advantage, lenders shy away from such transactions absent some form of redress because they expect to do no better than break even. In the worst cases, otherwise mutually beneficial trades simply do not occur.

Suppose that after a loan is made, the borrower invests the proceeds in projects that are riskier than the lender envisioned when the terms of the loan were set. In essence, the borrower's actions alter the terms of the transaction after the fact. This threat, referred to as *moral hazard*, arises when parties to a transaction can influence events that bear on their ability to carry out their obligations. Moral hazard is particularly common in the provision of guarantees or insurance. The purchaser of a fixed-price auto insurance policy, for example, essentially receives more insurance for his money by driving recklessly. Likewise, the insurer can reduce the insured's level of protection by recklessly investing the proceeds from the sale of the policy and thereby weakening its ability to make payments if the insured is involved in an accident.

Both adverse selection and moral hazard pose significant barriers to trade in financial markets; it is not surprising, therefore, that many of the institutional features of financial markets can be interpreted as responses to these problems. Lenders design covenants that constrain the borrower's ability to take undue risk. Deductibles require insurance buyers to share the cost of an accident. Insurance and other financial guarantees are made credible when providers set aside capital sufficient to cover their obligations as a performance bond.

Financial market performance also is compromised by the difficulty of restricting the costs and benefits of a transaction to the legally defined counterparties. For example, some over-the-counter (OTC) dealers match the price quotes of New York Stock Exchange specialists while paying a penny or two per share to attract order flow in NYSE-listed stocks. This copycat strategy is profitable because the OTC dealers reap the benefits of brokering trade without bearing the costs of price production. Economists refer to benefits that spill over from the immediate parties to a transaction as *positive externalities*. Externalities in financial markets tend to be informational.

Externalities can be negative as well as positive. In 1998, Long Term Capital Management (LTCM), a highly innovative hedge fund whose partners included two Nobel laureates, suffered a liquidity crisis that sent shock waves through the world economy. LTCM began the year with nearly $5 billion of heavily leveraged capital but lost nearly $2 billion in August 1998 alone as turmoil in the Russian economy created unexpected price disparities between many markets. By mid-September, LTCM's capital had diminished to $600 million. These losses strained LTCM's ability to meet contractual obligations to a number of money center banks and destroyed the capital they invested with LTCM. Fears for the financial well-being of the money center banks reverberated throughout world capital markets and caused a general decline in liquidity and prices.

Some argue that financial innovation commonly generates such systemic risk. Regardless of the merit of these arguments, other things being equal, one should expect excess production of products and services that generate negative externalities and underproduction of those that create positive externalities. NYSE specialists have less incentive to invest in price production when OTC dealers free-ride on their efforts. Likewise, financial innovation might be taken to excess if it carries costs that are not entirely borne by pioneering firms such as LTCM.

Are Financial Markets Special?

Surely these problems arise in other markets. But are there features of financial markets that magnify problems associated with asymmetric information and information externalities? This question is most easily addressed by contrasting financial markets with traditional markets in which buyers and sellers meet face-to-face to exchange goods of observable quality. The town markets still prevalent throughout Europe, for example, specialize in produce and hard goods whose quality is easily judged before a purchase is made. Where size, color, or texture are not fully revealing, as with a tomato, sellers offer samples so that buyers may verify quality. Cash is the usual medium of exchange, and all sales are final—sellers do not provide formal warranties against dissatisfaction. Finally, ownership is easily established and transferred in markets for physical goods. Mancur Olsen considered these sufficient conditions for "self-enforcing" transactions because they ensure that counterparties rarely fail one another.[5]

In contrast, financial transactions rarely involve face-to-face exchange, their quality often is judged over time and is contingent on future events and their costs and benefits can go well beyond the immediate parties to the transaction. Face-to-face exchange is rare because the capital demands of firms generally outstrip the lending capacity of any single individual or organization. Even when this is not the case, diversification considerations and physical distance often rule against a single lender fully satisfying the demands of a borrower. Financial intermediaries such as banks, mutual funds, and stock exchanges maintain a physical presence that serves as a focal point for borrowers and lenders and as a conduit through which capital can be bundled and exchanged.

Financial transactions often involve *experience goods* whose quality is apparent only after the transaction is completed. The quality of an investment bank's advisory services, for example, becomes clear after the service is provided. Likewise, a mutual fund's performance must be judged after the fact and relative to a benchmark. Financial intermediaries also make both formal and informal guarantees or commitments contingent on events that take place after the transaction. A bank's letter of credit is a legal instrument that commits the bank to satisfy a debt obligation in the event of default by the party purchasing the letter of credit. The quality of the commitment depends on the bank's willingness and ability to live up to its obligations, which in turn depend on future market conditions. Similarly, investment banks often prop up or "stabilize" the price of initial public offerings by purchasing shares in the secondary market. Although never a formal commitment, clients interpret the marketing of stabilization services as an implied warranty.

Experience goods are particularly susceptible to adverse selection and moral hazard problems. Intermediaries diminish the problems by building reputations for willingness to deliver on their commitments and by taking measures, such as holding capital, to enhance their ability to do so.[6] But the central role of reputation creates additional complications for financial intermediaries. We turn to this issue shortly.

Finally, financial products and services are easy to reverse engineer and are generally built on ideas that receive little protection from copyright, trade secret, and patent law. The registration of public securities offerings, for example, virtually guarantees the reverse engineering of the transaction's innovative features before the typically high costs of innovation to the pioneering bank are covered. In fact, Peter Tufano of Harvard Business School found that pioneers most frequently complete only one transaction before a new product is replicated by competitors.[7] Although the practice is historically rare, innovative financial firms such as State Street Global Advisors increasingly seek protection under intellectual property law. But absent credible evidence of its violation, State Street's June 1998 patent granted for a

neural net-based investment strategy does not compel rivals to reveal
details of their own successful strategies. Effectively, it only prevents
a rival from attributing success to the protected strategy. Because
money managers are judged by the profits they generate and not by
their source, State Street has little recourse against those who go qui-
etly about the business of mimicking the protected strategy.

When it is difficult to establish and enforce property rights over
products and services, the incentive to invest in their production is
weakened. Worse yet for financial firms, the necessary productive assets
largely take the form of human capital embodied in a notoriously mobile workforce. For example, Deutsche Bank's entire technology banking group (more than seventy bankers) left to join Credit Suisse First
Boston in the summer of 1998. Ironically, the departure of the team
built by Frank Quattrone, Bill Brady, and George Boutros came only
two years after Deutsche bid the three away from Morgan Stanley.

New Rules for a New Economy?

The preceding discussion parallels common explanations for what is
different about information markets and the new economy generally. In
Information Rules, Carl Shapiro and Hal Varian offer the succinct explanation that information is costly to produce but cheap to reproduce.[8]
Millions of man-hours may go into the development of a piece of computer software, but copying the final product costs little more than the
storage medium. Or, as Tufano observes, the typical financial innovation costs the pioneering firm millions of dollars in development but
can be reverse engineered rapidly and at little marginal cost to the pioneer's rivals.

But why does this feature of information appear to be a problem
for the laws of economics? On the surface, it sounds like a good thing.
If grain could be reproduced as cheaply as information, the problem
of world hunger would be eliminated. University of California at
Berkeley economist Bradford DeLong and University of Miami School
of Law professor Michael Froomkin both turn to the "old" economics
of Adam Smith for perspective on this question.[9] In Smith's world,
prices in a free market acted as an invisible hand coordinating the resources and actions of many individuals to serve the greatest good. But
a price system depends fundamentally on property rights over assets,

rivalry for scarce resources, and transparency—features that DeLong and Froomkin argue were central to Smith's world but less so to the modern world.

The invisible hand struggles with Stewart Brand's claim that "information wants to be free." It is difficult to reap benefits from information without sharing it, but once shared, it is difficult to prevent its future use. The inability to control information once freed undermines incentives for its creation in the first place. Most modern economies have responded with intellectual property laws (e.g., patents, trademarks, or copyrights) designed in large part to give exclusive rights in observable uses of information—a physical application—whether it be a machine, photograph, text, or musical performance. But increasingly, information is used to great effect in unobservable ways. Could we ever hope to parse every line of computer code being written to assure that it does not "plagiarize" the ideas of previous code writers? Can State Street enforce its neural network patent?

Likewise, the invisible hand provides fair guidance when buyers and sellers know what they're exchanging. But information, like most financial products and services, is an experience good. Finally, once created, information is not a scarce resource because it can be duplicated at little cost and used simultaneously and in many different capacities. In the parlance of economics, information is a nonrival good. The consequences of nonrivalry in financial markets are subtle, and so we leave a more detailed discussion for chapter 4. However, the point that DeLong and Froomkin make is that these features of information should give us pause in relying strictly on the invisible hand for guidance in economic matters.

These challenges to the invisible hand haven't suddenly appeared in the last decade. The printing press changed the world because it lowered the cost of disseminating large volumes of visual and written information by orders of magnitude. The radio, telegraph, and telephone vastly increased the speed of verbal communication, and television widened the pipeline to include visual information. It's true that the Internet, with its capacity for interactive verbal, written, and visual exchange of information, marks a profound step forward in driving the marginal cost of reproducing information toward zero. But it's just one phase in a long and bumpy, but relatively continuous process, alongside which various institutions and intermediaries have evolved to cope with problems that the invisible hand passes over.

Financial intermediaries are a prominent example. For one thing, the private gains to information in financial markets can be enormous but are usually fleeting. The Rothschilds' exploitation of their network of couriers and paid agents proved decisive while awaiting the outcome of Waterloo. As rivals responded with their own networks of human messengers, the Rothschilds innovated by employing courier pigeons to secure their competitive advantages, including the added advantage of preserving confidentiality from snooping customs clerks. By contrast, the economic benefits of most information are more easily realized in due time. The fleeting value of information in financial markets has pushed financial intermediaries to remain at the cutting edge of communications technology, and so often one step ahead of the rest of the economy. More important, much of the value of information in nonfinancial markets was, until fairly recently, embodied in physical assets over which property rights were relatively easily established. In contrast, the indispensable information in financial markets always has been embodied in people. This, we'll argue, is a complicating feature that only recently has received serious attention from economists.

So while many observers have suggested that a new economy demands new economic laws, most economists argue that the fundamental laws haven't changed. Rather, the environment in which they are applied is changing. From our perspective, what is perhaps new in the environment—namely, a more prominent role for information or intellectual capital—has long been central to financial markets; and so the experience of financial intermediaries is particularly useful to understanding the modern economy.

Intermediaries at Work: A Preview

If intermediaries respond to circumstances where the invisible hand struggles in its coordination function, J.P. Morgan's role in the late-nineteenth-century railroad industry offers perhaps the rawest example of this complementary function. Railroading presents the extreme of circumstances underlying natural monopolies: The high fixed cost of laying rails coupled with the relatively low marginal cost of using the rails implied enormous economies of scale. Thus the *total* economic benefits from serving a particular route are maximized by having only one line per route. Unfortunately, weak regulation of monopoly pricing provided a powerful incentive for independent lines to compete with one another for control of a route, so competitors built parallel lines in the hope of outlasting rivals in a subsequent price war. Although cutthroat competition resulted in temporarily low prices for rail services, it was grossly wasteful of scarce capital resources because it produced huge, unsalvageable investments in idle rails. In addition to undermining aggregate economic welfare, wasteful use of capital diminished confidence in the budding U.S. economy and contributed to a reduced flow of capital from Europe.

This example is reminiscent of the prisoner's dilemma frequently studied by game theorists and economists. If we assume for the moment that there are two routes and two railroads, net benefits are maximized if each route is served by one line. However, each railroad has an incentive to maximize its private benefits by seeking control of both routes. If one railroad pursues this strategy, the other survives only if it does the same. As a consequence, resources are wasted as the two railroads compete for a given level of tonnage or passengers—in other words, the largest piece of a fixed economic pie. But the game is not zero sum, because large fixed investments are reduced when the railroads share the two routes. In other words, it's sometimes better to have a smaller share of a larger pie.

The problem in this example is that neither railroad can make a credible commitment to cooperation, and so cutthroat competition is necessary to protect each railroad's interests. At root, the problem is informational in the sense that neither party is particularly well positioned to verify that the other has cooperated until it is too late. In the terminology of DeLong and Froomkin, there is insufficient transparency.

Enter J.P. Morgan. Commonly portrayed as a rapacious financial pirate, Morgan also recognized the waste in competition and had the power to force cooperation among industry leaders. Because Morgan was the key source of capital necessary for building a new line, he credibly monitored and threatened to cut off the lifeblood of a would-be predator's strategy. If all else failed, Morgan was known to isolate adversaries aboard his yacht, the *Corsair*, and refuse to return to dock until a cooperative agreement was reached. A prisoner's dilemma indeed!

What Can We Learn from the Financial Intermediaries?

We offer Morgan as our initial example to illustrate how, given sufficient power, an intermediary can balance the competing interests of two or more parties to their collective benefit. Rarely does an intermediary, financial or otherwise, have the leverage maintained by Morgan. Nor is it likely that society at large would desire one or a few individuals to have such power for long. This means that intermediaries generally must rely on less coercive means of promoting cooperation. Much of the remainder of the book is aimed at identifying these subtle practices and their supporting organizational structure in financial markets.

As the part of the economy that is "about information" grows and more economic activity takes place around assets that are relatively difficult to control, intermediaries should become more, not less, important figures in the economy. However, the same technological advances that are pushing information to the forefront of the economy also force us to think carefully about which intermediary functions might be more efficiently and credibly carried out by machines. Some intermediary functions remain dependent on human judgment, but others lend themselves to codification. By *codification* we mean the transformation of human behavior or knowledge into a precise set of instructions amenable to execution. For example, modern information technology already provides a capacity for disseminating, storing, and sorting information that far outstrips that of even the most skillful human intermediary. Where codification of intermediary practices is possible, machines will displace human intermediaries.

Before turning to a detailed analysis of this interplay between advances in information and communications technology and the economics of intermediation, we examine the structure and functions of a particular form of financial intermediary, the investment bank. The investment banking industry provides a concrete foundation for much of the discussion that follows. Within this market sector we give particular attention to Goldman Sachs, perhaps the preeminent traditional investment bank, and three pioneering Internet investment banks: Wit SoundView, OffRoad Capital, and WR Hambrecht + Co.

The Internet banks are noteworthy not only because of their pioneering efforts but also because collectively their strategies cut across an entire area of intermediary practice. Securities underwriting traditionally has depended heavily and to great effect on relationships maintained by banks with both issuing firms and institutional investors. These relationships provided banks with the leverage necessary to balance the many competing interests that arise in securities offerings. However, the embodiment of these relationships in key individuals limited their scale and scope and raised questions of fairness associated with the extraordinary level of discretion granted to the intermediary. The Internet investment banks have taken dead aim at these concerns and therefore shed considerable light on how advances in technology will reshape intermediary functions.

3

INVESTMENT BANKING

> Wall Street was built on the basis of creating proprietary in-
> formation that was then distributed through an oral tradition
> of sales and research people.... [T]oday, general information
> is made available in an instant, and proprietary information is
> becoming a commodity. The new value added ... is in com-
> pleteness of information to clients, and in quickly aggregating
> the feedback from them.
>
> Scott Ryles, CEO, Epoch Capital Partners

CHAPTER 2 PROVIDED a bird's-eye perspective on the functions of financial intermediaries. This chapter outlines the functions of one
type of financial intermediary, the investment bank, describes the traditional intermediary platform and challenges posed by the Internet, and
then describes in some detail how banks smooth entrepreneurial firms'
transition from private to public ownership.

The investment bank provides a useful vantage point on the industry for several reasons. First, the regulation of investment banks in the
United States generally has been less heavy handed than that of commercial banks. As a consequence, their evolution can more nearly be interpreted as being driven by technological advances reshaping fundamental intermediary functions. The evolution of commercial banking
practices, in contrast, reflects an endless cycle of give and take between
regulators and bankers as technology undermines regulatory constraints on banking practice.[1] In this setting, financial innovation often
reflects "regulatory arbitrage" rather than improvement in the execution of fundamental intermediary functions.

Second, U.S. investment banks are widely considered the most innovative among intermediaries in world capital markets and engage in
a far wider range of activities than other financial intermediaries. For
better or worse, intermediary practices in world capital markets are
converging to U.S. standards where local regulation does not stand in

the way. Finally, relative to U.S. commercial banks or European universal banks, investment banks depend more heavily on the human capital of key individuals. In large part, this is a reflection of the more sedate world of retail deposit taking and commercial lending, in which the former are more active. Be that as it may, investment banks provide a more useful laboratory for examining the tension between human capital and information technology.

Among investment banking functions, those in the private and primary equity markets have served as the most prominent point of entry for pioneers in Internet investment banking. In part, pioneers have chosen this market segment for its high visibility in spite of the well-established and enormous success of traditional intermediary practice. But certain dimensions of traditional practice, such as the pricing and distribution of securities, appear ripe for codification. We'll focus specifically on the mechanics of pricing and distribution in the IPO market. Not only does this market provide a useful vantage point from which to assess how technological advances will alter the traditional platform, but there is also a well-developed literature on the mechanics of IPO underwriting practices. We review the theory and practice of this function in some depth over the course of the next two chapters to provide a concrete foundation as we develop systematic design principles for online business models capable of displacing or reshaping traditional intermediary practices.

The Traditional Investment Bank

The banker's network of personal relationships is perhaps the distinguishing feature of the twentieth-century U.S. investment bank. Investor networks began to take shape in the 1870s as the scale of industrial production and the evolution of the public corporation surpassed the funding capacity of even the largest banks. Simultaneously, the development of tight-knit client networks was triggered by the growing presence of powerful financiers on corporate boards that gave rise to the new financial capitalism. At the center of these networks of investors and corporate clients stood the likes of J.P. Morgan—men who brokered and coordinated the massive flow of information that shaped both their own industry and the industries they served.[2]

This relationship-based, human-capital-intensive production technology proved to be a remarkably effective institutional adaptation to the information-intensive nature of the investment banking industry. We need look no further than the names and organizational ancestors of today's most prominent banks to appreciate the staying power of the technology. And with good reason—when financial relationships were suppressed in the wake of New Deal financial reforms, the activity and amount of capital raised in public securities markets fell dramatically. Indeed, it was not until the 1960s, when investment bank relationships with institutional investors were reestablished, that U.S. public debt and equity markets returned to their former prominence.[3]

The U.S. investment bank is an artifact of the Glass-Steagall Banking Act of 1933. This federal legislation separated for the first time deposit taking and lending (commercial banking) from securities issuance, distribution, and trading (investment banking). However, on October 22, 1999, a U.S. Congressional House-Senate conference committee reached agreement on legislation (H.R. 10/S. 900) removing the last major barrier to repealing the Glass-Steagall prohibitions separating commercial banks from investment banks. Thus, now more than ever, it is important that we define precisely what we think of as an investment bank.

Ron Chernow describes investment banking as the "Olympian world of high finance," an identity stemming from the investment banker's long-standing role as strategic financial advisor to senior management and government officials.[4] Discretion and efficiency considerations led bankers to bundle their advice with a capacity for execution of the proposed strategy. Most often this included some form of securities issuance requiring a variety of underwriting, trading, and investor support services. The broad range of capital market services delivered by investment banks is reflected in table 3-1, a snapshot of Goldman Sachs that was offered to potential investors prior to its 1999 initial public equity offering.

Goldman Sachs identifies three broad lines of business: investment banking, trading and principal investments, and asset management and securities services. Investment banking encompasses a variety of fee-based, strategic products and services offered to corporations and governments. The asset management and securities services category comprises fee-based services offered to institutional and high-net-worth retail investors. The trading and principal investment category reflects activities in which the bank puts financial capital at risk for profit. Banks often place capital at risk in support of client transactions, but they also

Table 3-1
Goldman Sachs: Primary Products and Activities by Business Line

Investment Banking	Trading and Principal Investments	Asset Management and Securities Services
Equity and debt underwriting	Bank loans	Commissions
Financial restructuring advisory services	Commodities	Institutional and high- net-worth asset
	Currencies	management
Mergers and acquisitions advisory services	Equity and fixed- income derivatives	Margin lending
	Equity and fixed- income securities	Matched book
Real estate advisory services	Principal investments	Merchant banking fees and overrides
	Proprietary arbitrage	Mutual funds
		Prime brokerage
		Securities lending

	Year Ended November		
	1996	*1997*	*1998*
Net revenues			
Investment banking	$2,113	$2,587	$3,368
Trading and principal investments	2,693	2,926	2,379
Asset management and securities services	1,323	1,934	2,773
Total net revenues ($ billions)	$6,129	$7,447	$8,520

Source: S-1 filing with the U.S. Securities and Exchange Commission, March 16, 1999.

take proprietary positions on the basis of information acquired, in part, by maintaining a broad presence in the marketplace. Obviously, there is overlap between these categories. For example, equity trading complements the firm's equity underwriting activities. Likewise, Goldman Sachs mingles its own capital (principal investments) with that of clients when making private equity investments. For managing the latter, Goldman Sachs receives merchant banking fees and overrides in addition to any return on its own invested capital.

In the three years preceding Goldman Sachs's IPO, the firm showed a pronounced increase in revenues from asset management and securities services as it sought to expand these less volatile, fee-based businesses.[5] Fee revenues from investment banking also rose sharply during the worldwide boom in securities offerings and mergers and acquisitions (M&A) activity. Revenues from trading and principal investments remained fairly steady considering the volatile nature of these businesses, which was reflected in the firm's enormous losses of 1994. Chapter 7 examines in greater detail the firm's business focus and how it has changed over the years. For the moment, note that the relative balance between the three business lines reflects a shift from Goldman Sachs's long-standing emphasis on (agency) activities that the firm places in the investment banking category, toward those activities that involve principal risk-taking.

For our purposes, it is useful to include venture capital within the realm of investment banking. Today, the difference between the two is more one of degree than of kind. Investment banks have always brokered private debt and equity investments and, in their "merchant banking" (or principal) capacity, placed their own capital at risk. More recently, investment banks have established venture units that provide an array of services to fledgling firms and serve as a pipeline for future securities transactions. Goldman Sachs, for example, raised a $2.8 billion private equity pool in 1998, followed more recently (August 2000) by a $5.25 billion private equity fund that will be devoted to investments in leveraged buyouts and early-stage technology companies. Goldman Sachs's commitment to private equity investment resulted in net revenue of $950 million in 1999, or 7 percent of the firm's total revenues.

As money center banks moved into the private equity arena, bringing with them substantial capital and distribution capacity, venture capitalists have been forced to reconsider a business strategy that revolved around small private partnerships providing specialized services to fledgling companies. An early but noteworthy reflection of their response to competitive pressure is the recently formed Epoch Capital, a San Francisco-based partnership including the prominent venture capital firms Kleiner Perkins Caufield & Byers, Benchmark Capital, and Trident Capital and the online brokerage firms Charles Schwab, Ameritrade, and TD Waterhouse. Chase Manhattan (now J.P. Morgan Chase & Co.) also provides an interesting example in light of its aggressive entry into private equity and its subsequent acquisition of The Beacon Group, which handed the reins of its investment banking business over to Geoff Boisi.

The Internet Investment Banks

Setting aside for the moment the large commercial and universal banks that increasingly lead or participate in capital market transactions, the most visible new entrants to the investment banking industry are the so-called Internet investment banks. Wit Capital, founded in 1996 by Andrew Klein, is usually credited with being the first Internet investment bank. Klein formed Wit Capital when he left the New York law firm of Cravath, Swaine and Moore in 1992 to found Spring Street Brewing, which based its first product, Wit beer, on a popular Belgian wheat-based recipe.

In the aftermath of the 1993 reforms to Section A of the Securities Act that streamlined the sale of private equity directly to the public, Klein set out, in 1995, to sell up to 2.7 million shares in Spring Street at $1.85 per share to fund expansion of the business. After raising nearly $1.6 million within a year, much of it from beer enthusiasts, Klein attracted attention from other small companies trying to reduce the costs of raising capital. With the support of Steven Wallman, a Securities and Exchange Commission (SEC) commissioner who had an eye for information technology's potential for ushering in securities market reform, Klein launched Wit Trade in 1996 to provide secondary market liquidity for small equity offerings.[6]

Wit Capital then set out to coordinate an "e-syndicate" of retail investors within which it could identify affinity groups for future equity offerings. Wit Capital committed to providing first-come, first-served access to IPOs on the condition that e-syndicate members refrain from immediate sale, or flipping, of their allocations in the secondary market.[7] This reliable network of retail investors made Wit Capital an attractive partner for deals managed by old-line banks with relatively weak retail distribution channels. In 1999, Wit Capital co-managed fifty-seven public offerings and was a syndicate member for an additional seventy-one. But by year-end 1999, Wit Capital had yet to lead an offering.

On January 31, 2000, Wit Capital merged with SoundView Technology Group, a private investment-banking firm founded in 1979, to form the Wit SoundView Group. Wit SoundView provides a full range of investment banking services to the Internet and technology sectors and boasts one of the largest research teams in these sectors. The alliance came on the heels of the sale of a 22 percent stake in Wit Capital to Goldman Sachs on March 29, 1999, and Wit's public offering on June 4, 1999. So in short order, Wit SoundView has joined the establishment.

WR Hambrecht + Co., founded in 1998 by William Hambrecht, effectively was spun out of the establishment. Hambrecht was a founding partner and chief executive officer of Hambrecht & Quist, the San Francisco-based investment bank that began in 1968 as a technology boutique and contributed to and flourished with the explosion of high-tech business development in Silicon Valley. Coincidentally, the enthusiasm of beer drinkers for specialty brews also drew Hambrecht's attention to the Internet. In November 1995, Hambrecht & Quist co-managed a $30 million IPO for the Boston Beer Company, the brewers of Samuel Adams beer. Boston Beer wanted to offer $10 million worth of shares to its customers, so Hambrecht & Quist printed the tombstone announcement for the offering on a bottle neckhanger and included it in about one week's worth of production.[8] Within a month, much to Hambrecht & Quist's surprise, they received about 120,000 requests for shares, totaling more than $50 million. Hambrecht observed that Hambrecht & Quist ultimately completed the transaction,

> but it was considered a great pain in the neck. We actually ended up doing $10 million with 30,000 people who sent money and sent back $40 million. I must admit, I'm enough of a businessman to think that sending back $40 million is not a really good idea. You ought to figure out how to use it. What it did for me, in a fairly dramatic way, was show me there was an unfilled market out there. That there were a lot of people who truly did want to invest in these kind of companies. . . . The obvious way to handle this is on the Web. Because there you can handle 100,000 people and handle them efficiently, but even more importantly, they become a valuable asset, because if you capture an account you have it for other deals.[9]

As a colleague from a prominent brokerage firm pointed out to Hambrecht, Hambrecht & Quist effectively declined nearly 100,000 new accounts, accounts that his brokerage firm paid anywhere from $100 to $200 per account in marketing expenses to acquire.

Rather than experimenting within Hambrecht and Quist, Hambrecht started the new firm because he "came to the conclusion that there was no way of changing the distribution pattern in an existing firm that relied on [business from] traditional brokerage" firms for revenue.[10] When key institutional investors are excluded from an IPO, they often place the bank in their penalty box. That is, the investors redirect some portion of their future brokerage business, and thereby their commissions, to another bank. The enormous profitability of flipping IPO shares aggravates the problem because investors request shares even when they have no intention of holding them for the long term. We'll see later that the symbiotic relationship between banks and their investors promotes cooperative use of information, but it clearly has the potential for stifling innovation. Moreover, retail investors complain because they are not similarly favored with IPO shares.

WR Hambrecht responded by creating an electronic auction platform called OpenIPO. The goal for OpenIPO is to produce savings for issuing firms by pricing their IPOs more accurately (and thereby avoiding the enormous first-day price increase so common to IPOs) and by narrowing the spreads paid to the underwriting syndicate. OpenIPO also places retail and institutional investors on an equal footing, discriminating only on the basis of price and quantity bids.

By year-end 2000, WR Hambrecht had auctioned four IPOs. Andover.Net's December 8, 1999, IPO illustrates the platform's potential.[11] Andover.Net paid WR Hambrecht 6.5 percent ($1.17 per share) of the $77.4 million raised in the offering instead of the traditional 7 percent fee. The auction resulted in a retail allocation of about 50 percent of the shares sold—well in excess of the typical 20 to 30 percent retail allocation when traditional selling methods are used. The only apparent failing was the 252 percent price increase from the offer price of $18 per share to the first-day closing price of $63.375. To be sure, the $45.375 per share ($208.7 million) that Andover.Net apparently left on the table is not small change. On the other hand, the 252 percent price increase was not unprecedented during the wave of dot-com IPOs—in fact, it is dwarfed by the 900 percent first-day price runup following globe.com's traditionally underwritten IPO (which was offered at $9, opened at $90, and closed at $63 on the first day of trading). Moreover, strict adherence to the auction rules in pricing the deal would have yielded an offer price well above $18. Rather than delay the offering to amend its prospectus, Andover.Net chose to price the offering at the $18 maximum suggested in the firm's prospectus filed with the SEC.

Although the entry strategies of these pioneering banks are in many ways unique, they are united in their challenge to the traditional practice of taking firms public. To understand why this line of business provoked an early challenge to the traditional platform, we take a closer look at the transition to public ownership carried out in the primary equity markets.

The IPO Market

The U.S. primary equity market has, until quite recently, been the exclusive domain of investment banks, and, in recent years, a very profitable one at that. In 1999, 563 companies went public in the United States, raising about $69 billion in equity capital.[12] At an average fee of 5.44 percent of the capital raised, investment banks earned about $3.8 billion just for underwriting IPOs. Goldman Sachs alone earned $730 million (or an average fee of about 5 percent) for the fifty-four IPOs it led and $2.1 billion (or 20.6 percent of the firm's total revenues) from underwriting all forms of securities. Relatively few banks compete for the lead management role that carries the largest part of the fees, and so profits are highly concentrated within the industry.[13]

IPOs are a profitable business for investment banks because they are difficult to carry out and require an infrastructure that is difficult to replicate in the short run. By definition, there is no existing market and therefore no price for an IPO. In essence, the bank's task is to create a market in very short order and use this market to "discover" a price at which the deal can be sold. In contrast, for firms that already have publicly traded securities, a market and price already exist and therefore the offering of new securities involves little more than distribution.

IPOs are usually one of two types. Bulge-bracket banks such as Goldman Sachs specialize in *firm commitment offerings* of larger deals involving more mature, less risky firms. Under the firm commitment contract, the leader of a syndicate of banks purchases the shares to be sold from the issuing firm at a discount (the underwriting spread) from the price at which shares are offered to investors. The lead bank therefore guarantees the firm a minimum amount of new capital regardless of the outcome of the offering. Regional banks more nearly specialize in *best efforts offerings*, in which they broker the sale of shares but make no commitment regarding the amount of proceeds delivered to the issuing firm. Traditionally, best efforts offerings involved younger, riskier firms. Clearly, this changed in recent years as the bulge-bracket banks led offerings by many highly visible but early-stage Internet start-ups.

The intermediary platform in U.S. primary equity markets is well established and highly standardized.[14] The process begins with the preparation and filing of a preliminary prospectus with the SEC. The prospectus represents findings from the investment banker's due diligence effort and, under Section 11 of the Securities Act of 1933, serves as the foundation for civil liability arising from omissions of material facts. With the filing of the registration statement, the firm faces a twenty-day waiting period before registration of the offering is effective. The SEC uses the waiting period to review and comment on the filing, and may delay the offering if it determines that amendments are required. If the SEC is satisfied that the registration statement satisfies full and fair disclosure requirements, it may accelerate the effective date of the offering's registration. The issuer generally requests acceleration when notified of SEC clearance of the registration statement.

As the preliminary prospectus circulates among potential investors, the issuer's investment bank organizes a series of investor presentations known as *road shows* to generate further interest. Based on these presentations and the information in the prospectus, including a suggested price range for the offering, participants provide non-binding indications of interest in the issue. Indications of interest take a variety of forms. Some investors indicate willingness to purchase a certain number of shares at the market price. Others indicate the number of shares they are willing to purchase at a particular price or range of prices. The collection of indications, referred to as the *book*, essentially forms a demand curve for the offering. Although indications of interest are legally nonbinding, they are collected in the context of an ongoing relationship between the bank and its network of institutional investors. Failure to stand by an indication can lead to an investor's exclusion from future deals managed by the bank. The book is then used to determine the price and other terms of the offering shortly before distribution begins.

Building a book for an IPO involves polling potential investors for information regarding their interest in the deal. Ideally, the bank would canvass the entire investor population. But historically it was difficult to assemble all interested parties at one time and place. Faced with relatively primitive information technology, bookbuilding methods economized on search costs by seeking the opinions of a relatively narrow but influential pool of institutional investors with whom the investment banker maintained long-standing relationships. In this respect, the investment banker is not unlike a political pollster seeking opinions from a representative sample of the population at large.

The information reflected in an indication of interest takes one of two forms. *Hard information* reflects insight about the issuing firm's future prospects or those of a competitor. Although it is counterintuitive that an investor might know more about the firm or industry than the issuing firm's management, portfolio managers devote considerable resources to fundamental analysis of firms and their competitors. This easily could translate into superior forecasts of the firm's future cash flows or greater access to information about the issuer's competitors. The latter is true if for no other reason than that firms more likely will yield information to a money manager who is considering the addition of the firm to her portfolio than to competitors.

Even if the command of hard information by potential investors is negligible, each investor knows his or her own demand for the issue. This *soft information* is valuable because in aggregate it represents the market demand for the issue. Moreover, some investors influence the thinking of other investors and thereby can make or break the issue. Fidelity Investments alone purchases about 10 percent of newly issued shares. Regardless of the merits of its analysis, a strong demand from Fidelity can provide a boost to the deal. Faced with the threat that the issuer's bank will use their interest to pump up the market, some management firms maintain an informal policy of withdrawing from offerings when they believe their indication of interest has been used to shop the deal with other prospective investors.

Regardless of the nature of the information obtained from prospective investors, it appears to have a substantial impact on the final terms of the transaction. Both the offering price and the number of shares offered commonly stray from the levels suggested in the preliminary prospectus. When investor interest is strong, the issuing firm often increases both the price of the offering and its size; firms take the opposite tack in response to weak interest. In fact, it was common among Internet-related IPOs for the offer price to be set at a huge premium to the price suggested in the prospectus. Netscape's 1995 offer price of $28 per share doubled the high end of the suggested price range.

The IPO Market as a Point of Entry

Although the historical success of this well-developed intermediary platform led to widespread adoption by even non-U.S. banks and issuing firms during the 1990s, several aspects of the bookbuilding process make it ripe for challenge from entrants promoting a new technology. First, the practice of face-to-face communication during road shows favors institutional investors because there are physical limits on the number of contacts the issuing firm and its bank can make. Communication with institutional investors has greater impact because institutions sweep together the capital and represent the interests of many individual investors. But the focus on institutional investors also leads to favoritism in share allocations. Institutional investors commonly receive more than two-thirds of the shares offered in an IPO in spite of generally overwhelming demand from individual investors. Even if there are good reasons for favoring institutional investors (and we explore this question at some length in chapter 4), criticism from retail investors and concern among policymakers has increased.[15]

Many also question the efficiency of the platform. Much has been made of the fact that investment banking fees are relatively high in the United States and tend to cluster around 7 percent of gross proceeds. The enormous first-day price increases, often taken as a positive sign by market observers, also mean that if shares are worth the higher price observed at the end of the first day of trading, then issuing firms are leaving a lot of money on the table. The average first-day price increase of 15 percent applied to a $50 million offering represents $7.5 million of equity that the issuing firm is not putting to work. In other words, issuers pay more for the equity they receive. These peculiarities of the market suggest to some observers that the relationships binding banks with one another and with their institutional investors corrupt the system and shortchange issuing firms. Economists, ever optimists, are more likely to wonder whether the relatively complicated process of bookbuilding could be replaced by a much simpler and less easily corrupted auction: Why not replace bank discretion with simple, enforceable rules that mimic positive behaviors?

Both Wit SoundView and WR Hambrecht take aim at fairness concerns by promoting their efforts to democratize the IPO market. And Wit SoundView, in particular, has gained the cooperation of traditional investment banks because its approach complements the status quo. As we'll see in chapter 4, retail investor channels provide a credible fallback for banks during (implicit) bargaining with institutional investors over the "price" of accurate indications of interest. For banks with relatively weak ties to individual retail investors, Wit SoundView offers its e-syndicate of individual investors at a price many traditional banks find attractive—simply include Wit SoundView in the underwriting syndicate. As the cost of communicating with individual investors plummets and institutional investor clout increases, bankers such as Ted Hatfield, managing director for equity capital markets at Credit Suisse First Boston (CSFB), are turning to online channels because they provide "the appropriate tension and excitement around our deals to create the best pricing for issuers."[16]

In addition to emphasizing the democratic aspects of its platform, WR Hambrecht appeals to concerns regarding the traditional platform's efficiency. Auctions, in their various forms, are widely considered a superior mechanism for pricing and allocating goods whose value is highly uncertain. Why then are they not a more prominent feature of securities markets? One reason is that financial assets are sold in large but divisible units, which means that ideally a large population of individuals would participate in the auction. In chapter 4, we describe the bookbuilding process as a relatively clumsy (by modern standards) albeit effective response to the difficulty of assembling many people at one time and place. But bringing together many people at one time and (virtual) place on the Internet costs little on the margin once initial investments in infrastructure are completed.

Upstream Competition

Wit SoundView and WR Hambrecht took aim at the highly visible and highly competitive point of transition between private and public ownership. By contrast, OffRoad Capital sought entry through the less competitive private equity markets that nurture firms from their founding to, ideally, their public offering. The Internal Revenue Service (IRS) estimates that approximately 400,000 private companies account for 35 percent of total employment in the United States and more than $2 trillion in book assets. In general, the securities issued by these companies, whether bank loans or other private debt or equity claims, are illiquid, resulting in a higher cost of capital. Illiquidity is related in large part to the absence of a regulatory body like the SEC that establishes reporting standards, monitors adherence, and promotes widespread dissemination of information among potential investors.

Were it a simple task to coordinate this enormous pool of firms and investors, venture capitalists and investment banks would have stepped forward sooner. In fact it was not, if only because of the prohibitive cost of communicating with such a diverse and geographically diffuse audience. OffRoad recognized that the Internet substantially altered the cost/benefit analysis and that within this segment of the financial marketplace there was no dominant platform to dislodge. OffRoad's founder, Stephen Pelletier, also learned in conversations with Steven Wallman that the private equity space was lightly regulated compared with public markets.[17] As Pelletier put it, "Putting hypertext in the S-1 [the document filed with the SEC upon registration for an initial public offering of equity] would require an act of Congress. The equivalents of that in private equity are by convention not regulation. If you can design from the ground up, you can do better than by just working within existing infrastructure."[18]

Finally, Pelletier, like Bill Hambrecht and Andrew Klein, held an abiding interest in the Internet's potential for democratizing financial markets. As he observed,

> The price of traditional intermediation is that you miss the opinions of a lot of smart people. Take the *New York Times* for example. As a newspaper it has the best writers, but do you think they have the best writers in the world? No. There's a lot of smart people out there who never get close to [writing for] the *New York Times*. When you rely strictly on the traditional intermediary, you miss out on these [people].[19]

OffRoad initially targeted later-stage, middle-market growth companies seeking financing in the $3 million to $15 million range. In further contrast to the companies typically funded by venture capitalists, they sought companies with experienced management and an operating history. OffRoad then developed the following tools for capital acquisition:

- Standardized online offering memoranda that promote easy evaluation and comparison

- A standardized online road-show format involving a series of interactive online meetings and e-mail exchanges

- A standard auction-like mechanism for pricing securities

- Standardized terms and conditions for five deal structures

- Mandated quarterly and annual performance reporting throughout the life of the investment[20]

OffRoad's strategy was designed to appeal to an online community of high-net-worth, "self-directed" individual investors but just as surely serves the interests of institutional investors that don't maintain an in-house capacity for evaluating private equity investment opportunities.

A key to success for OffRoad will be the credibility it develops for establishing and enforcing standards for behavior among investors and firms seeking capital. Building standards from the ground up is no simple matter. If nothing else, it requires a capacity for making a credible commitment to their enforcement. A firm seeking capital has little incentive to provide accurate information if it faces little risk of being found out by the fragmented membership of an uncoordinated investor network. Intermediaries add value beyond proposing a standard by making a credible commitment to its enforcement. *Credibility* is just another word for reputation, and reputations are established over time.

OffRoad overcame this reputational entry barrier by building on the reputations of key individuals from the outset. Pelletier had a reputation as a pioneer in online financial services and was well connected in the technology and venture capital communities. Other key members of the management team and the firm's board of directors included the following:

- John Forlines, III, co-president of OffRoad Capital, former managing director of J.P. Morgan and co-head of the firm's Technology and Telecommunications Investment Banking Group

- David Weir, co-president of OffRoad Capital, former managing director of J.P. Morgan and co-head of the firm's Technology and Telecommunications Investment Banking Group

- Susan Woodward, chief economist, former chief economist for both the Securities Exchange Commission and the U.S. Department of Housing and Urban Development

- Allen Morgan, board member, general partner of Mayfield Fund

- Michael G. McCaffery, board member, president and CEO of the Stanford Management Company, former chairman of Robertson Stephens

- Steven Wallman, board member, former SEC commissioner

The personal reputations of OffRoad's management team lend credibility to the firm's *ability* to enforce standards. But just as important is the firm's perceived *willingness* to enforce standards when doing so might damage relations with a client firm. A reputation is a valuable asset developed over time and usually at considerable effort, but it can be squandered in a moment of weakness. An intermediary with only a modest reputation has little to lose if it fails to deliver on a commitment. But OffRoad's principals have a powerful incentive to enforce standards because their reputations have substantial value in alternative uses. Thus a standard proposed by a highly reputable agent is *self-enforcing*.

Finally, the relative absence of regulation in the private equity markets provides OffRoad with far more room for experimentation than Wit SoundView or WR Hambrecht worked with in the primary market. From the outset, WR Hambrecht was concerned that institutional investors, because they know and communicate with one another, would have an upper hand in OpenIPO. To date, SEC guidelines have prevented WR Hambrecht from revealing detailed information about price and quantity bids as they arrive in the OpenIPO auction book or from rewarding bidders for early arrival. Sophisticated bidders tend to lay back as they try to gauge market demand through back channels before submitting their own bids. This potentially favors the relatively tight-knit group of institutional investors who invest repeatedly in IPOs. Retail investors, by contrast, are far less likely to be in communication with one another or institutional investors before placing their bids.

Reflecting Pelletier's view that investing is "fundamentally a social activity" and that the Internet is a powerful tool for fostering networks for lateral communication, members of OffRoad's investor community are encouraged to communicate with one another in online forums and even during the auction bidding process. As the following statement from the firm's Web site indicates, investors are encouraged (but not forced) to reveal their profiles (maintained by OffRoad under the investor's "community name") to other investors:

OffRoad's Investor Network has been designed to encourage discussion among the investors themselves. The members of our network form a community of like-minded investors, whose varying perspectives, geographical diversity, professional backgrounds, and investment experience help deepen individual insight as investors analyze, scrutinize, and debate the merits of each opportunity. When profiles are hidden from the community, investors have no way of getting to know each other. This, in turn, prevents them from forming smaller discussion groups within the larger community, or seeking out special areas of expertise as they conduct their own due diligence for an investment opportunity.[21]

The OffRoad auction represents the culmination of information production by establishing the price for the issuing firm's securities contingent on investor feedback. The auction is structured to encourage investors to bid early; their bids (although not the source) are shared with other investors, who then can revise their opinions based on the opinions of others. A complex and sometimes unwieldy closing period is maintained to promote further convergence of opinion among investors. During this period, no new investors are permitted to join the bidding, but those whose bids have been pushed aside by higher bids in the preceding twenty-four hours are permitted to submit a higher bid. In other words, early bidders are rewarded by protecting them from investors who otherwise might sit back and watch proceedings only to sweep in at the last possible moment, thereby never showing their own hand to other investors.

In its first full year of operation ending in September 2000, OffRoad completed eleven online private equity transactions totaling about $70 million in capital and built its investor network to more than 6,000 institutional and accredited retail investors. Over the same period, the firm entered alliances to leverage its technology platform with a variety of established financial firms, including Robertson Stephens, Mayfield Fund, Charles Schwab, and ING Barings. With the exception of Schwab, these alliances are noteworthy for having attracted the attention of traditional firms that see OffRoad's platform, designed with individual investors in mind, as a powerful vehicle for coordinating institutional investors.[22]

This chapter introduced a prominent financial intermediary, the investment bank, and discussed the role it plays in brokering a firm's passage from private to public ownership. This particular intermediary function provides an interesting vantage point from which to examine the industry because it was the point of entry for several upstarts who used the Internet to challenge existing intermediary practices. But in short order, as the upstarts mimic and partner with established firms, the distinction between the old guard and the new is blurring. This industry pattern of innovation by new entrants being merged into the traditional platforms of dominant firms is quite common; we'll explore it in much greater detail in chapter 6.

By introducing several pioneering Internet investment banks, we've also tried to draw your attention to what we believe is the basis for a sea change within an industry that always has been about information. In traditional industries, product and process innovations typically displaced existing physical assets with new, more effective physical assets. When intellectual capital was added or subtracted, it generally was embodied in physical capital—new machines embodied the ideas of their inventors. In the information-intensive industries that are so prevalent in the modern economy, intellectual capital takes the form of human capital, often remaining embodied within its originator. But here technological advances are creating the potential for both reshaping human capital and in some instances displacing it with physical capital. We believe that both will have profound implications for the organization of firms and their industries and that these implications already are apparent in the financial markets.

In Part II we develop this idea by drilling more deeply into the economics of information and organization. This will necessarily involve a somewhat higher level of abstraction. But we'll draw heavily on the experience of investment banks to provide you with an anchor in reality as we leap back and forth across the divide between academic theory and practice.

PART II

TRADE IN
INFORMATION
MARKETS

4

How Intermediaries Resolve Coordination Problems

FINANCIAL MARKETS provide for trade in information. Generally, broad and rapid dissemination of information is considered beneficial to the economy at large. Technically, it seems an easy goal to achieve if we recall Stewart Brand's contention that information wants to be free. And, unlike physical goods whose freedom is circumscribed by the cost of moving them about, the marginal cost of disseminating information is in sharp decline. Why then do institutions for filtering, vetting, and otherwise inhibiting the free flow of information persist? The short answer is that information is power.

Information can be used, or consumed, simultaneously by many people at little or no marginal cost to those who share. Knowledge of an impending heat wave, for example, if shared widely can ease the burden of many by enabling local authorities to arrange shelter for those who cannot avoid the heat. The same information placed in the hands of an electricity trader, however, can yield enormous private gains—but only if the information is not shared by the trader's counterparts. In other words, information can be both a nonrival and rival good simultaneously. Further complicating matters, the trader driven by hopes of private gain has the most powerful incentive to invest in the latest forecasting technology. Although sharing his forecasts with local authorities for planning purposes does little to undermine the trader's interests, the threat of his information being more widely disseminated does. Thus, a good deed might be left undone because the trader has little to gain but much to lose.

Although it might prevent the realization of a greater good, the pursuit of private gain here is not bad in and of itself. The trading firm and government agency are simply caught in a zero-sum game in which a non-zero-sum outcome is possible. Problems worthy of an intermediary's attention generally arise in instances like this in which information has both rival and nonrival features. Rivalry encourages investment in the production of information but undermines sharing. Nonrivalry cries out for sharing but can undermine incentives for producing the information in the first place. Intermediaries balance the interests in information production against those in sharing its benefits.

Thus, although intermediaries by some accounts obstruct the free flow of information, we side with John Seely Brown and Paul Duguid. They suggest that where others see burdens on information, they instead see solutions to information's burdens.[1] This chapter probes more deeply the frictions that arise in the exchange of information and how intermediaries, by promoting trust and cooperation, can better channel the self-interest that remains the primary constraint on the freedom of information.

Bilateral Coordination

The problem facing the electricity trader and government agency is fundamentally identical to our earlier example of cutthroat competition in the early days of railroading. Here, a public-spirited trader would happily share knowledge of a pending heat wave if doing so would not undermine strategic use of the information. Why prevent collective benefit if it leaves one no worse off? Likewise, why would two railroads build parallel lines if each could rest assured that the other would abide by an arrangement to share the market for their services?

Let's probe this question a bit more deeply by considering a simple example in which two people hold key remaining pieces of a puzzle. Clearly, sharing increases the total value of their information. But how can one who is willing to cooperate ensure that the other will? The problem is that someone must be the first to reveal her information. But as soon as she does, the other has incentive to express his gratitude and capture all the benefits from seeing the whole picture by not revealing his piece of the puzzle. What's worse is that the first mover cannot take her information back if the other withholds his—once free, information is difficult to recapture. As we discussed in chapter 2, this is a coordination problem in the sense that, left to their own designs, the two might not find their way to the cooperative outcome. As DeLong and Froomkin suggested, in the world of Adam Smith, the invisible hand guided parties to the best possible outcome. But Smith's underlying assumptions do not hold here.

Sometimes bilateral cooperation can emerge without an intermediary. In *The Evolution of Cooperation*, for example, Robert Axelrod describes widespread but selective mutual restraint between enemy units engaged in trench warfare during World War I.[2] In one instance, the simultaneous delivery of rations to the front as darkness set in created a focal point for coordination. Quite rapidly, an understanding spontaneously developed that aggression was off-limits during the delivery period. Within a few weeks, the level of trust was such that enemy soldiers were fraternizing with one another during their time-out from battle. As Axelrod observed, "What made trench warfare so different from most other combat was that the same small units faced each other in immobile sectors for extended periods of time." In other words, this life-threatening version of the prisoner's dilemma was resolved because the two parties repeatedly dealt with one another in a transparent setting. Good behavior was reciprocated, and the absence of anonymity assured severe punishment for violations of trust.

Similar opportunities exist in financial markets and markets for information generally. Most institutional investors deal repeatedly in the marketplace, often in a relatively transparent fashion—when you're managing tens of billions of dollars in assets, it's hard not to stand out from the landscape. On the other hand, instances arise when one or both parties are not active participants or are unwilling to sacrifice anonymity for strategic reasons. Here an active and transparent intermediary can credibly broker exchange without fully yielding the strategic advantage in anonymity. For example, even when influential mutual fund managers liquidate stocks merely to satisfy accountholder withdrawals, their actions might unduly influence market prices if the source of, but not the rationale for, their transactions were widely known. In such cases, a block-trading desk might add value by discreetly and credibly revealing the nature of a transaction to a select group of investors willing to provide liquidity on the intermediary's word. In general, bilateral coordination of information exchange should be easier to carry out, if only because there are fewer parties to monitor.

Network Coordination

It is more often the case that financial transactions involve multilateral exchanges of information among parties who because of the sheer breadth of their communication network have no choice but to be virtually anonymous. Moreover, balancing the competing interests of many rather than a few places greater information-processing demands on a would-be coordinator. Thus, network coordination of the kind carried out by most financial intermediaries is a more complicated undertaking than bilateral coordination and is not as likely to emerge spontaneously. But we need to be careful here. When network members have overlapping information, an individual's information is less valuable if others with similar information step forward first. In other words, if only one person holds a valuable piece of information, her bargaining power is great. If others hold the same or similar information, let the competition begin.

Network externalities provide another counterbalancing effect to the inherent complexity of multilateral information exchange. Membership in an information network often is more valuable to any single member as membership increases. A telephone network offers perhaps the simplest example of this principle. A telephone is of little value if the network has only a single subscriber. But as the number of subscribers grows, so does the value of the network to existing and potential subscribers, who now can communicate with more people. If aggregated information is generally more valuable than the sum of its parts, then an information network also benefits from network externalities. Network externalities present substantial barriers to entry for competing networks by locking people into the existing network. Thus members of a dominant network can expect to earn monopoly profits. By the same token, they are more likely to abide by the network's standards of cooperation if undesirable behavior leads to expulsion and sacrifice of monopoly profits.

The NYSE is an exclusive information network with both explicit and implicit constraints on member behavior. The membership voluntarily endows some traders with the power to sanction those who violate the rules and norms of behavior.[3] For example, the specialist responsible for making a market in a stock commonly provides price improvement and other services for cooperative floor brokers representing nonmember trades, and withholds these favors from brokers who violate behavioral norms. In turn, specialists are assigned new stocks, and therefore gain business, on the basis of floor broker evaluations of their performance. Failure to abide by certain formal rules can result in expulsion from the exchange. Judging from the price of an exchange seat, which remains near $2 million in the face of serious challenge from competing networks, membership remains a valuable asset and so the threat of exclusion from its benefits will not be taken lightly.

So while network coordination is a more complicated exercise than bilateral coordination, redundancy in the contributions of individual members and the threat of exclusion from the benefits of membership can thus provide an intermediary with considerable leverage if used wisely.

Mechanism Design Theory

How should intermediaries go about coordinating the exchange and use of information? In chapter 2, we described the coercive methods used by J.P. Morgan. Coercive methods are most common in the early stages of market development when standards for behavior are still evolving. Any parent of young siblings should be able to identify with this tendency. Rivalries develop that if left unchecked would leave everyone (including the parent) in a foul state. Ideally, we'd like to teach our children to cooperate with one another, but peace of mind often takes precedence in the short run. In such instances we use our parental authority to simply separate the rivals or hand down a solution rather than helping them work through their differences. Some, like Morgan, find themselves in the (enviable?) position of leveraging their parental experience to resolve the sibling rivalries of the commercial world.

As childish as these rivalries sometimes are, however, we generally are uncomfortable, and for good reason, with the idea of one or a few individuals or institutions having such coercive power. Moreover, it's human nature to strain at the leash of even the most benevolent dictator, if there is such a thing. Finally, there are many instances in which a benevolent dictator simply would not have the monitoring capacity to enforce his dictates—again, this point should resonate with parents. So brute force is perhaps not the most stable mechanism for promoting cooperation in the long run. And if we hope to codify and mechanize what intermediaries do, perhaps the Skinnerian prescription of rewarding desirable but not undesirable behavior would make for a more pleasant existence.

Mechanism design theory provides a powerful alternative to the benevolent dictator model. From the economist's perspective, "a mechanism is a specification of how economic decisions are determined as a function of the information that is known by the individuals in the economy."[4] We might think of a mechanism more concretely as a set of rules administered by a "discrete and trustworthy information-processing device."[5] In principle, the information processor could just as easily be a computer as a human intermediary. The purpose of the mechanism is to collect from interested parties all of their information and use the collected data to determine the set of actions that will make the best use of the information at hand.

In our example involving the completion of a puzzle, the mechanism's information processor would collect the remaining pieces of the puzzle, specify its completion, and recommend how best to divide the benefits from seeing the completed image among those contributing to its completion. The key to carrying out this function is whether the information processor, or intermediary, can be trusted to preserve the confidentiality of each individual's reported information. An absence of trust immediately leads us back to the prisoner's dilemma.

In the theory of mechanism design, the intermediary must sustain a property of the mechanism referred to as *incentive compatibility*. An incentive-compatible mechanism is one where, given the rules of the mechanism, participants find it in their individual interest to voluntarily provide an honest account of their information to the intermediary and behave according to the recommendations handed down. Thus an incentive-compatible mechanism provides for realization of mutually beneficial cooperative arrangements when they exist. In other words, if a benevolent dictator can force a mutually beneficial cooperative outcome, there is, in principle, an incentive-compatible mechanism that will elicit voluntary cooperation resulting in the same outcome. The trick is in specifying the rules that define an incentive-compatible mechanism.

At the risk of losing any credibility that we may still have with the reader, we examine this problem via a gross simplification of a highly stylized academic model.[6] Although it is precisely because of this kind of "toy modeling" that academics remain firmly lodged in their ivory towers, we hope to persuade readers that on occasion something can be learned from the mental gymnastics they engage in to while away their deservedly hard time. In this instance, our goal is to lay bare the strategy that an intermediary might carry out to induce investors to provide accurate indications of interest for an IPO. If we accomplish this goal, we take a first step toward codification of a practice that traditionally has relied largely on human judgment. If not, at least we will have taken a brief tilt at the windmills of the academic mind. Enjoy the ride.

The Traditional IPO Platform: A Toy Model

Recall from the discussion in chapter 3 that we compared the collection of indications of interest from investors to conducting a political poll. We misled you a bit by ignoring an important difference between polling potential investors and polling potential voters. Participants in a political opinion poll are more nearly (perhaps absolutely!) indifferent about the outcome of the polling effort. In contrast, institutional investors have a significant financial stake in the outcome of the investment bank's poll. The manager of a large mutual fund knows that a strong indication of interest drives up the offer price both directly and perhaps indirectly by influencing the beliefs of other investors. Simply put, investors have an incentive to understate their interest and thereby compromise the bank's effort to accurately assess market demand conditions.

Investors won't share their opinions freely if they expect that doing so will drive up the offer price. But issuing firms and their banks should be willing to compensate investors for providing accurate indications of interest if the net effect is to increase the expected proceeds from the offering. The trick is to compensate only those investors who are honest while penalizing or not rewarding those who are not. A capacity for bluffing is virtually a prerequisite for a successful career in the financial markets, so this is easier said than done. Be that as it may, we'll sketch out how to persuade an investor to show his hand.

Suppose (as the academic always does) that an issuing firm plans to sell 1 million shares of equity. To keep things simple, we'll also assume that the research conducted in preparation for filing with the SEC indicates that with equal probability the fair value for the firm's offering is either \$10 million (V_{high}) or \$8 million (V_{low}). This implies that the bank's best estimate of the value of the firm is simply the average of its high and low estimates, or $9 per share. To keep things concrete, think of this estimate as the suggested price included in the preliminary prospectus filed with the SEC.

Roughly speaking, demand for IPOs comes from two sources: individual retail investors and institutional investors. Although demand for shares in an IPO from each investor clientele often is substantial, even sufficient to take down the entire offering, the firm's bank generally will find it less costly to allocate shares among institutional investors. This is true if for no other reason than because it is cheaper to distribute 1 million shares among twenty institutional investors than among, say, 1,000 retail investors, each of whom demands 1,000 shares. Perhaps more important, institutional investors often maintain relationships with banks, cemented by regular, large-scale participation in a variety of transactions. So as a first approximation it makes sense to think of institutional investors as the more reliable source of demand. We represent this feature of the market in our example by assuming that institutional investors can take down the entire 1 million shares being offered, but that no more than 700,000 shares can be placed with retail investors.

In chapter 3 we suggested that if nothing else, investors know their own demand for an IPO. In this example, think of Fidelity's or some other influential investor's demand as representing the difference between the issuing firm realizing the $10 per share optimistic valuation or the pessimistic valuation of $8 per share. To keep things simple, we'll assume that institutional investors as a class know the fair value of the firm's offering (either $8 or $10 per share) and that retail investors can do no better than accept the $9 per share estimate reported in the preliminary prospectus.

Now consider the options facing the issuing firm and its bank if they choose to price the offering without knowing whether institutional investors are optimistic or pessimistic. One strategy they might consider is to simply set the offer price at the estimated value of $9 per share. If it turns out that institutional investors are optimistic, they will gladly purchase all 1 million shares offered. But the issuing firm would have then left $1 million on the table by selling its shares for $9 million rather than $10 million.

Conversely, if institutional investors are pessimistic, they'll refuse to buy at a price of $9 per share. Moreover, the firm might not even be able to count on the maximum retail demand of 700,000 shares at a $9 offer price. If retail investors believe that institutional investors know something that they do not, they'll expect to be crowded out of offerings that institutional investors think are underpriced and to be offered relatively large allocations in those perceived as overpriced. Kevin Rock of Citibank and MIT has argued that this *winner's curse* causes retail investors to buy IPOs only if they believe they will break even on average.[7]

If retail investors are crowded out of deals that look good to the smart money and are left holding the bag in others, then they will break even on average only if the offer price is less than $9. In fact, if oversubscription leads to pro rata rationing, the break-even price is $8.58 per share.[8] But this is still more than pessimistic institutional investors are willing to pay. So if the price is set at $8.58 per share and institutional investors are pessimistic, either the offering must be scaled back to the maximum retail demand of 700,000 shares or the firm's bank must be prepared to carry 300,000 shares in its own portfolio. Not an attractive choice, but it's the best the issuing firm can hope for.

If the bank knew whether institutional investors were optimistic or pessimistic, it could do better for the issuing firm on average by setting a high price in response to optimism and a low price in response to pessimism. The problem with this strategy is that if institutional investors understand that pessimism will yield a lower price, they have an incentive to feign pessimism even when they are optimistic about the firm's valuation. So if bookbuilding or any other mechanism for polling investors is to be effective, it must pay for institutional investors to be honest. This is the incentive-compatibility principle.

Simply put, an institutional investor must expect to gain more from claiming optimism (that V_{high} = $10) than pessimism (that V_{low} = $8). If the investor's rewards derive from share allocations, then algebraically, incentive compatibility means setting the offer price, P, and the share allocation, A, so that

$$A_{high}(\$10 - P_{high}) \geq A_{low}(\$10 - P_{low})$$

This inequality just says that the payoff to providing an optimistic indication of interest must be no less than the payoff to providing a pessimistic indication. Because any benefits accruing to institutional investors claiming to be optimistic come at the expense of the issuing firm, the bank's goal should be to minimize the benefits from claiming to be pessimistic. Unfortunately, the bank's options are limited. Institutional investors who are genuinely pessimistic will cooperate only if P_{low} is no more than \$8.[9] The best the bank can do then is to keep allocations to institutional investors who claim to be pessimistic (A_{low}) at a minimum. Here that means granting retail investors priority, leaving only 300,000 shares for institutional investors.

Conversely, a large share allocation (A_{high}) amplifies the incentive to be forthright with an optimistic forecast. Therefore, the bank should allocate the entire offering to institutional investors if they provide optimistic indications. This reasoning implies that the bank should commit to the following strategy on behalf of the issuing firm:

- If institutional investors claim to be pessimistic, price the offering at \$8 per share and allocate 700,000 shares to retail investors and the remainder to institutional investors.

- If institutional investors claim to be optimistic, allocate the entire offering (1,000,000 shares) to institutional investors at a price of P_{high} per share.

The highest possible value of P_{high} for which optimistic institutional investors will be honest is the level at which the algebraic expression of incentive compatibility is satisfied with equality, or

$$1{,}000{,}000\,(\$10 - P_{\text{high}}) = 300{,}000(\$10 - \$8)$$

Thus, institutional investors must expect the bank to set P_{high} equal to \$9.40 in response to an institutional show of optimism.

Because a show of optimism means that the fair value for the deal is \$10 per share, the strategy's success depends on oversight from an intermediary able to make a credible commitment to pricing the deal at \$9.40 even after learning this information. This "discount" is the quid pro quo for accurate indications of interest. It would be difficult for an issuing firm to make this commitment because once it learns that investors are optimistic, it will be tempted to hold out for a higher price, particularly if it doesn't plan to raise additional capital in the near future. But if investors expect this to happen, they'll refuse to play the game in the first place. An intermediary adds value by acting as a credible guardian of the rules of the game. Whereas the issuing firm may have little to lose by reneging on an implicit commitment to discount its shares, a bank doing the same would damage its credibility with investors and therefore its ability to represent future offerings.

The expected offer price of $8.70 (i.e., the simple average of $9.40 and $8.00) reflects the value of this commitment. In other words, the expected offer price under this strategy is 1.4 percent higher than the $8.58 expected share price had investors not been induced to reveal their perspective on the offering. We should emphasize that this is an *expected* benefit. A firm that learns of investor optimism might regret having its price set at $9.40 per share rather than $10.00, but really should not. Investors will only reveal optimism if they expect adherence to the implicit rules of the game. If they do not expect such adherence the best the issuing firm can hope for, on average, is to raise $8.58 per share. In other words, engaging an intermediary with a longer horizon eliminates any temptation the issuing firm may have to misbehave after the fact, and in doing so makes it a more attractive counterparty before the fact. This commitment to cooperation raises a firm's expectations for its share offering.

In practice, the degree of interest expressed by investors varies, and it is unlikely that the investor expressing the strongest interest in the issue would be willing to purchase the entire issue. In spite of these caveats, our toy model suggests two keys to a successful bookbuilding effort:

- Maintain a direct link between discounts and the strength and breadth of interest demonstrated during the bookbuilding effort.

- Give allocation priority to investors who provide the strongest indications of interest.

The Real World

A snapshot of the real world suggests that banks do follow the rules of thumb suggested by our toy model. First, because communicating with the entire investor community has, until recently, not been feasible, banks should focus most of their attention on the most influential investors. Institutional investors as a class more nearly fit this description if for no other reason than that they commit far more capital to research than individual investors. Indeed, virtually the entire IPO process is tailored to the interests of institutional investors.

Similarly, institutional investors are the primary source for indications of interest. Most people assume that share allocations strongly favor institutional investors, but we have little hard evidence. The available evidence indicates that on average institutional investors receive about two-thirds of IPO shares.[10] For example, figure 4-1 shows that for thirty IPOs managed by Goldman Sachs in 1993, institutional allocations ranged from 53 percent to 82 percent. On average, institutional investors received 68 percent of the shares offered.

Second, the model suggests linking investor allocations to the degree of optimism evidenced by indications of interest. Here again, the facts are consistent with the prescription—banks favor investors whose bids are more informative.[11]

Viewed in isolation, these characteristics suggest that banks and institutional investors benefit at the expense of retail investors and issuing firms. The true litmus test for the model is whether the predicted link between discounts and the level of interest holds in the marketplace. Goods usually are sold at discount when there is weak demand, and at a premium when demand is strong. But if discounted share allocations are the currency for acquiring information, the opposite should be true. Discounting deals that elicit strong demand and allocating the bulk of shares to investors who indicate the strongest interest provides a reward for those sharing valuable information. On the other hand, responding to disinterest with aggressive pricing destroys incentives for understatement. Institutional investors benefit little from fully priced shares. Using retail demand as a fallback can eliminate any remaining benefits.

On this point, the evidence is substantial and consistent. Hot IPOs generally are subject to larger first-day returns, or discounts from their fair value, than are cold IPOs. Figure 4-2 shows the link between initial returns and investor interest as it appears in the same thirty Goldman-

---

Figure 4-1   Institutional Allocations for Thirty Goldman Sachs–
Managed IPOs

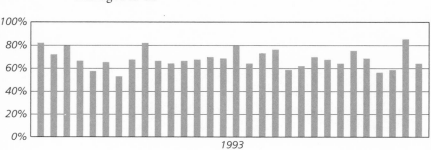

Figure 4-2   Initial Returns and Investor Interest

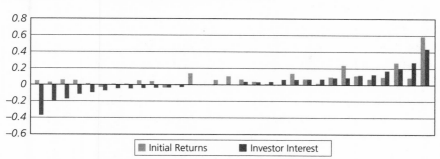

Figure 4-2 shows the link between initial returns and investor interest for the same thirty Goldman Sachs–managed IPOs that are shown in figure 4-1.

managed IPOs shown in figure 4-1. Here we've followed the approach of most researchers by measuring investor interest by the difference between the offer price and the price (range) suggested in the issuer's prospectus. In chapter 3 we suggested that this price range reflects the bank's best guess at a fair price prior to assessing market demand conditions. An offer price at the upper end or above the suggested price range typically reflects strong interest among institutional investors. Likewise, an offer price that is low relative to the suggested price range suggests weak interest. Thus we measure investor interest by the percentage difference between the offer price and the midpoint of the suggested price range.

At one extreme we see the maximum initial return of 57.5 percent associated with the offer price being set about 43 percent above the midpoint of the suggested price range. At the other extreme, the minimum initial return follows the offer price being set about 36 percent below the midpoint of the suggested price range. Although the relationship is not hard and fast, in general larger initial returns follow higher offer prices and smaller initial returns follow lower offer prices relative to the midpoint of the suggested price range. In other words, discounts follow our prescription for direct linkage to the show of interest among institutional investors.[12]

Taken together, figures 4-1 and 4-2 suggest that institutional investors benefit disproportionately from discounted offerings but also receive large allocations of fully priced offerings. The small initial returns on weak offerings probably do little to distort investor incentives.

But why are institutional investors such willing participants when profit opportunities are scarce? A likely explanation is that banks have sufficient leverage to prevent investors from skimming the cream from among the many IPOs brought to market. After all, IPOs far more frequently show positive initial returns than negative initial returns. Moreover, the positive returns are considerably larger on average. Therefore membership in an investment bank's network of regular IPO investors should be profitable even if investors participate indiscriminately.

The potential for persuading investors to approach IPOs as a bundle rather than as independent events introduces a new dimension to the design of an incentive-compatible mechanism. In essence, the bank's dealings with investors become a repeated game—a setting in which cooperation is more likely to thrive.[13] If investors expect future IPO participation to be profitable, the threat of losing the future income stream becomes a powerful inducement to cooperate in the exchange of information—so powerful, in fact, that investors might participate in a particular offering on terms that would be unacceptable in a one-time-only transaction. Thus, bundling current and future offerings and requiring all-or-nothing participation from investors reduces the cost of extracting information from investors and therefore lowers the issuing firm's cost of capital.

The last way in which the traditional IPO platform favors institutional investors, or discriminates against retail investors, is in the conduct of secondary market price stabilization of IPOs. The antimanipulation provisions of the Securities Exchange Act of 1934 permit banks to prop up an IPO's secondary market price in the face of heavy selling pressure. The act envisions this form of price manipulation as a legitimate means for banks to lay off the risk of distribution for a firm commitment IPO. However, the bulk of the evidence suggests that price stabilization takes place well beyond the now very brief period during which distribution of shares occurs.

Banks use a variety of means for absorbing or retarding the immediate sale of IPO shares. One important tool for preventing flipping is the *penalty bid*. Penalty bids typically require members of the IPO's selling syndicate to forfeit any fees they received for allocating shares to investors who flip their shares in the secondary market. Faced with the loss of selling fees, members of the selling syndicate threaten to exclude from future deals investors who flip current share allocations. Thus penalty bids cut to the heart of the matter by seeking to prevent price pressure before it occurs.

Of course, not all investors are equal. Any bank would find it difficult to impose its will on the most influential institutional investors, or even want to. Remember, these influential investors are the most valuable sources of information; their reward for sharing this information might include freedom from penalty bids. To see why this might be beneficial to investors, we need only recognize that banks grant put options to investors receiving initial allocations when they commit to stabilizing the secondary market. Investors can resell their allocations at the offer price if they choose, but they do not have to. Put options are valuable to investors, just as are opportunities for earning large initial returns on IPOs, and so investors should be willing to have the bank substitute one for the other in structuring the compensation package offered in exchange for their information. In other words, when a bank commits to stabilizing the secondary market price for an IPO, it provides initial investors with a package containing put options along with their share allocations.[14]

These options are an attractive substitute for discounting because banks can distribute them in a more discriminatory fashion. SEC regulations require that all investors pay the same offer price for IPO shares, so banks can only discriminate in the number of shares allocated to an investor. However, there may be instances in which the bank would prefer not to allocate discounted shares to a particular investor but needs that investor for a successful distribution. This is particularly true of retail investors, who contribute little information but often receive discounted share allocations. Banks effectively recapture some of the reward by imposing a penalty on, or withholding a valuable put option from, these investors. Here again, the evidence supports our prescription.[15]

Unless you have serious reservations about the correspondence between theory and evidence we've just described, the mechanism design perspective provides a performance benchmark for the traditionally human-capital-intensive approach to securities pricing and distribution. More important, mechanism design theory provides a blueprint for replacing human intermediaries with machines. WR Hambrecht + Co. and OffRoad Capital both followed this blueprint in the design of their Internet pricing and distribution platform; we'll examine their interpretation of the instructions a bit more carefully in chapter 5. But as we've emphasized here and in chapter 3, rules and standards are only as good as the perceived commitment to their enforcement. Because trust is so crucial to this perception, we spend the remainder of this chapter examining the formation and preservation of trust and the organizational demands it places on intermediaries.

Reputation and Relationships

According to J.P. Morgan, "character," more than any other quality, was the cement that bound together early merchant banking networks.[16] Morgan had many critics, but he spoke his mind and was a man of his word. Thinking of financial intermediaries as sponsors of incentive-compatible mechanisms draws into sharp focus the importance of communicating expectations and standing by them. The rules that define an incentive-compatible mechanism are meaningless if the sponsoring intermediary cannot be trusted to abide by and enforce them. This is not to say that intermediary behavior must be deterministic and thereby rule out human judgment. Unpredictability can be a source of leverage for intermediaries if everyone at least understands the potential consequences.[17]

Of course, if contracts addressing all possible contingencies could be written *and* enforced (what economists refer to as *complete contracts*), trust or a reputation for fair dealing would buy nothing more (or less) than the respect of one's peers. But if complete contracts were feasible, an intermediary would be unnecessary in the first place—people would contract their way out of problems such as the prisoner's dilemma.[18] In the real world of incomplete contracts, we can't specify all contingencies; even if we could, contracting is costly and characterized by rapidly diminishing marginal returns. Enforcement likewise is costly and in many cases uncertain. Under these circumstances, a reputation for fair dealing can substitute for a contract. This is the fundamental source of value in establishing a reputation.[19] For information intermediaries, this is true regardless of the quality of the communication network—it is the veracity, not the clarity, of information that is in question. It doesn't help to be able to hear a pin drop at the other end of a telephone connection if you can't be sure that, in fact, it is a pin being dropped.

In financial markets we often associate a reputation for fair dealing with an organization. Although there are important exceptions that we discuss later, names such as "Goldman Sachs" or "New York Stock Exchange" carry more weight than the names of individual employees and members. Individuals make commitments in the organization's name, but the organization ultimately is responsible for satisfying these obligations. An organization's reputation is thus a complex weave of the good (and bad) behavior of past and current members, and even the expected behavior of future members. At root, these interpersonal relations between representatives of the organization and outside parties are the basis for trust and its preservation. Reference to an organization's "relationships" provides a shorthand for these interpersonal connections with the outside world.

Financial relationships involve a series of transactions embodying a variety of products, services, and information and depend on a sort of institutional memory focused on making the most of a series of transactions rather than squeezing the last penny from individual transactions. This might even mean accepting a loss on one transaction with the expectation that it will be more than compensated in the future. As the old sales adage goes, sometimes the best way to win business is to lose business.[20]

The management of a financial relationship often becomes the responsibility of one or a few individuals. As such, the individual's human capital embodies the relationship. This is a double-edged sword. On the one hand, an interest in protecting one's human capital enhances the credibility of the relationship manager. If the relationship manager understands that she cannot simply walk away from a client's problem, she is more likely to make every effort to avoid problems with the client in the first place.[21] Moreover, if the relationship manager looks out for the client's interests, the client will more freely share the strategic information the intermediary organization seeks. This clearly is good for the client, but also, at least in part, is to the benefit of the organization.

On the other hand, the tendency of a relationship to attach to one or a few individuals diminishes the incentive for others within an organization to make investments that further enhance the relationship and therefore the organization's reputation. The problem is that human capital is mobile. It is quite common, for example, for senior investment bankers to leave their current firm, taking with them both members of their team and the client relationships they maintained. In an extreme case, Bruce Wasserstein and Joseph Perrella walked away from First Boston's top-ranked M&A business in 1988 and virtually overnight

First Boston fell from the ranks of serious contenders for new M&A business.

Managing relationships, and therefore developing and preserving reputation, is a balancing act. When the relationship manager's interests are too nearly aligned with the client's it is difficult to persuade senior management and product specialists to invest resources in the relationship. Conversely, gaining the client's trust is difficult when the manager's interests are closely aligned with his organization's. Over the next few chapters we examine these organizational considerations in greater detail. For now, recognize that the trust so crucial to the success of an intermediary organization has its roots in interpersonal relationships. This key asset of the intermediary organization is thus a form of human capital, and managing such assets presents a variety of problems in its own right.

The Jekyll-and-Hyde character of information impedes its exchange. On the one hand, its joint-use capacity cries out for sharing. But sharing information undermines incentives for its production or exposes the originator to exploitation because, once shared, information is difficult to control. On the other hand, rivalry encourages investment in information production but undermines sharing. Keep in mind as we proceed that the same argument often applies to information that costs nothing to produce. For all practical purposes, personal preferences and characteristics are costless to develop and can be beneficial if shared. But widespread dissemination of this information can be costly—at minimum yielding an avalanche of direct marketing material. Thus the argument cuts directly to the debate over privacy on the Internet.

Intermediaries promote trade in information by balancing these competing interests. In this chapter we've attempted to outline precisely how intermediaries go about performing this balancing act. From the perspective of mechanism design theory, intermediaries commit to collecting strategic information from potential trading partners, maintaining its privacy, and then establishing and enforcing ground rules for its best use. But once we identify these rules, in principle we can displace the human intermediary by having the rules executed by a machine *if* credibility for the mechanical process can be established and preserved.

This perspective suggests that the intermediary's competitive advantage lies not so much in identifying the "right" rules as in making a credible commitment to their enforcement. After all, rules for promoting trade in information are themselves just a form of information. Once made explicit, preventing others from competing in their use is difficult and undermines incentives for their development in the first place. In other words, information intermediaries struggle with the same problems that face the parties they serve. Traditionally, financial intermediaries were successful in bundling the design and execution of rules and their credibility in the human capital of key individuals, but technological advances are shifting the boundary between human judgment and codifiable rules or explicit knowledge. Chapter 5 examines the tension between human capital and information technology and sets the stage for understanding its influence on the evolving organizational structure of information intermediaries.

5

THE DEATH OF THE BANKER?

Bank of America Corporation said its move to eliminate 9,000 to 10,000 jobs, or 7% of its work force, by next summer, will save $550 million a year . . . it will spend $70 million more than planned on electronic commerce systems the rest of this year.

The Wall Street Journal, July 31, 2000

THE TRADITIONAL investment banking platform bundled the functions of disseminating information to clients and investors and eliciting, aggregating, and storing feedback from them. Information was exchanged by word of mouth in the context of long-standing personal relationships, and people formed the physical infrastructure underlying investment banking products and services. Now information technology dominates the physical infrastructure of financial markets. Recent experience in online securities brokerage suggests that in the capacity of information dissemination, the traditional banker's demise is imminent. Modern information technology simply provides a lower-cost and more reliable means of disseminating, aggregating, and storing information.

What remains of the human dimension in financial intermediation reflects subtle human behavior that promotes information sharing but eludes codification. Michael Polanyi argues that codified or *explicit* knowledge is useless without this *tacit* knowledge or human judgment.[1] But in chapter 4 we took a step toward separating the two in an investment banking practice traditionally dependent on human judgment. Members of both the new and the old guard are actively exploring this and similar opportunities.

Before we bury traditional investment banking practice, however, we should examine the process of codifying human capital a bit more carefully. In this chapter we'll see that codification has both costs and benefits as well as obvious technological limits. In some areas of investment banking, information technology is displacing human capital at a rapid pace and will continue to do so. In others, such as corporate restructuring and advisory services, displacement of the traditional platform remains unlikely in the foreseeable future. However, the increasing capacity for unbundling what now are mundane tasks from those requiring higher-order human judgment will have a profound effect on industry structure. To jump the gun a bit, we believe not only that reports of the banker's demise are premature but that some bankers could, in the absence of new regulatory constraints, regain the power and visibility of their nineteenth- and early-twentieth-century predecessors.

Intellectual Capital: A Taxonomy

Before we examine the changing role of intellectual capital in financial markets, it is useful to develop a consistent language for describing the various forms that intellectual capital can take.[2] All intellectual capital derives from human creativity and so begins as human capital. The information embodied in human capital is valuable when it suggests a set of actions that create value either by reacting to or altering the environment. Some of this information can be written down or codified.[3] This explicit element of human capital has the potential for being disembodied from its originator and put to use by any person or machine capable of following instructions. The remainder of human capital is poorly defined, or tacit, and does not lend itself to codification; it is therefore valuable only in the hands of its originator or originators.

We might think of tacit knowledge as taking two forms in financial firms. The first encompasses the unwritten rules of internal engagement among the members of an organization. In some instances, tacit knowledge is distributed broadly throughout the organization. In others, key individuals, or *culture carriers*, embody and transfer this tacit knowledge through their interactions with others. The second form of tacit knowledge comprises similar rules of engagement with the outside world. Reputation and trust formed around these rules of engagement cement client relationships. Client relationships and the information they embody, in turn, are central to carrying out intermediary functions.

Historically, it was difficult to codify, and therefore separate from their originators, the relationships defining a bank's information network—perhaps its key intangible asset. The wide recognition of names such as Rothschild, Barings, Morgan, Baker, Schiff, Gould, and so on, beyond financial circles speaks to this point. In contrast, with the exception of Michael Milken, it's difficult to identify a modern-day banker who so captured the public's imagination. This admittedly simplistic measure suggests that modern banks have been successful in converting human capital into intangible assets that more nearly attach to the firm at large.[4]

As we suggested in chapter 2, the centrality of reputation to intermediaries derives from the experience-good nature of information and the impracticality of writing and enforcing complete contracts. In chapter 4 we emphasized the role reputation plays in supporting incentive-compatible mechanisms for information sharing. Although we examine its development in some detail in chapter 7, it is worth emphasizing now that reputation in its various forms defines the frontier of tacit and explicit knowledge in financial firms and intermediary firms generally. We know a reputable person or organization when we see one, and we know that a reputation is worthy of protection. We might even have some ideas as to how it can be developed. But separating a reputation from an individual or collection of individuals (i.e., codifying that reputation) and transferring it is a far more complicated matter. Failure to do so guarantees the demise of a reputation with its originator. The abundance of financial intermediaries whose lineage can be traced through several generations speaks to the feasibility, if not the means, of transferring reputation.

Codification of human capital produces an *intellectual asset*. Codification of information diminishes control by the individual in whom it was previously embodied because he or she can no longer prevent others from using the information by simply not sharing it. However, codification does not prevent the originator from making use of the information, perhaps even in another capacity. If simultaneous use of the information is nonrival, then the conversion from human capital to intellectual asset improves social welfare at no cost to the originator. But if the value of information largely is strategic, rivalry in the use of an intellectual asset undermines incentives to invest in information production in the first place unless some capacity for exclusive use enables the originator to capture a fair return on investment.

Ownership, or the capacity to exclude others from using information, depends on the establishment of intellectual property rights. This might occur through any one or a combination of trade secret, copyright, or patent laws, in which case we refer to the intellectual asset as a piece of *intellectual property*. By this definition, financial intermediaries maintain little intellectual property. In the only systematic analysis to date, Josh Lerner of Harvard Business School recently identified only 445 financial patents awarded between January 1971 and the end of February 2000.[5] By comparison, IBM was granted 2,778 of the 169,153 total patents awarded in 1999 alone.[6] Despite the disparity in absolute numbers, Lerner observes that during the 1990s interest among financial intermediaries in patenting their ideas and practices skyrocketed. However, as we mentioned earlier, the enforceability of financial patents remains an open question.

In summary, all intellectual capital has its roots in human capital. Some elements of human capital, those amenable to codification, evolve into intellectual assets. Among intellectual assets, intellectual property is the subset over which the capacity for exclusive use is reestablished. At the extremes of this continuum, property rights over intellectual capital are strong. In the first case, the originator controls whether to share his human capital. In the second, the state enforces limits on the use of intellectual capital. The real action takes place in the middle ground where intellectual capital takes the form of an intellectual asset, either because it is in transition to intellectual property or because establishing property rights is too costly or technically infeasible. Traditionally, intermediary functions depended heavily on human capital—banking was more nearly an art than a science. Advances in theory and information technology are shifting the balance, however. As property rights weaken with the disembodiment of human capital, financial intermediaries are reconsidering both strategy and organization.

The Codification of Information Dissemination

The impact of information technology thus far is most profound in functions involving little more than information dissemination. Retail securities brokerage provides a particularly striking example of the pattern (see Box 5-1).

Box 5-1 The Thundering Herd Brought to Market

In little more than five years, over 5 million retail investors have opened online brokerage accounts (as of March 2000). The number of securities firms offering online trading to their customers increased from thirty-seven at the end of 1997 to 160 by July 1999. About 500,000 trades now take place online each day. This number represents approximately 37 percent of all retail trades of equities and options at an average commission of about $15.75 per trade. Compare this to the $53 to $55 per trade commission charged by online firms in 1996; these were already far below commissions of $200 per trade that bundled investment advice with execution—a common pricing strategy for full-service firms—typically paid by full-service brokerage clients. If we take a look at the recent experiences of Charles Schwab, the largest online securities brokerage, and Merrill Lynch, it brings the consequences of this shift into sharp relief.

Merrill Lynch, traditionally among the largest and most powerful retail operations on Wall Street, maintained a herd of 17,000 retail brokers (out of 65,000 total employees) in 1997. In the same year, Charles Schwab's market capitalization hovered in the neighborhood of $10 billion, less than half that of Merrill Lynch. Charles Schwab, a market leader in discount brokerage with 7,000 retail brokers, was just beginning the transition from telephone discount brokerage to online brokerage, having already de-emphasized the aggressive selling of research and advisory services that Wall Street brokers had for so long grazed on.

Charles Schwab's online unit, *eSchwab*, ran in parallel with traditional discount brokerage until January 1998, when the firm consolidated operations around an online platform. By December 28, 1998, Charles Schwab had closed the market capitalization gap with Merrill Lynch when its $25.5 billion market capitalization topped Merrill Lynch's $25.4 billion (Charles Schwab currently maintains a market capitalization of $25.6 billion, compared to Merrill Lynch's $52.8 billion).

Initially, the full-service brokers, who had the most to lose to a technology that enabled unbundling of these services from execution, countered the competitive threat by bundling trade execution with a new menu of "financial planning" services. But by 1999, with investors apparently not persuaded of the benefits of

(continued)

the new services on offer, John "Launny" Steffens, the head of Merrill Lynch's brokerage operations, felt compelled to announce that "the do-it-yourself model of investing, centered on Internet trading, should be regarded as a serious threat to Americans' financial lives."[7] Setting aside this deep concern, Merrill Lynch introduced its own online brokerage service, *Merrill Lynch Direct*, in December 1999.

The Online Road Show

In our running case study of the IPO market, the most prominent example of information technology providing for the separation of human judgment from mundane tasks arises in the context of the road show. The issuing firm's investment bank orchestrates road shows featuring the issuing firm's management team for the benefit of institutional investors. In theory, road show presentations should offer little insight beyond that available in the prospectus filed with the SEC. The prospectus is meant to contain the information pertinent to an investor's review of the firm's offering and therefore determines the issuer's liability in disputes over the accuracy of information provided to potential investors.[8] Statements that deviate from the substance of the prospectus risk being interpreted by the SEC as having been made for the purpose of stimulating market interest. A firm's legal counsel generally advises management to steer clear of such statements because the SEC can then use its discretion to delay the effective date of the offering while the firm prepares a revision to the prospectus.

In practice, during road shows management occasionally shares information, particularly with regard to earnings estimates, that does not appear in the prospectus. Retail investors, who rarely are included in road shows, therefore claim a disadvantage in their evaluation of IPOs. Broadband Internet access should diminish the technical arguments for exclusivity, but differences in the rules bearing on written and oral communication have thus far blunted challenges to the traditional road show. As early as 1996, firms such as NetRoadshow began petitioning the SEC for permission to conduct online road shows. To date, the SEC has responded with a series of no-action letters outlining parameters within which firms can act without interference from the Commission. Most recently, the SEC issued a no-action letter to

Charles Schwab that would allow participation in online road shows by individuals, but only those with $500,000 in investment assets or extensive trading experience.

Established banks were slow to adopt this technological advance but more recently have used it as a complement to the traditional platform.[9] The demand for Internet road shows is growing rapidly, and banks now routinely schedule online presentations in conjunction with the traditional road show. If nothing else, less time spent marshaling senior management through repetitive presentations to analysts and fund managers permits greater leveraging of the banker's judgment on behalf of the issuing firm. Information technology will continue to displace human capital in similar functions that involve little more than information transmission, even deeply entrenched functions, because it vastly extends the breadth and precision of information dissemination and releases human judgment for higher value-added functions.

Codification of Storage and Retrieval

In part, the financial intermediary's heavy dependence on human capital reflected not so much an inability to write down or make knowledge explicit as it did a limited capacity for nonhuman storage and retrieval of information. Data warehousing and mining are buzzwords of the day, but the concepts are not really new to financial markets. In the traditional investment banking platform, for example, individual bond traders warehoused in their own memory data regarding the interplay between past market conditions and the bonds they traded. They mined the data and applied its implications when their experience or judgment guided future trading decisions. Likewise, stock exchange specialists have long memories for those who exploit their willingness to quote sharper prices, and bankers dealing IPOs routinely exclude investors or other bankers who have broken implicit rules of engagement in the past.

This distributed data warehousing and mining model reflected the technology of the day. Even if many traders agreed to record their experience in a common language, rapid retrieval of relevant information in summary form—that is, data mining—would have been difficult and time consuming in the absence of digital storage and retrieval capacity. But distributed storage was costly because it inhibited sharing of information among traders. In other words, it did not take full advantage of the nonrival nature of information within the organization.

Recent advances in digital storage and retrieval are making feasible the sweeping together of decentralized knowledge within an organization to provide for broader application. For example, the management consultancy McKinsey & Co. maintains an internal information market that supports contribution of "practice" documents by over 70 percent of the firm's consultants and internal exchange of nearly 5,000 copies of these documents weekly. Similarly, John Seely Brown and Paul Duguid suggest that Xerox's Eureka database, which collects, vets, and refines tips from sales representatives, has already saved the corporation $100 million.[10] In short, advances in storage and retrieval technology are driving codification of what previously was narrowly applied human capital.[11]

Feasibility implies neither straightforward codification of data storage and retrieval nor assured success. In fact, Brown and Duguid argue that there is an inherent tension between coordinated use of information (process) and the unstructured environment in which ideas blossom through experimentation (practice). This tension leads to a hard balancing act:

> Lean too much toward practice, and you may get new ideas bubbling up all over the place, but you'll lack the structure to harness them. (And in the modern business world, worthwhile ideas that you don't harness end up in your competitors' hands.) Lean too much toward process, and you get lots of structure but too little freedom of movement to strike that initial spark.[12]

Perhaps the greater threat in codifying information retrieval and storage capacity is destruction or loss of information and knowledge embodied in existing networks and communities of practice. For example, both Wit Capital and WR Hambrecht + Co. built capacity for monitoring and storing bidding and secondary market trading behavior into their IPO platforms. The framework developed in chapter 4 suggests that such information can be put to good use in extracting private information from investors. Brown and Duguid suggest that inflexibility in the storage format might compromise the quality of such information going forward. But more problematic is the dilemma facing well-established banks considering a transition to an electronic platform. If the electronic platform substitutes for traditional, informal practice, then what remains tacit in the marketing and distribution of IPOs is at risk of being lost. Worse yet, a productive team of bankers recognizing that its human capital will soon be captured or otherwise devalued will simply defect. Wasserstein and Parella leaving Credit Suisse First Boston and Frank Quattrone and his technology banking team subsequently joining CSFB upon leaving Deutsche Bank are just two examples of what has become commonplace within the industry of late. Regardless of the role of information technology (or the lack thereof) in these particular defections, the capacity for codifying what previously was human capital creates new tension between the human capitalists and the organizations in which they reside.

Advances in Theory and the Codification of Information Processing

Just as digital storage and retrieval capacity is exploding, so too the apparent steadfastness of Moore's Law—the doubling of microchip processing capacity approximately every eighteen months—is driving nonhuman information-processing capacity forward at a similarly rapid rate. The last forty years have also witnessed extraordinary advances in the economic theory of financial markets. Advances in processing capacity and economic theory work hand-in-glove to amplify one another's effects. As portfolio theory and financial engineering become standard fare in the training of every M.B.A., the computer has become invaluable to traders, market makers, and money managers. These areas of practice are vastly more systematic as decisions increasingly are guided by theory embodied in computer code. In the extreme, decision making and execution are entirely automated in practices such as program trading. And as processing power increases, the capacity for monitoring and coordinating trading in real time across many different marketplaces amplifies the value of the codified theory.

Recent experiments with the IPO process owe much to simultaneous developments in processing capacity and the theory of auctions. In 1961 William Vickrey reached the remarkable conclusion that under fairly general circumstances, English, Dutch, first-price sealed-bid, and second-price sealed-bid auctions are equivalent in both the bidding strategies they induce and the expected revenues they generate for the seller.[13] Vickrey's analysis, for which he was awarded the 1996

Nobel Prize for economics (along with James A. Mirrlees), opened the floodgates to a body of research explaining when and why different auction rules alter expected revenues. This example of what Daniel Bell refers to as *codified theoretical knowledge* has few equals within the social sciences. Over the last twenty years, the theory has found application in auctions for everything from radio frequencies to mineral rights.[14] Now we see its application taken for granted in the online auctioning of everything from used tools to airline tickets. Even *The Economist*, the reliable voice of reason in the business press, recently joined the ranks of the believers with its recent pronouncement that we've entered "the heyday of the auction."[15]

In most instances, applications of auction theory involve indivisible goods for which there are relatively few bidders. By contrast, securities offerings represent fractional, identical claims on a single firm's assets and typically are purchased by thousands of individuals and institutions. Until very recently, it would have been quite costly, if not impossible, to entertain bids from all interested parties. Traditional bookbuilding practices relaxed this technological constraint by seeking the opinions of a relatively narrow but influential group of institutional investors who represented the interests of many smaller investors.

For retail investors collectively, the rise of the institutional investor was a good thing. Mutual funds and the like provided access to markets that, for efficiency considerations, otherwise would have been closed to retail investors. But from the perspective of any single retail investor, the informal auction conducted via bookbuilding and similar practices amplifies the voice of institutional investors to the point of drowning out smaller competing bids. The Internet essentially resolves the technological problem of assembling all interested parties at one time and place and providing them with equal capacity for being heard. At minimum, there now seems little reason not to cast a wider net across the investor community. This was the essence of Wit Capital's initial foray into Internet investment banking. However, if we can express the informal, discretionary behaviors that elicit accurate indications of interest from investors as a set of well-defined rules, as our "toy model" in chapter 4 suggested, then there seems to be little preventing even the rules' disembodiment and mechanization. WR Hambrecht's OpenIPO Dutch auction represents the first serious attempt along these lines (see Box 5-2).[16]

Box 5-2 Rules versus Discretion

Traditional discretionary practices and the OpenIPO auction rules are perhaps more similar than they first appear. If nothing else, mechanism design theory has taught us that there are many equally effective means of skinning a cat. In fact, two French economists, Bruno Biais and Anne Marie Faugeron-Crouzet, recently have shown that bookbuilding practices and the auction-like mechanism used for many French IPOs present fundamentally similar incentives to potential investors and therefore should result in similar outcomes—an argument borne out by the data.[17]

The similarities in the incentives created by bookbuilding practices and various auction mechanisms shed light on the fact that the first four OpenIPO auctions exhibited first-day price behavior not unlike that of traditional offerings. But as Bill Hambrecht observed, "We're not trying to get rid of a 15 percent discount. We're trying to get rid of the 50–100 percent discount. . . . I think probably the best answer is to run an auction, run a clearing price and discount, modestly, from that price." Hambrecht's intuition squares with the academic literature that suggests that if the pricing rule is too aggressive, then the incentive to bid aggressively (i.e., to reveal information) in the first place is weakened and that therefore proceeds from the auction might be diminished.[18]

Codification of bookbuilding practices, perhaps along the lines reflected in OpenIPO, offers the potential for a more efficient response to the boom and bust nature of the IPO market. The IPO market in 2000 saw sharp swings in both issuance and performance. Four hundred and twenty-nine IPOs were completed in 2000, but the first half of the year was more vigorous in almost every category. In February, March, and April 2000 alone, more than 350 offerings were filed.[19] However, as one industry source noted, "for a year that began with optimism and confidence, caution and concern became the prevailing sentiment . . . ".[20] In August alone seventy deals (out of 201 for the year) were withdrawn and taken off the table. "By year's end, nearly two-thirds of all IPOs completed in 2000 closed the year trading below their offer price."[21]

The traditional human capital-intensive implementation of book-building does not support rapid scaling up to meet these sudden bursts of demand in the marketplace. In fact, references to backlogs are common in the financial press. Scaling back during cold markets also is difficult. Even with most of their pay coming from year-end bonuses, bankers carry high fixed costs. But laying off bankers during cold markets sacrifices human capital that is difficult to replace in the short run when the inevitable but unpredictable reversal occurs. An OpenIPO-like platform addresses this problem because the marginal costs of rescaling in the face of changing market demand conditions are minimal.

Setting aside the obvious efficiency gains that arise when mechanizing what previously required human judgment, there remains another important dimension to the debate regarding rules versus discretion. Intermediaries work as agents who presumably balance the interests of competing parties. But when granted considerable discretion and lack of transparency, intermediaries have incentive to favor parties from whom it is easier to extract a payback for their efforts. It is widely believed, for example, that first-day price runups in the IPO market reflect, at least in part, corruption arising from investment banker pricing and allocation discretion—recall Hambrecht's concern that OpenIPO could not be introduced alongside existing institutional investor relationships within Hambrecht & Quist. Investment bankers deal regularly with institutional investors but infrequently with firms going public. As a consequence they have incentive to tilt the scales in favor of institutional investors.

The incentive for bankers to place the interests of investors ahead of those of issuing firms is a byproduct of the concentration of power in the hands of a relatively small group of institutional investors. But the technical hurdles to investors speaking as individuals rather than through the common voice of an institutional representative are few and rapidly shrinking. The rules-based technologies developed by Wit Capital and WR Hambrecht + Co. provide means of dividing and conquering the institutional investor network at the core of this agency problem.

Surely there is merit in the argument that investment bankers, and intermediaries generally, use their discretion to favor some clients over others. In fact, this bias could be to an intermediary's benefit even in the long run, despite its corrosive effects on the intermediary's integrity, if potential competitors face serious barriers to entry. But is anything lost in the translation of discretionary practices to rules-based systems? Almost certainly there is, if for no other reason than it is unlikely that a discretionary practice can be fully reduced to a set of rules. If the approximation is close, however, efficiency and integrity might favor rules over discretion.

More serious is the risk that rules-based systems will adapt less effectively to a changing environment. OpenIPO might fare well against a bookbuilding effort under the range of circumstances envisioned by its underlying set of rules, but should issuing firms turn over the controls to a machine knowing that market conditions might arise for which the machine has no good response? In other words, where the intermediary's role is poorly defined or more fluid, rules are a less effective substitute for discretion. In this regard it is noteworthy that WR Hambrecht exercised discretion in pricing Andover.Net's IPO below the clearing price established by OpenIPO. Can WR Hambrecht have the best of both worlds? If the primary benefit of the online auction is its relative efficiency, then perhaps it can. But if discretion is sacrificed in the name of integrity, any deviation from the rules puts the firm on a slippery slope.

We'll return to this question later in the chapter, but for the moment we can sum things up by recognizing that the boundary between explicit and tacit knowledge even in functions involving higher-level reasoning clearly is shifting. Electronic auctions and clearing networks, program trading, financial engineering and recent financial market applications of expert systems, neural networks, and autonomous agents ("bots") reflect a confluence of advances in theory and machine processing power that show few signs of leveling off soon.

Collateral Consequences of Codifying Human Capital

The preceding discussion of the conversion of human capital into intellectual assets suggests at least three primary consequences:

- Codification unbundles human judgment from mundane tasks.
- Codification of intellectual capital provides for wider use and larger-scale application.
- Codification commoditizes previously monopolized assets.

Each has important collateral effects that we now explore in greater detail.

Codification Increases the Supply of Human Capital

By definition, human judgment or tacit knowledge is not scalable beyond the processing capacity of the originator. Unless the best use of tacit knowledge is always in conjunction with a particular form of explicit knowledge, having the two remain bundled in their originator's human capital makes poor use of tacit knowledge. For example, traders forced to attend to both mundane and complex trades do not make the most of their judgment. Trading support systems that handle mundane transactions free judgment for the transactions where it adds greater value. Generally, advances in theory and information technology that promote codification of human capital unbundle explicit and tacit knowledge. Unbundling of tacit and explicit knowledge amplifies the value of judgment by freeing it for application to its best use (see Box 5-3). Consequently, codification increases the relative supply of the truly scarce resource—human judgment.

Codification Amplifies the Value of Intellectual Capital

Intellectual capital locked in the mind of its originator may better serve the originator's private interests, but at considerable social cost. Application by the originator is physically limited by the number of hours in the day and by his or her imagination. When knowledge is codified, its nonrival character permits a larger scale and wider scope of application. Wider use also promotes efficiency by way of standardization. Finally, wide use of intellectual capital can promote the critical mass necessary for the generation of increasing returns to scale or network effects. In these ways, codification amplifies the value of *existing* intellectual capital to society at large.

Codification Promotes Competition

Explicit knowledge that remains uncodified provides its originator with monopoly power over the asset. The ability to exclude others from its use can have the effect of making a relatively mundane but not widely known element of knowledge quite valuable to the originator at the expense of social benefits gained from wider use. Although simultaneous

---

Box 5-3 Amplifying Human Judgment

Vic Simone, managing director for fixed-income e-commerce at Goldman Sachs, estimates that bond dealers traditionally have spent about 60 to 80 percent of their time and resources on information dissemination and order execution. Simone expects that with Goldman Sachs's new e-commerce initiative (outlined in chapter 6), 70 to 80 percent of their time and resources will be freed for more human capital-intensive and higher value-added activities such as new content creation and relationship management.

---

use of explicit knowledge by someone other than the originator does not prevent the originator from its continued use, it can diminish the benefits derived by the originator. If applications for the knowledge are sufficiently narrow as to present a zero-sum game, any benefits derived by copycats come at the expense of the originator. Thus, codification of explicit knowledge can diminish its private value while increasing its social value.

In financial markets and more generally, it is often the case that the application of intellectual capital is not a zero-sum game. The potential benefits from broad application of an idea may therefore warrant constraints on the originator's ability to control its use in the first place. Intellectual property law in the United States recognizes a need to balance the originator's interests with those of society at large by granting exclusive rights to intellectual property for only a limited time. Patent law only permits control over narrow applications. "Fair use" and "first sale" doctrines limit control from the outset. In most respects, it appears that this body of law, in the United States at least, strikes a useful balance.

Some observers are concerned that recent technological advances will upset this balance. On the one hand, Lawrence Lessig suggests that advances in information technology will permit the originator to maintain more control than is socially beneficial as the cost of metering and billing for use of information distributed over the Internet diminishes.[22] Mark Stefik, a principal scientist at Xerox PARC, provides a blueprint for a "trusted system" that accomplishes what Lessig has in mind. As he observes, "the use of trusted systems to enforce terms and conditions provides a much finer grain of control than copyright law, and it moves the legal basis of protection toward that of contracts and licenses."[23]

On the other hand, Tom Bethell argues that the embodiment of knowledge in physical forms, along with the priority afforded by intellectual property law, was sufficient to support costly creative effort in the past but may not be in the future. Increasingly, Bethell argues, productive knowledge is not embodied in machinery or other physical goods and so is more difficult to protect. If so, the economic value of knowledge to the originator becomes precarious and the incentive to produce such knowledge is undermined.[24]

Our purpose is not to enter this debate but rather to suggest that financial markets provide a long case history of value being created with knowledge embodied in human rather than nonhuman physical assets. Moreover, financial markets have not in the past benefited substantially from the protections of intellectual property law. Rather, as we argue in chapter 6, financial intermediaries have protected their intellectual capital through a combination of organizational and industry structure. But this delicate balance is also under pressure from technological advances.

Implications for Content Originators, Distributors, and Consumers

The same advances in theory and technology that promote codification also shift the balance of power among originators, distributors, and consumers of knowledge or content. To take a nonfinancial example, consider that the early musician's following was mostly local because transportation was slow and recording technology nonexistent. This limited the scope of application for the musician's human capital and also limited consumers' access to alternative forms of entertainment. As transportation and recording technology advanced, the reach of individual musicians expanded and distribution was separated from production. The unbundling of distribution from the tacit function of composition and performance enabled the musician to leverage his or her human capital and provided consumers with a wider menu of entertainment.

As the recorded music industry evolved, radio and television expanded the scope of distribution. However, the marginal costs of reproduction and distribution remained high because content storage required a physical medium and because there was a growing difficulty in standing out from the crowd. The dominant distributors were large, specialized organizations that exploited scale economies in physical distribution and maintained creative marketing talent. Thus the economics of the industry favored musicians who captured a large share of attentive ears by appealing to a mass market. "Stars" crowded out the "village musician," who survived on demand for live performance or idiosyncratic tastes.[25]

Until recently, the highly idiosyncratic musician, no matter how accomplished, was the proverbial starving artist. But the Internet coupled with digital recording and compression offers virtually costless reproduction and distribution and therefore greater potential for the starving artist to reach would-be patrons directly. The primary cost remains in matching patrons to artists. This is no small consideration in a world of infinite variety and so it might still support a specialized matchmaker or intermediary. But lower technological barriers to entry and reduced distribution costs suggest that the life of the average record producer will be less glamorous. Artists (content providers) and their patrons (content consumers) will benefit accordingly.

This does not mean that intermediaries will disappear or be less well compensated. Rather, modern distribution technology appears tailor-made for extending the reach and power of the most creative intermediaries while sharply diminishing demand for the less creative. In other words, we foresee a world in which major labels and independents coexist, but perhaps in an even more segmented fashion than at present. This is a good thing for the artist because it diminishes the all-or-nothing approach to distribution that often forced those with narrower appeal to compromise their art. For the consumer this implies wider variety. Both will likely benefit economically as fringe intermediaries fall by the wayside.

A similar pattern has emerged in the financial markets in recent years and is most easily seen in the rise of star money managers and analysts, such as Peter Lynch in the 1980s or Mary Meeker during the dot-com boom of the late 1990s. But simultaneous with the rise of stars whose names shone above their firm (the distributor of their content) there has been massive growth in the amount and variety of content. In the United States alone, there are now more than 8,200 mutual funds on offer, representing investment styles that range from simply matching the performance of a market index to those seeking to carve out a unique risk profile through the use of complex derivative trading strategies. Likewise, the number of portfolio managers has risen to over 10,100 with over 7,000 assistants.[26]

Producers of financial content are no longer so dependent on armies of brokers to disseminate their content. This will mean an even wider gap between the returns to content provision and distribution than currently exists. Again, this is not to say that brokers are dead. Rather, there will be fewer, and their aggregate earnings relative to those of content providers will diminish. The reason is simply that pure, physical dissemination of information is now trivial. Distributors will retain power relative to content providers if they maintain a comparative advantage in gaining ever-scarce attention for the content provider. The most likely sources of this comparative advantage will be a capacity for certifying the quality of content and for maintaining large-scale communications and data-processing networks that collect and process feedback regarding consumer preferences. Both functions suggest consolidation as distributors of financial content seek scale economies in information technology and to leverage a brand or reputation through cross selling. The question that remains is whether content origination and distribution can be successfully melded within a single organization as they so often have in the past. This question will be the focus of much of chapters 6 and 7.

The Limits of Codification

Technical limits to further codification of the functions of financial intermediaries have less to do with the state of processing capacity and more to do with our understanding of how financial intermediaries process information. Economic theory has gone far in the areas of relative asset pricing and security design. To a first approximation, financial engineers have clear guidelines for designing securities to meet *well-defined* needs. Likewise, the Black-Scholes formula and its many derivatives and the capital asset pricing model (CAPM) provide portfolio managers and traders with a fairly clear understanding of how these securities ought to be priced relative to one another.[27]

By contrast, corporate finance theory, which seeks to provide the underpinnings for the corporate restructuring and general advisory side of the investment banking business, remains relatively immature.

The typical corporate restructuring is a poorly defined problem with no clear solution or solution strategy. Thus, we should expect corporate finance advisory services to remain dependent on a human-capital intensive technology for the foreseeable future.

Even if corporate restructuring becomes highly systematized, the division of any value created through restructuring will be determined by bargaining among the various interested parties. Mechanism design and auction theories provide general guidelines for carrying out this bargaining, but application to the myriad special cases that face intermediaries daily is less systematized.

We might think of theoretical developments in security design and pricing, mechanism design, and corporate finance as providing the basic tools of the financial intermediary's trade. Independently, each is being codified, albeit at its own pace. How these tools complement one another to promote cooperation in the production and sharing of information is less well understood. For example, take the simple case of a firm that wishes to alter its capital structure. There is almost certainly some element of reasoning among the firm's senior management as to how restructuring will benefit the firm (or perhaps themselves) that will not be apparent to the firm's current and potential funding sources. As we suggested earlier, this generally results in outsiders assuming the worst about management's intentions. Corporate finance theory provides some guidance as to how security design can help to alleviate this problem.

Likewise, it is just as surely the case that management would like to learn more about potential reactions to restructuring before committing to a specific plan. We've seen in the case of the IPO, at least, how such information might be extracted from the marketplace; it's probably safe to assume that most of what we've learned here is fairly general. However, we know very little about how an intermediary might use the security-design and selling mechanism design guidelines to complement one another. So as the individual tools are being codified, their joint use should be as well. As things stand, this aspect remains largely within the realm of human judgment.

Finally, and perhaps most important, intermediary functions, as with any human function, lean heavily on adaptive behavior, or learning. The cognitive sciences are making great strides in understanding human learning, but the state of the art in autonomous agents, for example, poses little immediate threat to intermediaries whose livelihood depends largely on subtle behaviors that promote trust and cooperation among self-interested parties.

The Dark Side of Codification

The preceding discussion highlights the benefits of codifying human capital. Although the benefits appear substantial, the transformation of human capital in financial firms raises at least three areas of concern:

- Maintaining incentives for continued innovation
- Preserving collective interests in existing networks
- Preserving the balance in competition policy

In some instances there almost certainly is an inherent trade-off to be weighed. In others, careful attention to the transformation process might prevent realization of unnecessary costs. Before turning our focus to competition policy in chapter 6, we outline some trade-offs and opportunities associated with financial innovation and the preservation of existing tacit knowledge.

Financial Innovation

Historically, the design of new financial products was more an art than a science—an undertaking that Robert Eccles and Dwight Crane of Harvard Business School suggest benefited from day-to-day client interaction and experimentation.[28] This in turn led to long-standing client/bank relationships based on an informal understanding that a banker's time spent evaluating and responding to a client's needs would eventually be rewarded with an opportunity to execute a transaction for the client. The symbiotic relationship between banks and clients provided for sharing the high costs of research and development (R&D) and protected against clients taking their bank's ideas to others who might then execute the strategy for a smaller fee.

In spite of the declining importance of relationships (see Box 5-4), financial innovation has flourished. In part this reflects the codification of financial engineering practices and the resulting decline in learning by trial and error. Moreover, an increasingly wide array of publicly traded securities provides a highly liquid set of building blocks for fashioning new financial products. In other words, the basic inputs to

---

Box 5-4 The Demise of the Relationship

During the last twenty years, relationships between investment banks and their corporate clients have been strained as corporations increasingly placed securities underwriting services up for competitive bidding. But even against this background, a recent attempt by Ford Motor Company to take back some of the benefits that bankers capture from securities offerings stands out. Ford made a highly publicized demand that potential underwriters make commitments of low-margin credit lines in exchange for future underwriting business. J.P. Morgan, Lehman Brothers, and Merrill Lynch capitulated, but Goldman Sachs, Ford's long-standing lead banker, and Morgan Stanley Dean Witter rejected the demand.[29]

---

production—the capacity for making claims on future cash flows liquid and the knowledge required for organizing them in novel and productive ways—are being commoditized.

But codification of product design also contributes to undermining client relationships and so promotes greater competition among banks.[30] Systematized financial engineering practices provide a foundation for reverse engineering new products and practices. As a consequence, corporate clients can be more confident that one bank will execute a transaction as effectively as another once the blueprint is drawn. In turn, this heightens the threat that innovators who produce the original blueprint will fail to recover investments in R&D.

We believe that recent interest in patenting financial products and services reflects the loss of control banks are facing as traditionally human-capital-intensive functions are codified. Intellectual property law has the potential for balancing the resulting incentive distortion, but the nature and scope of intellectual property law as it applies to financial products and services remain in a nascent state. Since 1908, business methods had been widely considered unpatentable in spite of the U.S. Patent and Trademark Office's occasional willingness to do so. But everything changed with a 1998 appellate court decision that explicitly rejected the notion of a "business method exception" in a finding handed down on State Street Bank's effort to invalidate a 1993 patent obtained by Signature Financial Group for software used to

value mutual funds.[31] The decision triggered exponential growth in fil-
ings for financial patents and for patents on business methods generally.

However, concerns about the merits of these patents and the patent
office's oversight of the new terrain are leading even beneficiaries of the
system, such as Amazon.com's Jeff Bezos, to call for examination of the
apparent latitude being given business-method applications. Among
the ideas percolating in the United States are suggestions for reforms
that would mimic the European patent system's capacity for challenges
from competitors before the patent is granted, at least for business-
method patents.

In areas such as semiconductor design and fabrication, where
patenting is the norm for protecting intellectual capital, the competitive landscape is so heavily patented that competitors commonly
infringe one another's patents. The usual outcome according to *The
Economist* is "a cross-licensing agreement, with or without cash thrown
in," depending on the relative number of competing claims.[32] In
essence, these cross-licensing arrangements take on the character of industry consortiums empowered by the government to exclude competition from nonmembers (see Box 5-5).

In sum, as more of the intellectual capital of financial intermediaries finds its way into the no-man's land between human capital and
intellectual property, intermediary firms are exploring new ways of sustaining a level of protection for intellectual capital necessary to support
investment in its development. Where protection was traditionally informal, the trend is toward seeking formal protection. As we'll see in
the course of chapters 6, 7, and 8, the shift in the status quo has implications both for how intermediary firms organize themselves and how
their regulators interpret and promote competition.

Preserving Existing Networks

Finally, it is worth considering from a slightly broader perspective how
the codification of intermediary practice might undermine information
sharing. We've already discussed the immediate consequences of the
threat to key individuals as intermediary firms seek control over their
human capital. The threat of losing institutional knowledge through
employee mobility should give pause to any human-capital-intensive
organization considering an aggressive strategy for gaining control over
the human capital it harbors. We'll examine this issue in a bit more detail in our case study of Goldman Sachs in chapter 7.

Box 5-5   A Bias toward Formal Protection of Intellectual Capital?

As we'll see in chapter 6, informal arrangements such as the underwriting syndicate lead to a similar outcome of exclusion of competition in the investment banking industry. These temporary consortiums dissolve upon completion of a transaction but exhibit a high degree of continuity in membership across transactions. Gaining entry to a syndicate depends on a capacity for offering access to one's own deals to other syndicate members. This capacity is a function of reputation and relationships—the key elements of any investment bank's intellectual capital. Ironically, as banks have attempted to formalize such exclusive arrangements in online business platforms, they've drawn attention from the antitrust division of the U.S. Justice Department. Is there an obvious reason to prefer industry consortiums formed under threat of litigation with property rights protected by the state? If so, then expect more memos like the one Bill Gates circulated after Microsoft lost a patent-infringement suit to IBM. Gates's answer? Microsoft should be "patenting as much as we can."[33]

But even when organizations avoid driving away human capitalists by being judicious in how they parcel out benefits from intellectual capital, we might consider whether efforts to more fully codify and mechanize intermediary practice are consistent with long-term preservation of the tacit elements representing the best of traditional methods. In our examination of the IPO market, we've tried to illustrate the existence of a delicate ecology that balances the interests of the many competing parties. In several dimensions, we've highlighted the fact that success in maintaining this balancing act is associated with, if not dependent on, an element of cooperation. But one man's cooperation is another's collusion. WR Hambrecht's OpenIPO is the current antithesis of this long-standing dimension of U.S. primary equity markets. In the event that OpenIPO or something like it prevails, can it complement and thereby sustain the benefits of more relationship-intensive mechanisms? Or do electronic mechanisms, perhaps more efficient on net, sacrifice certain benefits of traditional practice?

On a slightly different note, we've suggested that one consequence of codification in financial markets will be a shift in the balance of power in favor of individual investors. But what if this diminishes their incentive to delegate asset management to institutional investors? Delegating responsibility for research to institutional investors reduced duplication of effort. It also provided more powerful incentives for information production than would be likely to exist in a more fragmented market wherein each individual would have incentive to free-ride on the research efforts of others. Thus, as financial markets became more institutional, they probably became more efficient mechanisms for allocating scarce investment capital. The gap between relatively informed and uninformed investors was likely wider, creating more opportunities for exploitative use of information, but a variety of intermediary practices served to balance the tension.

The tension is very much like that surrounding intellectual property. Democracy in the marketplace sounds like a good thing, just as does sharing information and knowledge. But if taken to an extreme, both undermine incentives for information production in the first place. As online platforms for discount brokerage and access to securities offerings upset the status quo, effectively providing the foundation for a wealth transfer from institutional investors to retail investors, they might also undermine the public interest in efficient capital markets. Although we suspect this is not precisely what Mr. John "Launny" Steffens of Merrill Lynch had in mind when he warned of the serious threat Internet trading posed to the financial lives of Americans, this potential consequence of codification warrants serious consideration in light of the increasingly active and independent role of individual investors and events such as the extraordinary market volatility surrounding recent dot-com IPOs.

We began this chapter by asking whether bankers, or financial intermediaries generally, are on a path to extinction. In some capacities the evidence does not bode well. But forecasts of their demise are premature and in fact likely to be wrong. Where traditional intermediary practice is being displaced, generally technological advances are enabling the separation of the mundane from higher-order functions that require human judgment. Roughly speaking, content development is being unbundled from distribution. The tying of the two functions endowed traditional intermediaries with great power and wealth. J.P. Morgan had a strong reputation as a creator of financial content, but he also controlled a large fraction of the distribution network for such content via his network of relationships. In essence, technology is promoting competition by enabling conversion of what once was perhaps un-necessarily embodied in human intermediaries into explicit rules that lend themselves to mechanization.

Property rights over the intellectual capital of intermediaries, the real source of competitive advantage, are being upset during this transformation. Historically, the practice of financial intermediation—content creation and distribution—was dominated by human capital, and property rights were strong. As pure distribution becomes more of a commodity, one source of bankers' leverage is being challenged. In response, bankers are scrambling to reestablish their power through legal claims and experimentation with new organizational structures. This struggle is the focus of chapter 6.

6

HUMAN CAPITAL
AND INDUSTRY STRUCTURE

Control over nonhuman assets leads to control over human assets.

Oliver Hart

CHAPTER 5 SKETCHED OUT how advances in economic theory and information technology are driving the codification of human capital in financial markets. This chapter links the codification of human capital to the massive restructuring of world financial markets that is currently underway. Obviously, this is not the only force at work. In the United States the demise of the Glass-Steagall Act has unleashed a mad rush to identify the limits of scale and scope in both retail and wholesale banking. Likewise, the integration of world financial markets is creating unprecedented competition among alternative intermediary and regulatory platforms.

But as important as deregulation and market integration are to the reshaping of financial markets, we contend that their impact is largely a function of the more fundamental forces we've examined thus far. As economic theory and information technology advanced, banks found new ways to pierce the regulatory firewall between commercial and investment banking, often spurred on by regulators' best preventive efforts. Likewise, in a world of primitive information technology, geography presented a significant boundary to market integration that supported government efforts to isolate their markets. Today, distance no longer props up isolationism.

Restructuring is taking place at the level of markets at large and within individual intermediary firms. This chapter focuses on how codification is altering the way investment banks collaborate and compete with one another. We also take a first cut at understanding organizational structure by thinking a bit about what determines the boundaries of firms and how this might be changing with advances in theory and information technology. Our case study of the Goldman Sachs IPO in chapter 7 focuses on the motivation for and consequences of organizational change within the industry.

Throughout this chapter we use the investment banking syndicate as a unifying theme in thinking about how industry structure is changing. Syndication has a narrow meaning and a well-developed form in the securities underwriting function. But the syndicate also serves as a metaphor for a variety of less formal cooperative practices as well as for the e-commerce platforms blossoming throughout the industry.

Syndication

Kevin Werbach argues that for the same reason syndication has traditionally occurred only at the margins of the economy, it will be the business platform of choice for e-commerce.[1] Broadly speaking, syndicates coordinate content origination with distribution capacity when the players on both sides of the equation are highly fragmented. The film industry provides an obvious and long-standing example. A large and highly fragmented community of artists develops discrete units of content (feature films), and a variety of physically diffuse channels—ranging from first-run theatres to a variety of channels for home viewing—provide for their distribution. Traditionally, large studios bundled content according to local tastes and other considerations and thereby coordinated the interaction between content providers and distributors.

Figure 6-1 places the syndicate in the framework developed in chapter 4. The focal point of the syndicate is a standardized set of contracts that coordinate origination and distribution. Think of these contracts as a bundle of codified knowledge and rules forming an interface between the tacit-knowledge-intensive functions of content origination and distribution. The platform lends an element of stability to the more fluid community of content originators and distributors.

Content originators deal primarily in highly specialized human capital—gray matter, if you will. Distribution involves a combination of human capital (marketing talent and networks of relationships) and the explicit knowledge embodied in the physical distribution network. In contrast to their cousins in the investment banking industry, the conti-

Figure 6-1 Syndication in the Film Industry

Figure 6-1 is a representation of the syndicate framework developed in chapter 4. The focal point, or stable interface, is a standardized set of contracts that coordinate content originators and content distributors. The relative permanence of the arrangement is reflected by the solid lines linking the originators and the distributors to the interface.

nuity provided by the syndicate arises from a relatively long-lived set of formal contracts. In figure 6-1 the relative permanence of the arrangement is reflected in the solid lines linking originators and distributors to the interface. Originators and distributors may come and go or evolve with technology and consumer preferences, but the basic interface or business platform is stable. As such, the syndicate structure provides continuity and order to an environment where flexibility and experimentation are in the nature of the game.

Investment Bank Syndication

Investment banks always have engaged in fragmented production and distribution of information goods.[2] From the outset, the industry comprised relatively small organizations headed by dominant individuals such as J. P. Morgan—the content originators, or artists, of the industry. Organizations were small for two reasons. First, the knowledge underlying the information goods produced by investment bankers was mostly tacit; a form of knowledge whose scale and scope of application was limited by the physical capacity of the individual in whom it was embodied. Second, even where codification was possible, monitoring one's peers in the application of shared intellectual assets was difficult.[3]

At the turn of the twentieth century, fragmentation of the industry prevented individual banks from meeting the needs of governments and the large-scale industrial concerns spawned by the second industrial revolution. This led content producers and distributors to coordinate informally, often through family connections or within well-defined social networks such as the German-Jewish banking community in New York.[4] In the case of securities offerings, a formal syndication platform evolved. Jay Cooke, dubbed the "modern Midas" for his role in marketing Civil War bonds, is credited with introducing the underwriting syndicate to U.S. markets after having observed its application in France. Prior to 1890, syndicates most commonly formed in the United States to handle massive bond issues for railroading concerns. The syndicate *temporarily* brought together the resources of many banks to purchase securities from the issuing firm or government and then orchestrated their distribution through the combined networks of the syndicate members.

The underwriting syndicate has changed little since its inception. Modern syndicates have a lead manager or perhaps several comanagers who advise the issuer in structuring the transaction and are responsible for coordinating the sales and distribution effort of other syndicate members—often upward of twenty banks. Chief among the sales efforts is responsibility for managing the book for the offering. The lead bank also is responsible for allocating securities among the selling members of the syndicate and so effectively determines the commissions earned by other syndicate members. Whether the offering is successful or not, the codified elements of the underwriting syndicate are formally dissolved upon completion. The price of admission to underwriting syndicates is a proven ability to admit others to one's own deals. As a consequence, banks tend to work repeatedly with one another so that syndicate composition across deals is quite stable, with only the lead manager or managers varying.

Although syndication takes its most explicit form in securities underwriting, coordinated efforts and repeated dealing through complex networks of relationships are pervasive in the investment banking industry. Foreign exchange markets might be thought of as syndicates composed of the many dealers in the market bound by a tacit but clear understanding of each other's capacity for analysis of market conditions (content) and for putting capital at risk (distribution capacity). Similarly, in their corporate advisory role, investment bankers repeatedly work with one another for a single client or negotiate with one another on behalf of adversarial clients. In doing so, banks make unique contributions, usually involving tacit knowledge, to the bundle of content defining a particular deal. Content might involve only advice, but more typically it includes the execution of securities transactions necessary for financial restructuring. Distribution capacity might come bundled with advice from one or more banks or might just as likely be provided, at least in part, by other banks. But again, the coordination among intermediaries tends to be transaction specific.

Figure 6-2 reflects these unique features of the investment banking syndicate. The interface itself is smaller in scale and fluid relative to the general platform described in figure 6-1. In the extreme case of the underwriting syndicate, the transaction-specific platform is defined by a relatively small set of standardized contracts that make up the agreement among underwriters. More generally, we can think of the syndicate platform as comprising the evolving knowledge of past dealings among the participants that guides behavior in circumstances where formal contracts are silent—less black and white perhaps than the general syndicate platform described in figure 6-1.

Similar to figure 6-1, we think of content origination as being intensive in tacit knowledge, or judgment, relative to distribution. Although investment banking distribution networks remain bound by relatively tacit personal relationships, advances in information technology provide for greater codification of distribution than for origination. The dotted lines reflect the syndicate's temporary linkage of both origination and distribution to the transaction-specific platform.

On the surface of things, investment banking syndicates appear rather inefficient. Why, for example, are syndicates—virtual firms, if

Figure 6-2 Syndication in the Investment Banking Industry

This example of a syndicate in the investment banking industry is based on the same principles presented in figure 6-1. This type of syndication, however, incorporates a smaller and more fluid interface relative to the general platform described in figure 6-1.

you will—formed around a transaction only to be dissolved and then re-formed for the next? Why didn't the highly fragmented banking indus-try simply collapse into a smaller core of behemoths each capable of in-dependent execution of the largest transactions? Alternatively, why weren't more permanent, formal syndicate arrangements established? Before addressing these questions, it's useful to take a brief detour into the thinking of economists on what exactly determines the structure and boundaries of firms.

The Theory of the Firm

Why do firms exist? As trivial as the question might appear to those who spend their working lives within firms, the firm poses a significant challenge to the economist's fundamental trust in markets. The seminal work of Adolf Berle and Gardiner Means suggests that firms effectively remove certain transactions from the open marketplace.[5] In principle, nothing prevents unbundling of the contractual relationships that de-fine transactions within a firm and then executing them as arm's-length transactions in the marketplace. Why, for example, should we write long-term employment contracts? Why not daily contracts? For that matter, why not contract with employees on a minute-by-minute basis? This would provide for more flexible production, if nothing else. Posing the question in this way leads immediately to the answer arrived at by Ronald Coase: Although markets may be efficient mechanisms for carrying out economic activity, they are not costless.[6] Arm's-length con-tracts are costly to negotiate, write, and enforce. Bundling transactions within firms economizes on these transaction costs.

Of course, organizing economic activity within firms also has costs. In large partnerships where it is difficult to link individual contributions to the bottom line, there is incentive for partners to free-ride on one another. Similarly, Michael Jensen and William Meckling argue that "agency costs" arise when ownership is separated from control of the firm's assets, as in the modern publicly owned corporation.[7] CEOs who own little or no equity in their firms might place their own interests ahead of the firm's owners by overinvesting in corporate jets, acquiring firms and assets to enhance their own power rather than maximizing re-turn on equity, and the like. Jensen and Meckling suggest that the firm's debt/equity structure and management employment contracts, among other things, reflect an interest in aligning the interests of shareholders with the interests of those managing their assets.

Sanford Grossman, Oliver Hart, and John Moore challenge this perspective by observing that, in principle, shareholders could write contracts with employees that rule out self-interested behavior.[8] But in practice contracts are ambiguous, difficult to enforce, and otherwise incomplete. So when circumstances arise for which a contract is ambiguous or silent, how should they be dealt with? Grossman, Hart, and Moore suggest that careful assignment of property rights over physical assets can help to resolve this problem.

To see why, it is useful to recognize that a firm is nothing more than a collection of human and physical assets. Contracting over physical assets is relatively straightforward, but not so with human assets. A mind cannot be enslaved. However, if human assets are most productively used in conjunction with certain physical assets, then the control that resides with owners of the physical assets can be used to shape behavior in circumstances in which contracts are ambiguous— that is, control over nonhuman assets leads to control over human assets. Physical assets thus are the glue that binds the collection of human assets defining a firm, and the assignment of property rights over physical assets determines how effectively the firm's assets are used (see Box 6-1).

The example in Box 6-1 highlights what is for our purposes the central insight of the property rights perspective on the firm offered by Grossman, Hart, and Moore. That is to say, production efficiency is served when control over physical assets is in the hands of those who bring the most valuable human assets to a project. But what if physical assets contribute little to the value of products or services that nevertheless require a team production effort? This is more descriptive of the setting in which investment banks as well as most other professional services firms operate. Advances in information technology have led to a substantial physical infrastructure in financial markets, but at the turn of the twentieth century the physical infrastructure of financial markets was virtually nonexistent. In such instances, Oliver Hart observes, "it is not clear what keeps the firm together, or what defines authority within the firm."[9] So the Grossman, Hart, and Moore view of the firm suggests one reason why the investment banking industry remained so fragmented for so long—physical assets, the glue that binds human assets to one another, were inconsequential.[10]

Box 6-1   The Property Rights Perspective on the Firm

We can make the discussion a bit more concrete by considering the production of a piece of software that depends on a combination of unique computing capacity (the physical asset) and the design and coding capacity of a team of programmers (the human assets). The computing capacity might be a prohibitively costly supercomputer or have a unique architecture that is not easily replicated. The key is that it must be an asset that is central to the best use of the programming team's skills and something from which individual members of the team can be excluded. In other words, a standard-architecture PC will not satisfy the latter condition because it can be replicated at low cost. The problem is how to get members of the design team, who almost surely differ in their ability and energy, to work productively with one another.

   Now suppose that a wealthy but dull member of the team owned the physical asset while the software's chief architect had no ownership stake and simply worked under a fixed compensation arrangement. Ownership of the physical asset enables the dullard to take his toys and go home if the development contract is incomplete and he does not like the way things are progressing. This effectively permits him to "fire" the architect after capturing whatever element of the architect's human capital is thus far codified in the development process. Facing this threat, a talented architect is not likely to join the project team in the first place. A more plausible employment contract for the architect is one that provides an equity stake in the project—in other words, a partial, or even complete, transfer of ownership over the physical asset. This provides the architect with more bargaining power relative to the dullard in circumstances in which the team's development contract is ambiguous. This should increase the architect's willingness to put forth her best effort, which after all is more important to the team than the dullard's financial capital, for which there are probably many close substitutes.

Form Follows Function

The success of an underwriting syndicate is determined in large part before the syndicate is formed.[11] Obviously, the marketing and distribution of a securities offering must be conducted in a professional manner, but the capacity for doing so lies in the tacit knowledge and relationships developed independent of the transaction at hand. Likewise, the quality of a banker's advice to a client that is considering acquiring a competitor or otherwise restructuring derives more from experience in other transactions than from the sheer effort exerted in the moment. In other words, bankers bring human capital to transactions.

In light of the grueling pace of their work, it is perhaps a statement of the obvious to say that the development and preservation of the banker's human capital requires considerable effort. Unfortunately, measuring the quality of this effort on a day-to-day basis is difficult. One can shed light on the quantity and quality of a banker's effort by measuring the frequency of client contacts (call reporting) and encouraging cross evaluations among bankers who work closely with one another.[12] Going one step further, one can link these evaluations to compensation and promotions, thereby diminishing the incentive for bankers to free-ride on each other; but only if the evaluations are truly meaningful.

The problem is that anything more than a superficial review process consumes an enormous amount of energy in nonhierarchical organizations. For example, a two-person partnership demands at most two cross-evaluations. But a five-person partnership in which each partner works with the other four calls for twenty cross-evaluations. For those inclined to mathematical patterns, the number of cross-evaluations that can be conducted in a group of n individuals is $n(n-1)$. Obviously, as organizations grow, there will not be direct contact between each member. But this progression makes clear how easily evaluation can begin to take precedence over performance. For example, when Goldman Sachs went public in 1999, it reported in its S-1 filing with the SEC that its "360-degree" evaluation system involved over 140,000 performance evaluations (in a firm with fewer than 15,000 employees) in 1998 alone. At some point, the balance between evaluation and performance begins to favor a more decentralized form of organization; this tension, we think, essentially determines the limits of formal organization in the investment banking industry.

But collaborative efforts, like the underwriting syndicate, that cut across formal organizations present their own problems. Syndicate members do not work with one another on a day-to-day basis and therefore have limited opportunity for monitoring the current state of a collaborator's human capital. Observable outcomes, such as the number of deals carried out and the banker's role, provide some insight. In a business where reputation is everything, however, even modest effort can disguise slow but steady decay in human capital. In other words, potential collaborators must consider the threat that their peers are resting on the laurels of past success. If there was a physical asset central to the collaborative effort, one party's control over that asset might serve to diminish the problem by threatening potential slackers with exclusion from future use of the asset. But again, the role of physical assets in the traditional banking platform was minimal. Likewise, if reputation attached to the syndicate rather than its members, control over this intangible asset might be assigned to a key member. But the syndicate is short lived.

Against this background, let's reexamine the structure of underwriting syndicates. Banks compete aggressively for the lead manager's role because it carries larger fees and enhances the bank's reputation (and therefore future earning power). But the lead manager designation also puts one (or a few) syndicate member's feet to the fire. Responsible or not, the lead manager is usually held accountable for the highly visible outcome of an IPO by the issuing firm and the market in general. Thus banks have an incentive to protect their reputations by putting forth the ongoing effort necessary to make the most of such opportunities.

The incentive for bankers to free-ride on one another is further blunted by the relatively exclusive but informal working relationships they maintain. Exclusive working relationships essentially create a barrier to entry for potential upstarts and therefore support fees in excess of competitive levels. If transactions are beyond the capacity of any single bank, there is no way for a single competitor to break into the market by undercutting the existing fee structure. Many would argue that this is the reason that underwriting spreads in the United States for medium-sized IPOs have clustered so persistently around 7 percent of the money raised. But if spreads exceed competitive levels, dominant banks will have a powerful incentive to preserve access to such opportunities. So although there is no physical asset of the kind imagined by Grossman, Hart, and Moore, similar incentives are created if slackers can be excluded from sharing in particularly attractive profit opportunities.

Placing one or a few banks in the spotlight provides a crude means of judging a bank's ongoing efforts that bear so heavily on their contribution to the team. The informality of banking relationships, embodied in the limited formal life of the syndicate, eases the exclusion of apparent slackers from future deals. If underwriting syndicates were longer-lived legal entities, the threat of exclusion would have less bite. Seen in this light, the form of the underwriting syndicate reflects its function as an organizational structure that reduces the threat of shirking among bankers who do not work closely with one another on a day-to-day basis but depend on one another for success in large-scale transactions.

Exclusivity

The syndicate's very reason for being is to link otherwise fragmented elements of a network more or less permanently. Sustaining competing arrangements of the same network membership traditionally involved maintaining idle capacity at high marginal cost—think of the railroading example offered in chapter 2 or imagine many local versions of the NYSE for trading listed stocks. By nature, therefore, these networks tend to favor exclusive arrangements. Exclusivity can be a good thing because it's easier to build trust when one deals repeatedly with known counter parties. Exclusivity in financial markets diminishes the threat of exploitation by individuals who would violate community standards for short-term gain. As we saw in chapter 5, exclusivity also can be an important ingredient in fostering innovation.

But taken to an extreme, exclusivity stifles innovation and competition. A concrete example arose recently in the interdealer segment of the bond markets. Broadly speaking, these markets provide for interdealer or dealer/customer trade. Interdealer trading platforms are the more arcane and opaque consolidators of liquidity that provide the scaffolding for the more visible dealer/customer trading platforms that provide a point of entry for retail and most institutional investors. In the United States, the interdealer market is dominated by a small cast of characters, most of which maintain dominant positions in other segments of the investment banking industry. Without pointing a finger at particular firms, let's just say that by now you shouldn't need a scorecard to identify most of the key players.

Like the IPO markets, the interdealer market has long been criticized for engaging in mutual back scratching behind a curtain of secrecy, with the end result being that outsiders incur unnecessarily high transaction costs. The vignette in Box 6-2 outlines the experience of an outsider, InterVest, bent on upsetting the status quo.

Box 6-2   InterVest's Attempt to Join the Interdealer Bond Market

In November 1992, the SEC provided InterVest with a no-action letter enabling it to trade corporate bonds through an electronic system that would compete with the traditional interdealer network without requiring the firm to register as a securities exchange under Section 6 of the 1934 Securities Exchange Act. In August 1995, a similar letter opened the door for InterVest's electronic platform for municipal bond trading.

With tacit approval from the SEC, InterVest sought to provide access to their platform through the widely used Bloomberg information and communications network. InterVest's platform was distinguished not only by its technology for streamlining the negotiation of bond transactions but also by the firm's willingness to publicly display market bid, offer, and transaction prices to Bloomberg subscribers. Bloomberg initially denied InterVest's request but in July 1995 agreed to connect InterVest's platform with the Bloomberg Electronic Transaction System (BETSY). BETSY enabled selected broker-dealer subscribers to trade various categories of securities with other Bloomberg subscribers or to route trades to securities exchanges through their Bloomberg terminal, but did not provide the level of price transparency InterVest offered.

Following protracted negotiations, InterVest filed a $100 million lawsuit with the U.S. District Court for the Eastern District of Pennsylvania in November 1999 against eight major broker-dealer firms, alleging that Bloomberg repeatedly delayed access to BETSY and ultimately refused access. The complaint also alleged that Bloomberg's refusal followed demands from prominent dealers that Bloomberg not permit InterVest to display the current bid and offer prices and transactions to Bloomberg subscribers. Bloomberg claimed that dealers feared for their profits if they were forced to negotiate with subscribers armed with more accurate price information.

As the deadline for settlement approached, InterVest's technology had already been sold to GFInet, a dominant player in the international wholesale currency and over-the-counter derivatives markets. The lawsuit itself was viewed as sufficiently strong to attract funding from a group of private equity investors who hoped to share in the settlement or jury award.

Shortly after InterVest's filing, a flurry of activity occurred in the marketplace as the established dealers marked their initial forays into e-commerce with several January 2000, offerings sold at least in part over the Internet. In the future, InterVest will be noteworthy only for its absence. In other words, although InterVest appears to have sparked innovation, for all practical purposes it was forced to sell its technology to the existing network. As Alec Petro, managing director of Gamma Investors (a private equity partnership with stakes in GFInet and the InterVest lawsuit), observed, "The guys with deal flow have the power. Without liquidity something like InterVest is just another piece of software. The bond dealers' view is 'Great, we'll pay you a license fee.' "[13]

InterVest's experience sheds light on why WR Hambrecht + Co. chose the IPO market as a point of entry for its electronic auction platform. WR Hambrecht's decision was surprising because in spite of the fairness and efficiency concerns discussed in chapter 4, other developed economies are rapidly assimilating U.S. underwriting methods in hopes of achieving similar levels of technological innovation and entrepreneurial activity.[14] Moreover, the informational conflicts facing intermediaries in IPO markets are far more severe than in bond markets, where estimation of future cash flows is relatively straightforward and investors (mostly institutional) are more nearly on equal footing. One would think then that the bond markets would be a more natural point of entry. But WR Hambrecht was aware of the major dealers' stranglehold on the bond market and also recognized that any attempt to break it would take place out of the public eye. Therefore WR Hambrecht took the indirect approach of exploiting the high visibility of IPOs and opening the prospect that generating publicity through auctions for IPOs might provide traction for simultaneous but less visible efforts to break into the bond markets.

Thus far, having focused most of their energy on the IPO markets, the impact of the Internet investment banks on the structure and function of underwriting syndicates has been nominal. OpenIPO has auctioned shares for only four firms to date, and Wit SoundView has become a complementary member of the traditional order. Some would argue that several recent IPOs (most notably, the Goldman Sachs self-underwritten IPO) in which the bulk of the syndicate's responsibility has been borne by one bank presage the demise of the traditional syndicate. But as recently as the three-year period from 1996 to 1998, the average syndicate membership for the approximately 1,300 IPOs brought to market in the United States remained at about eighteen banks.[15] So why have investment banks been so slow to change?

Why Incumbents Drag Their Feet

InterVest's experience suggests that entrenched intermediaries have little incentive to be early champions of technological advances that promote efficiency. But why, with their deep pockets, valuable brand names, and reputations, must incumbent intermediaries have their backs forced to the wall? In *Mastering the Dynamics of Innovation*, James Utterback makes an observation that we think is particularly relevant to understanding why threats from upstarts like Wit SoundView, WR Hambrecht, and InterVest are necessary to promote innovation in the coordination of information networks.

> One reason for the lethargy of well-established competitors in a product market in the face of potentially disruptive innovation is that they face increasing constraints from the growing web of relationships binding product and process together. At the start of production of a new product, general-purpose equipment, available components, and highly-skilled people may suffice to enter the market. As both product and market increase in sophistication more specialization is generally required in equipment, components, and skills. Thus change in one element, the product, requires changes throughout the whole system of materials, equipment, methods, and suppliers. This may make changing more onerous and costly for the established firm than for the new entrant.[16]

This description appears tailor-made for the relationship-intensive nature of investment banking, where the boundaries between transactions and even the inputs to production can be quite blurry. As Bill Hambrecht observed, changes in the pricing and allocation mechanism for IPOs would upset the balance in a finely tuned web of existing expectations among the bank's clients and investors. So even as the traditional banks joined the fray, their efforts were aimed less at transforming than at enhancing the efficiency of their existing platform. According to WR Hambrecht's chief operating officer, J. D. Delafield, "What you're seeing on the Street today is mainly automation and information delivery, not something new." Similarly, Scott Ryles, of Epoch Capital, observes that "Wall Street firms are using the Internet to extend their existing service model, the research and sales force," not for distributing information directly to clients.[17]

How Innovators Gain Traction in Networked Markets

It thus appears that the pioneers developing new technology outside existing networks are having a tough time of it. Given the circumstances, can they reasonably expect to succeed? Perhaps the better question is how they should define success. Suppose that Wit SoundView's or WR Hambrecht's technology actually promotes efficiency and gains widespread acceptance. They would have proved their point. But what prevents Goldman Sachs from letting them do the heavy work of cutting a new path in the jungle and then sweeping in afterward to dominate use of that path? Goldman Sachs's investor network surely is more difficult to replicate than either entrant's physical infrastructure. In fact, as we go to press, Goldman Sachs is acquiring Epoch Capital for its technology and distribution system, and is expecting to retain few of Epoch's employees.

Posing the question in this way casts things in a different light. Rather than concentrating on what's wrong with the incumbent market setting, perhaps innovators are better served by setting out to at least preserve what's right. As awkward or anticompetitive as they might appear to the e-commerce entrepreneur, the tight-knit personal networks at the heart of many financial and product markets promote a high level of cooperation in the production and use of information. The relationships and trust that bind these networks are valuable assets that not only are worth preserving but also, by their nature, are not replicable in the short term.

As we look back on the strategies followed by the Internet investment banks described in chapter 3, OffRoad Capital's approach appears most consistent with this perspective. Rather than seeking to displace an existing network, OffRoad identified a market segment that as yet was not heavily intermediated and set about building a network of highly diffuse investors and firms likely to benefit from an ongoing relationship with the capital markets that extends beyond their existing commercial banking relationship. Part of the strategy from the outset involved making it easy for incumbent intermediaries to serve their own interests by connecting with OffRoad's network, hence the large number of strategic alliances formed in short order between OffRoad and key members of the traditional venture, investment banking, brokerage, and money management industry segments. OffRoad's strategy from the outset can be interpreted as designed to enhance the intermediary function rather than to displace it.

Both Wit SoundView and WR Hambrecht are developing detailed data on the preferences and behavior of their investors. The capacity for linking investor bidding behavior with personal characteristics and secondary market behavior and storing this information in an easily accessed digital format could prove a powerful marketing and bargaining tool both for their own purposes and those of other banks. WR Hambrecht in particular has taken a more independent approach with OpenIPO and OpenBook, using them in part in an attempt to, "build up a base of . . . 100,000 angel accounts doing $1,000 a year brokerage business" each.[18] In most instances, presumably, this would involve attracting business from existing brokerage firms as opposed to broadening the scope of the market by bringing new capital to the marketplace—that is, capturing a bigger slice of the existing pie rather than increasing the size of the pie. Effective coordination of the distributed knowledge residing in these accounts might prove to enhance its value as independent bits of information. But to date neither Wit SoundView nor WR Hambrecht appears to have fully exploited this opportunity presented by the new technology (see Box 6-3).

The Incumbents: Co-opting or Innovating?

Are the incumbents faring any better in their struggle to adapt to the new technology? The bond markets provide a useful setting for addressing this question. Although slow off the mark, U.S. banks have sought to recast themselves virtually overnight as January 2000, debt offerings by Freddie Mac, Fannie Mae, and Ford Credit Co. opened the floodgates of a variety of e-commerce initiatives for issuing and trading fixed-income securities. The market is evolving even as we write, but if we focus, for example, on just the dealer/customer initiatives being pursued by Goldman Sachs (not a party to the InterVest

---

Box 6-3   Fast Forward

On August 15, 2000, WR Hambrecht launched OpenBook, an
auction platform for investment grade bonds, with a $300 million
offering for Dow Chemical. Similar to OpenIPO, OpenBook sets
the price for a bond issue when demand expressed in the auction
clears the market and allocates the issue in a non-discretionary
fashion according to a ranking of investor bids. Unlike OpenIPO,
it provides all institutional investors with real-time price discovery,
which they can use to observe the book building for the offering
and adjust their bidding strategies accordingly. The minimum
quantity investors can bid is $1 million but the system provides for
online brokers to sweep together the bids of retail investors in
order to clear this limit. In contrast to Dow Chemical's usual
offering clientele of fifteen to twenty institutional investors,
the OpenBook offering allocated bonds to at least fifty-five
institutional investors some of which, like WR Hambrecht, used
the capacity to bundle smaller quantity bids to bid on behalf of
retail investors.

---

lawsuit, by the way) as of May 2000, they can be classified as supporting research and analysis, primary sales and distribution, and secondary
trading (see table 6-1).

In each case, codification of intermediary functions is occurring on
two levels. At the proprietary level the goal is to use information technology to enable bankers to spend less time in pure information dissemination and more time managing relationships and originating new
ideas and analysis—in other words, to focus their energy on the development and marketing of content rather than pure distribution. For example, Goldman Sachs's Financial Workbench provides institutional
investors with analytical models made possible by recent advances
in fixed-income pricing theory. Computer programs that embody this
codified knowledge reduce duplication of effort both within Goldman
Sachs and among the investors it serves. The platform also provides for
online order entry and trading, thereby freeing salespeople from the
mundane task of accepting simple orders from clients who need no
additional guidance. In the parlance of this chapter, Financial Workbench, as well as the other proprietary initiatives, is designed to leverage or amplify the firm's human capital.

Table 6-1

Goldman Sachs Fixed-Income E-Commerce, May 2000
(Dealer/Customer Initiatives)

	Proprietary	*Joint Venture*

Research and Analytics	Financial Workbench
	Information
	Online analytics
	Online order entry
	and trading
		Bond.Hub
		Commingled nonproprietary content
		Links to proprietary content of each
		  member dealer
		Partners: Morgan Stanley Dean Witter,
		  Citi/Salomon, J.P. Morgan Chase & Co.,
		  Lehman Bros., Merrill Lynch

Primary Sales and Distribution	E-Syndicate
	Electronic information
	  dissemination
	Electronic order entry
	and allocation
	Electronic secondary
	trading
		Syndicate.Hub
		Commingled content
		Links to member dealer sites for
		  prospectuses, electronic roadshows,
		  etc.
		Partners: Morgan Stanley Dean Witter,
		  Citi/Salomon, J.P. Morgan Chase & Co.,
		  Lehman Bros., Merrill Lynch

Secondary Trading	Web.ET
	Goldman's real-time bids
	and offers for auto-
	execution
		TradeWeb
		Commingled indicative dealer prices
		Electronic negotiated trading
		Partners: same as other joint ventures, plus
		  Credit Suisse First Boston, Deutsche
		  Bank, Barclays, Greenwich Capital

Perhaps more interesting are the joint ventures: Bond.Hub, Syndicate.Hub, and TradeWeb. Each forms part of a scalable electronic platform for price quote dissemination, electronic order execution, and the dissemination of analyst research reports and other nonproprietary codified knowledge. In other words, they provide for large-scale distribution of goods and services that are more like commodities. But the joint ventures also serve a different purpose. As the costs of information dissemination decline, the primary barrier to being heard is the difficulty of standing out from the gathering crowd. By sweeping together research from six of the most prominent fixed-income broker-dealers, Bond.Hub, for example, encompasses a critical mass of research that is more likely to attract the attention of institutional investors than that offered by any single broker-dealer. Thus both the competitive pressures posed by a commodity market and the need for having one's voice heard in an increasingly noisy marketplace argue for scale. The argument gains further weight from network effects in trading and price discovery, where large-scale participation leads to sharper pricing and more liquidity.

But if scale is the order of the day, we might ask why these joint ventures are so exclusive and whether they will remain so. The tension between content and distribution comes into play here. On the one hand, there is little marginal cost to posting the prices or research of an additional participant, and a bit more competition to stand out from a crowd of content providers is a good thing. On the other hand, the distribution platform or portal need not be just a pipeline. If it also vets the quality of content or other experience goods, it takes on the role of an intermediary balancing the competing interests of the parties it serves.

Against a noisy background, a reputable portal serves content providers by setting them above the din and thereby increasing the returns to investment in high-quality content. Consumers benefit from delegating responsibility for monitoring quality to the portal. But content providers will always have the incentive to either misrepresent the quality of their content to make their way into a reputable portal or, once in, to curb the investment that made their content quality high enough to gain entry in the first place. Limited membership reduces the dimension of the portal's vetting and monitoring responsibilities and leaves open the door to exclusion of those who do not measure up. Joint ownership of the portal by key content providers serves the function envisioned by Grossman, Hart, and Moore of placing control over nonhuman assets in the hands of those contributing key human assets.

Joint ownership of the portal presents its own problems in the sense that it is more difficult to break ties with a partner in the venture who fails to bear his share of the load than in the traditional syndicate structure, where formal ties were weak. But here advances in information technology can help by providing direct links from the portal into an interface for proprietary content for each partner in the venture. For example, upon entering Bond.Hub a Goldman Sachs client has the option to click through directly to any partner's proprietary area. This exposes Goldman Sachs to the risk of losing value-added business to partners in the portal unless it contributes the high-quality nonproprietary content that might persuade a client to consider its proprietary offerings. With each partner facing the same incentives, Bond.Hub's structure promotes high-quality nonproprietary content that will serve as a magnet for a larger share of market attention, which might then be attracted to proprietary goods and services. The threat of losing one's clients to competitors can substitute for the frequent recontracting in traditional syndicates that was a costly but perhaps necessary means of assuring commitment from syndicate members.

So although both syndicate structures might serve the same function, they differ in form because technological advances have made possible the creation of a physical asset, the portal, that extends the formal boundaries of the firm. Whereas the traditional syndicate might be thought of as a virtual firm that temporarily linked human distribution networks, modern electronic networks lend themselves to large-scale, long-lived business platforms. The scope of these platforms, or their degree of exclusivity, will be tied directly to the difficulty of monitoring the quality of the content for which they provide distribution. Where quality is observable or can be sampled, as in the case of books and other physical goods, expect the likes of Amazon.com to extend their brand or reputation broadly. In financial markets, where content is a true experience good that depends on unobservable investments in relationships or other forms of human capital, scalable distribution platforms will tend toward preserving exclusivity.

In sum, Goldman Sachs's fixed-income e-commerce initiatives suggest that something interesting is in the offing. The emerging structure preserves the received relationships embodied in the traditional syndicate. However, it appears that the modern equivalent to the syndicate will involve more permanent shared distribution and price discovery platforms through which content providers will compete with one another for the market's attention. Co-opting or innovating? That essentially is the question regulators must be asking themselves.[19]

An Evolutionary Perspective on Financial Innovation

Let's step back for a moment and take stock of the implications of chapters 4 and 5 and see if they can help shed light on the massive reorganization underway within the financial markets at large.[20] We began this book by arguing that intermediary functions are stable but that how they are carried out varies with the regulatory and technological environment in which they are embedded. As both vary, we should think of the execution of intermediary functions, and institutions generally, as following an evolutionary path.

In financial markets there is a natural attracting barrier for the evolutionary path of intermediaries. Economists define a *complete market* as one in which it is possible to trade on any potential future state of the world. We might imagine a very simple world in which the future is either good or bad and economic welfare is determined by the efforts of ten industries whose performance differs with the state of the economy. In other words, there are twenty elements of uncertainty, or states, in the future (ten each for the good and bad economic states). A complete financial market provides for buying or selling a claim on any one of these states. A risk-averse investor might hedge his bets by spreading wealth across each of the states, perhaps investing a bit more in industries expected to perform well in the bad economic state. As long as markets are incomplete, opportunities for financial innovation exist because there remain elements of risk that cannot be traded. The primary barriers to market completeness are frictions that outweigh the benefits of new products that contribute to market completeness. Intermediaries diminish these frictions.

Intermediaries also follow an evolutionary path over the life cycle of most financial products and services. Initially, intermediaries serve as catalysts for a previously nonexistent market. At this stage of market development, the intermediary is active in promoting trust and balancing interests in privacy and openness. In this capacity, intermediaries can be thought of as deploying human capital in the creation of new content. OffRoad Capital's use of its principals' reputations as the foundation for community building and establishing trust provides a good example of the central role of human capital in jump-starting a new market. Michael Milken's stranglehold over the junk bond market at its inception provides another, perhaps more ominous, example.

As community standards evolve, members develop their own reputations and relationships, and best practices become apparent. Consequently, human-capital-intensive intermediary functions diminish in importance. The remaining intermediary functions are predominantly aimed at sustaining trade. These include maintaining distribution and communications networks and the like. Because these functions are more like commodities, profits diminish. In effect, content originated by the intermediary enters the public domain. On the one hand, this di-

minishes the intermediary's control over intellectual capital that it originated. But on the other hand, the transformation enables unbundling
of human capital from the now mundane functions, freeing human capital to serve as a catalyst for higher-margin products that lend themselves to further market completion. And the process goes on.

Advances in technology or theory whether continuous or abrupt,
compress the product life cycle by promoting codification and widespread application of what once was tacit knowledge. This, in turn,
heightens competition. At this point, the game is one of scale and scope
economies that pose a threat to intermediaries that lag in redeploying
human capital. Where application of human capital persists, we might
think of lags in technology or theory as delaying the redeployment of
human capital. In some instances, as in pure advisory services, the lag
might for all practical purposes be indefinite.

Codification of human capital provides for its redeployment in the
development of new products and thus promotes convergence toward
market completeness. Technological advances speed the process by
providing for more rapid deployment of human capital. Therefore,
human capital is less central to production in mature financial markets.
But as long as markets are incomplete and there is thus room for financial innovation, there will be demand for the catalytic role of human
capital.

Prior to the many advances in information technology over the
last half century, intermediaries got stuck in a human–capital-intensive
mode of production. Standards developed, to be sure, but many mundane functions still required human beings for execution. This meant
that production in investment banks, as in the traditional underwriting
syndicate, remained human capital intensive. As information technology further enables unbundling of codifiable or mundane functions,
we'll see a shift to larger-scale and longer-lived platforms for carrying
out these functions. Organizational emphasis then begins to shift from
human capital to the financial capital necessary for building permanent
physical infrastructure. The modern analogue to the syndicate begins
to look something more like the e-commerce platforms taking shape
in the fixed-income markets. This does not portend the decline of
the human side of intermediation. Rather, freeing human capital from
mundane functions and coupling it with large-scale physical infrastructure vastly amplifies its power.

So where do we stand now? We believe that recent decades have witnessed financial markets in the midst of continuous theory-driven technological advance supported by rapidly declining costs of computer processing. This has driven firms to seek greater scale as profit margins narrow. The Internet represents a profound shock whose impact has only begun to surface. It has the potential for converting many traditionally human-capital-intensive functions into pure commodities. As this is taking place, investment banks are redeploying human capital in a number of novel directions, including larger commitments to private equity and venture capital and the development of markets for trading energy, Internet bandwidth, and other nonfinancial goods. Connected with the former, bank balance sheets are growing not only from investments in new technology but also as they take equity stakes in firms they previously only provided with advice.

The nature of dealings between functions that remain human capital intensive and those that depend more on physical and financial capital is also changing. In many instances, we've seen leveraged buyout (LBO) groups, for example, being spun off from large, full-service banks. Even when these human–capital-intensive functions are not formally spun off, the increasing mobility of entire teams of bankers suggests widening informal divisions. As these human capitalists use technology to extend their reach, we expect to see more key individuals or small teams whose stature approaches that of J.P. Morgan's at the turn of the twentieth century. There may be fewer bankers than we've seen through the course of the twentieth century, but the rewards to these key individuals will remain substantial. It is less clear that the rewards to the industry at large will be so great.

From this perspective we see two questions that remain to be answered before we can fully understand how the reorganization of markets is likely to proceed:

- Can human–capital-intensive and financial–capital-intensive functions coexist peacefully within vertically and horizontally integrated organizations or will independent content boutiques and large-scale distribution platforms mark the industry? If the latter, what form will cooperation between the two take?

- What implications does the path of reorganization have for regulatory policy?

These questions lie at the core of our case studies of the Goldman Sachs IPO and of the competition between traditional exchanges and electronic communications networks in chapters 7 and 8. Having probed these questions a bit more deeply, we'll return to broader issues of industry reorganization and their implications for other information-intensive markets in chapter 9.

7

WHY GOLDMAN SACHS WENT PUBLIC

What matters to Goldman Sachs long-term? People and culture, culture and people, people and culture.

Stephen Friedman, 1993

We've been looking very hard at the impact of technology in all our businesses, looking at where the markets are headed, and electronic trading is going to have a big impact . . . . [O]ur assumption [is that] when you look at the U.S. markets, they will move the way Europe has gone [toward all-electronic trading].

Henry Paulson, July 1999

THE JUNE 1999 INITIAL public offering of equity by Goldman Sachs marked the end of an era in banking. The first investment banks, like most industrial concerns of their day, formed around a small, tight-knit group of individuals, often from the same family. But even as large-scale production drove industrial concerns to the publicly owned, corporate form of organization, investment banks retained the private partnership form. Only in the 1970s did investment banks begin to reorganize as publicly owned firms. By the late 1980s Goldman Sachs remained the lone holdout among the bulge-bracket banks.

Goldman Sachs's commitment to the partnership became a distinguishing feature of the bank; the culture it fostered, emphasized in 1993 by Stephen Friedman (Goldman Sachs's co-senior partner along with Robert Rubin), was given substantial credit for the firm's steady rise to the top of league tables. The partnership culture comprised a mentoring and patronage process that placed the team squarely ahead of the individual. Furthermore, the retirement of active partners to limited partnership at a relatively young age created opportunities for the junior members they had mentored. If these features of the organization were indeed central to the bank's success, it is important to understand why Goldman Sachs sacrificed them by going public.

Goldman Sachs's offering prospectus identified three motivations for dissolving the partnership:

- The need to share ownership more broadly among employees

- The need to secure permanent capital

- The need for publicly traded securities to finance acquisitions

Although each factor has merit in its own right, collectively they beg a series of deeper questions. At the very least, it is worth examining the timing of Goldman Sachs's IPO. A common explanation for the IPO is that the partners simply wanted to cash out as the market went through a period of irrational exuberance. If so, what held the partnership together in 1986, when many of its peers went public shortly before the 1987 crash? More important, can the fraying of the firm's culture during the late 1980s and early 1990s teach us anything about the profound reorganization occurring within the financial markets at large?

In this chapter, we offer an explanation for the long-standing dominance of the investment banking partnership and its recent demise as the organizational form of choice. Partnerships carry both costs and benefits. On the one hand, they are constrained by the wealth and risk-bearing capacity of their partners. On the other, they appear to foster the development and preservation of human capital. We argue that the demise of the partnership, in large part reflects technological advances that displaced and reshaped traditional human-capital-intensive intermediary functions. As these functions became more competitive and dependent on scale economies for profitability, the premium on access to financial capital rose and the *relative* importance of human capital declined. This perspective sheds light on the industry's ongoing reorganization as well as helps us to understand why the Goldman Sachs partnership lasted so much longer than others did.

A Brief Organizational History: 1869–1986

Partnerships have a long and storied history in banking. Early banking partnerships typically formed around one or more family members who were previously engaged in some other form of commercial activity that provided the partnership's initial capital base. These early "merchant banks" expanded their information networks by scattering partners in key commercial and financial centers. With primitive communication and reporting technology making remote monitoring of one's partners virtually impossible, the trust engendered by family ties provided for a scale of operation that would otherwise have been inconceivable.

The House of Rothschild provides a striking example of this type of organizational structure. By 1815, the Rothschilds had offices in Frankfurt, London, Paris, Vienna, and Naples, each manned by one of Mayer Rothschild's sons.[1] Although each maintained separate accounts, the partnership agreement regulated activity and reporting and defined each brother's share of capital and profits.[2] The partnership agreement also had a limited life that permitted periodic renegotiation of terms as economic circumstances and the relative performance of the offices changed.

Like the House of Rothschild, family ties provided the foundation for Goldman Sachs. The firm was founded in 1869 when Marcus Goldman moved to New York and began dealing commercial paper. Like his many predecessors, Mr. Goldman accumulated his initial capital stake elsewhere (in this case, from a highly successful men's clothing store in Philadelphia). Mr. Goldman's first partner, Samuel Sachs, joined the firm in 1882 with a loan from Mr. Goldman after marrying Mr. Goldman's daughter, Louisa. The firm continued to expand strictly through interfamily relationships, marriages, and their offspring until 1915, when the first nonfamily member joined the partnership. The first partner from outside the family's German-Jewish social group, Waddill Catchings, joined the firm in 1917.[3]

The Goldman Sachs kinship group was embedded in a larger web of relationships among bankers of German-Jewish extraction and the banks they founded, which included, among others, Kuhn, Loeb & Co.; Lehman Brothers; Speyer & Co.; and J. & W. Seligman & Co. A common culture that resulted in frequent personal interaction and intermarriage bonded these relationships, and the trust they engendered supported transactions that were beyond the scope of any single partnership.[4] For example, Goldman Sachs's initial foray into securities underwriting in 1906 came when Lehman Brothers and Speyer & Co. supplemented Goldman Sachs's capital base of $3 million to underwrite offerings by United Cigar Manufacturers and Sears, Roebuck totaling more than $15 million. Goldman Sachs and Lehman Brothers "continued to cooperate and the informal partnership headed 144 issues for fifty-six issuers, largely concentrating on firms engaged in distribution or light manufacturing."[5]

As the scale of transactions increased, underwriting syndicates became the norm. These virtual firms that formed around individual transactions brought together the capital necessary to underwrite large offerings. But as we suggested in chapter 6, they also mitigated conflicts of interest created when banks organized information and distribution networks beyond the scope of those bound by family ties. Banks were included in syndicates only if their reputation warranted the expectation that they could (and would) return the favor in the future. The short-term syndicate contract provided for lower-cost exclusion of those who rested on the laurels of past success.

When Catchings's infatuation with trading nearly brought Goldman Sachs down during the 1929 market crash, Sidney Weinberg took over and began to steer the firm from its capital-intensive trading origins to the agency function of advising major corporations. During his thirty-nine-year reign as senior partner, Weinberg oversaw the development of a culture that served its own interests by placing the client's interests first. Weinberg's emphasis on building client relationships by serving in an agency capacity received support from the 1933 Glass-Steagall Banking Act that separated deposit taking and commercial lending from securities market transactions and thereby created the uniquely American distinction between commercial banking and investment banking. This distinction had the effect of separating relatively capital-intensive principal activities such as commercial lending from agency functions such as corporate advisory services and securities underwriting.[6] Because the primary weakness of the partnership is that its capital base is limited to the wealth of the partners, the exclusion of investment banks from deposit taking and commercial lending probably contributed to the viability of investment banking partnerships through the mid-twentieth century.

Investment banking partnerships evolved on a large scale in the 1950s as a number of firms reorganized as private corporations. In 1950, 28 percent of all broker-dealers registered with the SEC (most quite small) were incorporated; by 1960, the proportion had increased to almost 42 percent.[7] Merrill Lynch was an early mover among large banks with its 1959 incorporation, followed by E.F. Hutton in 1962 and Dean Witter in 1968. However, the 95 percent holding of the Bear Stearns Companies Inc. common stock by the Bear, Stearns & Co. limited partnership suggests that incorporation was more a response to liability concerns than to capital or organizational considerations.

Prior to 1970, the NYSE required member firms to be organized as partnerships. In fact, Morgan Stanley, incorporated in 1935 at its founding, liquidated and reorganized as a partnership in 1941 to gain membership in the exchange.[8] In 1970, the NYSE, with the SEC's approval, opened the door to public ownership of member firms. Donaldson, Lufkin & Jenrette was the first bank to go public, on April 9, 1970, followed by First Boston and Merrill Lynch in 1971 and Dean Witter and E.F. Hutton in 1972. A second wave of public offerings occurred in the mid-1980s with the 1985 Bear Stearns IPO, followed by Morgan Stanley's 1986 offering.

Goldman Sachs's capital base in 1986 was about twice that of Morgan Stanley's (pre-IPO) capital of $500 million. The firm's general (active) partners controlled over 80 percent of this capital, with the remainder contributed by the firm's limited (retired) partners.[9] Although the firm's management committee gave serious consideration to a public offering at the time, the partners agreed instead to supplement their capital by accepting an offer from Sumitomo Bank of $500 million in private equity. This investment increased Goldman Sachs's capital by about 50 percent in exchange for only 12.5 percent of the firm's annual profits and any appreciation in equity value. The Bank Holding Company Act of 1956 further precluded Sumitomo from having voting rights or any influence over day-to-day operations.

So by 1986 we see an advisor to Fortune 500 firms that evolved from origins in the financial-capital-intensive world of trading facing increasing demands for financial capital commitments in conjunction with its advisory services. The partnership strained under these capital demands, but it helped to curb incentives for excessive risk taking by ensuring that those taking the risks were playing with their own money. During the period when Goldman Sachs shifted its energy to agency functions that depended more heavily on the organization's human capital, the partnership began to play an additional role.

Developing and Preserving Human Capital

Up to this point in the book, we've taken knowledge, culture, reputation, and relationships—the human capital of investment banks—for granted. But we've also suggested that investment in human capital requires an expectation of a fair return and that financial intermediaries rarely received protection from intellectual property law. Even if we set aside these concerns, there is a more fundamental problem. As Jack Morgan (J.P. Morgan Jr.) observed, a banker's reputation is "neither quickly nor easily acquired" and comes only after "years of fair and honourable dealing."[10] Worse, reputation is acquired by proving oneself in circumstances that most often present themselves only to the most reputable individuals and organizations. In other words, inexperienced bankers do not attract complex deals, and yet only through the successful completion of such deals can one gain the reputation necessary to attract them. Developing a reputation thus poses a Catch-22. Much the same can be said for other elements of the banker's human capital. How then do bankers develop human capital? Are there organizational strategies that assist in jump-starting the process?

Once developed, a reputation or client relationship is amplified by bringing less reputable parties under the umbrella. A senior banker's reputation for fair dealing or for providing valuable advice often presents more opportunities than the individual banker can pursue regardless of his work ethic. But if the senior banker delegates mundane tasks to underlings while ensuring that they are carried out at a level consistent with his reputation, his human capital is freed for tasks where it has greater impact on the margin. Perhaps more important, delegation of the mundane (or, to put it more politely, *mentoring*) transfers human capital—tacit knowledge encompassing reputation, relationships, and culture—to the next generation of bankers.

Mentoring in financial markets may be no less altruistic than elsewhere. But we think it's safe to assume that mentors envision a quid pro quo associated with their efforts (see Box 7-1). Leveraging one's human capital by delegating mundane tasks to subordinates provides its own payback. However, it's rare that enough blood can be wrung from a junior banker to match the benefits gained from working under the auspices of a banker of, say, Geoff Boisi's stature. Worse yet, as with information assets generally, once the junior banker is exposed to the mentor's human capital, it can be difficult to exclude the junior banker from future or excessive benefits. Wall Street bankers are infamous for job hopping, and clients often follow bankers in spite of long-standing associations with the banker's firm. Thus, exposing junior bankers to private information or client relationships might come back to haunt the mentor. Taking on less ambitious subordinates diminishes this problem but increases the risk that the mentor's reputation will be squandered through the subordinate's laziness or incompetence. In

Box 7-1   Life-Cycle Considerations in Human
             Capital Development

When human capital is developed through cooperative effort and
mentoring, it is often the case that junior employees are net
consumers while senior employees are net producers. Regardless of
the crushing workload imposed on the junior banker or new law
associate, it is not likely to offset the benefits derived in the short
run from joining a highly reputable organization. In principle, this
would argue for a *negative wage* for entry-level employees and a
wide gap between net consumers and net producers.

In a perfect capital market this might be implemented by
having junior employees borrow against future earnings to pay for
mentoring. This is impractical because an outside lender would
find it difficult to assess the employee's future earnings, and the
security for the loan—the human capital the employee seeks to
develop—is intangible and therefore provides poor collateral.
Alternatively, we might imagine mentors taking on the highest
bidders for their services. But again, it's not clear that bidding
capacity would be closely linked to the qualities being sought
for mentoring. Instead we see junior bankers and law associates
jump-starting the development of their human capital with "loans"
from their employers that are "paid down" by putting in long
hours at relatively low pay.

An "up or out" policy coupled with comparatively low pay for
nonpartners complements this alternative to negative wages. We
might think of nonpartners as having part of their current earning
power withheld to fund a "bet" on their prospects for gaining
partnership. The withholdings are then pooled and used to reward
the few who gain partnership. This further heightens incentives for
individual effort and promotes uniformity among the firm's
workforce over time by discouraging less talented candidates who
recognize that the bet does not favor them. And while there is no
shame in failing to gain entry to a prestigious partnership such as
Goldman Sachs, being asked to leave diminishes any undeserved
positive halo.

short, delegation of responsibility is limited by the mentor's capacity for
direct monitoring and for maintaining incentives that balance the talent and ambition of subordinates. Overreaching these limits leads to
degradation of the mentor's human capital.

Decay and rivalry are not usually considered threats to information assets. In principle, an idea is not diminished in the hands of a fool, nor does the fool's work preclude other useful applications of the idea. But this perspective presumes codification of the asset. Some elements of the investment banker's human capital, however, are difficult to codify and therefore are virtually inalienable. By *alienability* we mean the capacity for both transferring exclusive decision rights over an asset or piece of knowledge and its economic consequences to another party *and* capturing the benefits from doing so (see Box 7-2). It may be possible for a senior banker to nurture the transfer of a client relationship to a junior banker but more difficult to command fair compensation for doing so. If the latter were possible, the value of the relationship would be enhanced by its liquidity and would thereby heighten incentives to invest in its development in the first place.

Consider the case of George Peabody as he neared the end of his banking career in the middle of the nineteenth century after developing George Peabody & Co. into the premier American bank in London. Despite its prominence, Peabody & Co. was little more than Peabody and his clerk, G. C. Gooch. Had Peabody retired or died at this point, the firm's hard-earned reputation would likely have passed with him. In principle, Mr. Peabody could have auctioned his firm to the highest bidder. Had he done so, unless clients perceived the highest bidder to be Mr. Peabody's equal, their history with the firm would have had little influence on their future dealings. Recognizing this, potential bidders would have found bidding for the asset less attractive, and some fraction of the intangible asset's value would have been destroyed. In other words, Mr. Peabody's reputation suffered from limited alienability. Seen in this light, Mr. Peabody's 1854 offer of partnership to a relative unknown by the name of Junius Spencer Morgan represented an attempt to preserve an asset that could not be exchanged through an arms-length transaction. The partnership set in motion the transfer of human capital that remains at the foundations of J.P. Morgan Chase & Co., Morgan Stanley, and (Deutsche) Morgan Grenfell today.

In the case of human capital, suppression of alienability appears to be in its nature rather than a voluntary act. Keep in mind that alienability of decision rights involves the capacity for both exchange and capturing the benefits of exchange. Decision rights over human capital can be exchanged either through the simple act of disseminating information or, in more complex situations, through mentoring others in

Box 7-2 Inalienability and Organizational Structure

From the economist's perspective, alienability of a decision right encompasses both the right to sell or transfer the decision right and the ability to capture benefits in exchange. In other words, decision rights over a machine tool are alienable because our legal system provides for establishing and enforcing title over the asset and therefore supports its sale by providing legal transfer of the title. Property rights generally are understood to combine decision rights—how the tool will be used—with the right to alienate those rights.

Michael Jensen and William Meckling argue that organizational structure represents an evolved response to the voluntary suppression of alienability that comes with the separation of ownership from control.[11] In the extreme, it is unlikely that financial capital and the knowledge or capacity for putting it to its best use will reside in a single individual. I may have capital enough to purchase a lathe, but have little capacity for turning parts to precise specifications. Separation of ownership from control, as in the large public organization, enables specialization in the provision and application of financial capital. Shareholders delegate control, or "decision rights," to employees, but generally not the right to alienate their "positions or any other assets or decisions under their control."[12] Delegation of control rights to a machinist means that he controls how capably he uses the lathe, but it does not provide him with the right to sell the lathe or let others use it.

Suppression of alienability means that employees working under a fixed salary, for example, may have little incentive to make the best use of the assets or decision rights under their control. The machinist benefits little on the margin from an exquisitely turned part and shares the costs of a poorly turned part with his machine's owner. Jensen and Meckling see the various control systems that define organizations—employment contracts, performance measurement, compensation schemes, and so on—as means of diminishing this incentive distortion that effectively is the cost of specialization.

the use of that information. Capturing benefits from exchange is more difficult, however. Intellectual property law provides some relief by establishing and enforcing title over intellectual assets. But, as Oliver Williamson points out, law firms, for example, are organized as private partnerships for a reason—there is nothing to sell to the public.[13] A law firm's value depends on information concerning clients that can neither be separated from attorneys nor prevented from departing with those who leave the firm. In such instances where the law is silent or difficult to enforce, organizational alternatives are likely to develop. In this spirit, we argue that the Goldman Sachs partnership structure was a reflection of the intrinsic inalienability of human capital.

The Goldman Sachs Partnership

Culture

The Goldman Sachs partnership had a number of features that supported the development and preservation of human capital. Like most top investment banks, the firm maintained an exceptionally aggressive screening process for new hires. The need for high standards and aggressive screening of new recruits is obvious when the quality of goods and services is directly linked to the level of talent within an organization. Less obvious are the benefits that arise when the organization's members are *uniformly* talented. Uniformity of talent reduces the threat that less talented people will expropriate or free-ride on the human capital of more talented peers and thereby heightens incentives to invest in further development of the human capital residing within the organization. Unlike less human-capital-intensive organizations, where recruiting rarely involves senior management, even senior partners at Goldman Sachs participated in the screening of new associates. This is less surprising than might first appear when one considers that partners placed considerable human and financial capital on the line and therefore had a powerful incentive to think carefully about who would share it.

Upon joining the firm, several elements of the firm's culture discouraged junior bankers from free-riding. Mentoring essentially began with the first interview. Becoming a partner required the patronage of a partner, and patronage was earned by generating benefits for others. Junior bankers put in extraordinarily long hours at comparatively low hourly wages under the experienced and demanding watch of mentors

who drove home the firm's commitment to teamwork. John White-
head, co-chairman from 1976 to 1984, is said to have responded curtly
to a new associate's reports of (trivial) personal triumphs, "At Goldman
Sachs we say *we*, we never say *I*."[14] As the firm grew, basing annual
compensation on extensive internal reviews of both junior and senior
peers as well as cross-discipline reviews reinforced incentives to produce for others.[15] The emphasis on mentoring and peer review, apparently common throughout the industry at one time, effectively subordinated individual interests to those of the firm.

The emphasis on teamwork made the contributions of individual
bankers more opaque to the outside world. In fact, the primary visible
recognition of the individual's contributions to the firm was the offer
to join the partnership. Other things being equal, this limited an individual banker's ability to defect with client relationships and other intangibles that might be used in competition with the firm because it
made more difficult a credible claim to having been responsible for
their development and effective application.[16] Thus the relative lack of
transparency supported the trust necessary for the cooperative development and use of human capital in the first place (see Box 7-3). The
flat organizational structure that put junior and senior bankers in direct
contact with one another on a regular basis further assured that knowledge and relationships were handed over to the next generation of
bankers.

Compensation

New M.B.A.s have always found investment banking opportunities
quite lucrative. But bonuses tied to profitability generally account for
the bulk of total compensation. Until the early 1990s, Goldman Sachs
based bonuses on the overall performance of the firm rather than on
profits generated by individuals or small teams. But as it became commonplace for competitors to reward individuals with astronomical year-
end bonuses, the firm began to lose top performers and surely failed to
attract some in the first place. The firm responded to the threat in two
ways. First, although a star performer earned less at Goldman Sachs in
the short run, the lure of partnership provided a substantial counterbalance. Particularly after the other bulge-bracket banks dissolved their
partnerships in favor of public incorporation, the offer to join the Goldman Sachs partnership represented a unique and highly visible honor
within the Wall Street community. The financial rewards were also

Box 7-3   Hierarchy and Transparency

University of Chicago economists Raghuram Rajan and Luigi
Zingales argue that a hierarchical organizational structure serves a
similar trust-building function by buffering strategic knowledge or
relationships from employees who have not proven their
commitment to the organization.[17] Their argument appears tailor-
made for software development and similar settings where
exposure to strategic blocks of codified knowledge poses a threat of
expropriation but where the codified knowledge is sufficiently
modular to support arm's-length development of complementary
assets. We might imagine, for instance, the case of a computer
operating system where property rights over fundamental
principles of operation might be difficult to enforce but can be
protected by wrapping the system in a general interface that
permits arm's-length development of application software. In the
typology developed in chapter 5, such firms are best classified as
intellectual asset intensive in their operations.

We think it is no accident that *human-capital-intensive* firms
generally are less hierarchical simply because direct exposure of
inexperienced employees to the human capital of senior employees
appears to promote both its further development and its
preservation. Thus the optimal organizational structure might be
more nearly transparent or cooperative internally but highly
opaque from the perspective of outsiders—a structure consistent
with an emphasis on teamwork involving both experienced and
inexperienced members of the organization and limited
communication of individual contributions to the outside world.

generous. In 1993 first-year partners had 0.25 percent of the firm's
more than $2.6 billion in pretax profits, or about $6.5 million, contributed to their capital accounts.[18]

Second, Goldman Sachs sought to "do the ordinary things extraordinarily well."[19] Although Wall Street regarded the firm's people as
exceptionally able, it did not regard the firm as among the most daring
or innovative. Instead, Goldman Sachs relied on cooperation among
highly talented people to deliver existing products and services at a
higher level of quality than its competition. Presumably, no matter
how talented, an individual's long-run private benefits from exceptional

team performance outweighed those she could expect in a more star-oriented system.

But by the mid-1990s, with foreign banks aggressively bidding for banking talent, even the lure of the partnership did not stem defections by many top junior performers. Prior to creating the rank of managing director in 1996, Goldman Sachs lost about fifty mid-level vice presidents and analysts to Deutsche Morgan Grenfell alone. In 1997, as the partnership stood at about 200 members, the firm named 126 new managing directors. Aimed at likely partners, the managing director rank essentially narrowed the large gap in earnings between partners and the highest-ranking nonpartners. Although the designation was not a guarantee of joining the partnership in the future, it did offer greater opportunity to share in the firm's profits and thereby brought total compensation more nearly in line with the competition. If opacity was a key element of the partnership's capacity for developing and preserving human capital, then the pre-IPO designation of managing directors probably undermined incentives by revealing information about the individual's perceived contributions. With the public offering visible on the horizon, however, introduction of the managing director rank protected the firm's human capital during the transition.

Ownership Structure

A final noteworthy feature of the partnership had to do with its ownership structure and the transition from general partnership to limited partnership. Prior to Sumitomo Bank's 1986 private equity investment, general partners owned about 80 percent of the firm's equity, with the remainder held by limited partners. Moreover, as recently as 1980 the firm had only 2,000 employees, although the workforce increased to about 6,000 by 1986. In other words, ownership and day-to-day control of the firm were closely linked, as Williamson suggested they should be where production is largely dependent on human capital. But by 1994 the general partners owned less than one-third of the partnership's equity (although the agreements with private equity investors still entitled them to the majority of profits).[20] By the time the firm went public, only about 200 general partners and 160 nonpartner managing directors of the firm's 13,000 employees shared in the dwindling equity stake.

The firm's team culture apparently survived the declining ownership stake of the partners. But this was likely related to the tendency for senior partners to retire to limited partnership status at a relatively early age. In other words, partners effectively turned over equity and control to the next generation of partners at a fairly rapid pace. For example, when the firm went public, the names and ages of its directors and executive officers were as shown in table 7-1.

With the exception of former chairman John L. Weinberg, the age of directors and executive officers ranges from the early forties to the early fifties. Weinberg retired to limited partnership in 1990 after a five-year transition period during which control of the firm was gradually passed on to Stephen Friedman and Robert Rubin. Similarly, when Geoffrey Boisi left the firm in 1991, he was only forty-four. Although this was still considered young for a partner "going limited," it was part of a pattern of decline in the average duration of general partnership from eight years in 1986 to five years in 1994. By 1996, over half the general partners had less than three years tenure with the firm.[21]

While partnership had its rewards, there were severe limits on withdrawals by active partners. In a 1973 interview, Gus Levy (then chairman of the management committee) pointed out that only the management committee had the right to authorize a withdrawal of capital by an active partner.[22] Such withdrawals might be approved for the purpose of buying a house or insurance, but otherwise the firm paid partners a 6 percent annual return on their capital and paid the partner's taxes on the firm's profits. Partners were prohibited from borrowing money outside the firm for any other purpose. This strict commitment

Table 7-1
Names and Ages of Goldman Sachs Directors and Executive Officers

Name	Age	Title
Henry M. Paulson Jr.	52	Director, Chairman, and Chief Executive Officer
Robert J. Hurst	53	Director and Vice Chairman
John A. Thain	43	Director, President, and Co-Chief Operating Officer
John L. Thornton	45	Director, President, and Co-Chief Operating Officer
John L. Weinberg	74	Director
Robert J. Katz	51	General Counsel
Gregory K. Palm	50	General Counsel
Robin Neustein	45	Chief of Staff
Leslie M. Tortora	42	Chief Information Officer
David A. Viniar	43	Chief Financial Officer
Barry L. Zubrow	46	Chief Administrative Officer

Source: S-1 filing with the U.S. Securities and Exchange Commission, 1999.

to capitalizing the ongoing operations of the firm provided a powerful incentive for partners to remain focused in their oversight of junior bankers as well as of one another.

Upon stepping down to limited partnership, partners could withdraw capital from the firm, but only incrementally. Until 1996 the withdrawal rate varied between 25 percent and 50 percent of capital within the first year, with the remainder withdrawn over five years.[23] However, at the discretion of the firm's management committee, the payout schedule could be extended to preserve capital. The firm exercised this option in 1996 in response to problems created by the large number of partners going limited in the wake of large trading losses racked up in 1994. Biannual renegotiation of the partnership agreement also provided a mechanism for increasing or reducing a partner's claim on future profits in response to changes in productivity. The threat of both immediate and delayed consequences encouraged partners to remain vigilant and put forth their best effort on behalf of the firm even as they approached retirement.

The Demise of the Partnership: 1986–1998

Following the 1986 Sumitomo investment, the *relative* importance of human capital began to diminish as the firm sharply increased principal risk-taking activities both to leverage human capital in agency functions and to exploit advances in theory and technology in securities trading, particularly in the fixed-income and derivatives markets (see Box 7-4). We see the former reflected in the firm's 1988 principal investments of $1.1 billion in bridge loans and $250 million through a leveraged buyout fund while falling short in a bid (led by Geoff Boisi) for RJR Nabisco that would have involved substantial additional bridge lending. Shortly after Kohlberg Kravis Roberts & Co. (KKR) closed its leveraged buyout of RJR Nabisco in February 1989, Goldman Sachs invested $250 million of partners' capital in BroadPark, a joint venture with Citibank formed to provide syndicated bridge financing for deals that would later be refinanced with long-term debt.[24]

The firm took a controversial step in the fall of 1990 with the opening of Water Street Corporate Recovery Fund. Goldman Sachs formed the $783 million fund to invest in the debt of firms in financial distress, with the goal of squeezing out profits during restructuring. Goldman Sachs liquidated the fund after only one year because these "vulture

---

Box 7-4   Principal Investments as a Substitute for
Client Relationships

Principal investments in support of traditional advisory functions
enabled banks to recapture benefits associated with human capital
that diminished with the weakening of bank/client relationships.
Recall that exclusive relationships supported R&D in spite of the
ease of reverse engineering financial innovations by assuring banks
of handsome rewards for their efforts. The decline of exclusive
relationships in the 1980s put pressure on fees, meaning that
dealmakers faced a greater threat of having the value of their ideas
expropriated by competitors. Taking an equity stake in a deal
enables the bank to compete more aggressively on fees while
maintaining a strong claim on any human capital contributed to
the deal. Although principal investments also expose the bank to
risks not previously borne, the enormous returns expected from
these investments (typically in excess of 30 percent annually)
almost certainly reflect a return on the bank's investment in human
capital.

---

investments" put off both institutional investors who faced the firm
during restructuring negotiations and distressed firms who otherwise
might have sought the firm's representation during negotiations. The
firm followed with a series of four private equity funds in the 1990s.
At its August 2000 closing, the $5.25 billion Goldman Sachs Capital
Partners IV fund was the second largest LBO fund ever, trailing only
the $6 billion fund closed by KKR in 1996. Goldman Sachs employees
and employee investment funds provided $1.6 billion of the funding.

At this point, in the minds of many of Goldman Sachs's corporate
finance specialists, the firm remained a partnership in name only as
it substantially expanded proprietary trading activities under the leadership of Stephen Friedman and Robert Rubin. The firm's culture
strained under tension between bankers and traders. On the one hand,
bankers saw their wealth put at risk by traders who shared little in the
pain of failed trades but shared richly, through performance-based
bonuses, in successful trades. Traders, on the other hand, saw themselves as increasingly central to the firm's profitability. For example,
Larry Becerra, a high-profile trader in London, made more than $70
million for the firm in 1993 alone, and the London office accounted for

approximately $800 million of the firm's $2.6 billion in pretax profits. The firm responded by altering its compensation strategy to pay some traders as much or more than junior partners who placed their own wealth at risk in the firm.[25] But in 1994 the London office lost virtually everything it made in 1993, and partnership capital declined by 10 percent. About 30 percent of the partners who signed the (two-year) partnership agreement in 1992 left the firm prior to the December 1, 1994, closing on the new partnership agreement—thirty-six in 1994 alone.

In the aftermath of the 1994 debacle, the firm reorganized as a private limited liability partnership, thereby shielding partners' private assets from exposure to business risks, and did away with title of partner. All partners and several hundred vice presidents became managing directors, with the former retaining their ownership stakes in the firm but now with limited liability. After several false starts the firm went public in June 1999. Priced at $53 per share, the offering valued the firm at about $25 billion and raised $3.66 billion in new capital by selling 16 percent of the firm's equity.

Why Goldman Sachs Went Public

Against this background, our central thesis is that the three motivations for going public outlined earlier reflected a declining relative importance of human capital as the investment banking industry became more dependent on physical and financial capital. We now consider each motivation in greater detail.

Broadening Employee Equity Ownership

As the firm grew rapidly in the 1980s and 1990s it depended more heavily on leadership from employees who had little hope of joining the partnership, and the breadth of equity ownership was not keeping pace with the firm's growth rate. Or so it seemed.

In fact, nonpartners captured an increasing share of the firm's equity in the form of bonuses. This was nowhere more striking than in the proprietary trading business. Lisa Endlich, a former Goldman Sachs vice president and foreign exchange trader, offered the following insider perspective of the business's state in the early 1990s:

> Compensation for a successful proprietary trader [could] be as high as or higher than that of the newer partners—without the personal risk of unlimited liability or the requirement that earnings be rein-

vested in the firm until resignation or retirement. Traders were paid out everything in the year in which they earned it. If a proprietary trader earned $60 million for the firm one year and lost $50 million the next, he would still be well compensated for the two years, with a bonus of perhaps $2 to $3 million the first year and maybe $100,000 in salary the next.[26]

Sharing the gains with traders but not forcing them to endure losses was tantamount to giving them a call option. Option theory demonstrates that a call option is equivalent to a leveraged equity stake. In other words, traders implicitly received equity stakes by way of a "heads I win, tails you lose" compensation schedule. In principle, there is nothing wrong with distributing equity via options, but in practice it can be like letting children play with matches. The problem is that traders can unilaterally increase their implicit ownership stakes by taking on more risk unless strict guidelines prevent them from doing so. With options, greater risk translates into more leverage on the equity stake, and in this instance the trader effectively gains leverage on the backs of the partners, whose equity is lost when a trade goes sour.

The only real downside risk is the threat of being fired. The firm repeatedly laid off people in response to poor earnings during this period, but it's not clear that this was a substantial disincentive to risk taking. Wall Street bankers have an uncanny ability to move seamlessly from one opportunity to the next regardless of problems they may have left in their wake. Other things being equal, having spent time at Goldman Sachs might only have helped in this regard.

But Goldman Sachs may have had little choice in the matter. By the early 1990s Goldman Sachs's competitors began to recognize that they had a problem on their hands. In a few instances, they tried to hold the line by forcing traders to "bank" their bonuses so that they might be used to offset future losses associated with their risk taking. Salomon Smith Barney was a noteworthy case in that immediately upon introducing this type of new bonus scheme, competitors swooped in and bid away their best people. This forced the firm to return to the old bonus scheme almost immediately. Thus, had Goldman Sachs not offered large bonuses to traders, they would have lost even more traders to competitors willing to do so.

So why didn't the firm just extend partnership to a larger fraction of employees? In effect, it did so with the first class of managing directors in 1997. Managing directors received participation shares in the firm whose value was tied to firmwide rather than individual or departmental performance. But a deeper point is reflected in the pre-IPO battle over the division of spoils that pitted senior general partners against limited partners, junior partners, and nonpartners. The firm embodied the collective reputations of past and current partners; client and investor relationships; a culture that for some time had promoted good use of these intangibles; and a growing pool of tangible assets, including the contributions of financial capital by nonpartners. Historically, the intangible assets were the primary source of value and were the partners' province. Limited partners viewed their contributions to the intangible asset base as tantamount to being placed in a sacred trust. They handed down relationships and reputation to the next generation and expected the beneficiaries to do the same. No single generation had greater rights to these assets than another.

The IPO presented a problem very much like the game of musical chairs. The music stops when the firm goes public and the intangible assets are monetized. The active partners with the most influence over the division of spoils grabbed the empty chairs, leaving limited partners and nonpartners on the sidelines. But were the limited partners correct in claiming that the general partners wanted something that wasn't theirs to take?[27] Well, if the nature of the business hadn't changed, probably so. But as client relationships eroded, spreads from securities underwriting narrowed, and the firm's profits increasingly came from putting financial capital at risk, they may have been off the mark.

Human capital remained important, to be sure, but in many instances it was being leveraged with financial capital, increasingly contributed by nonpartners. In other words, investment banking was moving away from a pure content model in which most bankers created content to a model in which many bankers now managed the human and financial capital that others placed at their disposal. In the old model, bankers owned the firm because they *were* the firm. In the new model, ownership, spread more widely, improved incentives for those who managed the assets of others. In other words, investment banks, with the exception of their pure advisory businesses, began to look more like (God forbid) their commercial banking brethren. And the banking teams at the core of these advisory businesses increasingly operated more like free agents. From this perspective, the active partners were seeing the firm through a regime shift in which the value of past contributions was eroded and development of a new mode of operation became necessary. Because the firm's public valuation reflected market expectations regarding future income streams, the active partners might then argue with some force that their contributions carried greater weight and therefore warranted a larger share of the spoils from going public.

In the event, limited and junior partners and nonpartners gained relative to initial proposals, but active senior partners ultimately commanded the lion's share of the firm's value on a per capita basis. Retired limited partners exchanged their partnership interests for a combination of cash (24 percent), common stock (68 percent), and nontransferable subordinated debt (8 percent).[28] Active partners received equity stakes subject to a vesting period and various noncompete agreements. We'll return later to the significance of each structure.

The Need for a Larger and More Stable Capital Base

A common explanation for investment banks' increasing demand for financial capital is the sheer magnitude of deals in the global marketplace. Without question, both the international privatization movement and the rise of huge multinational corporations produced eye-popping transactions. The billion-dollar IPO is commonplace, as are mergers and acquisitions of similarly extreme magnitude. But on a relative basis, it's not clear that these transactions are any more extreme than, for example, nineteenth-century railroad transactions. Moreover, this view begs a larger question: Why are investment banks shifting from their more traditional agency role to the financial-capital-intensive principal role?

As we've emphasized throughout this book, the agency role was quite profitable to banks in a world of primitive communications technology. But now spreads for agency functions, in the debt markets at least, are under severe pressure. As *The Economist* observed, "Competition is fiercest outside America, where very few firms even earn their cost of capital. Merrill Lynch, for instance, won a recent mandate to lead-manage the sale of a stake in Brazil's national oil company, Petrobras, with fees of just 0.45 percent of the amount raised, about one-tenth of the amount charged for similar deals a few years ago."[29] Codification of agency functions is promoting unprecedented competition.

Likewise, the erosion of client relationships is squeezing advisory fees. Investment banking fees at Goldman Sachs generated 35 percent of the firm's profits in 1989 but only 16 percent by 1993, with M&A fees declining from 40 percent of investment banking revenues to 17 percent by 1993.[30] As we saw earlier, banks are countering this trend by taking equity stakes in the deals they advise on. Increasingly, however, they're also pressured to make low-margin loans in support of transactions.

Finally, codification of asset pricing and portfolio management coupled with enormous increases in computer processing capacity is enabling new capital-intensive trading strategies. These trading strategies, in large part, responded to inefficiencies in the marketplace. Widespread implementation wrings out the inefficiencies and narrows the spreads that made the strategies attractive in the first place.

The experience of LTCM, previously discussed in chapter 2, provides a case in point. Early on, LTCM had more opportunities than it knew what to do with. But their early arbitrage successes picked off the low-hanging fruit and forced a shift to either lower-return or higher-risk alternatives. Eventually, for want of attractive opportunities, the firm returned a portion of its capital to investors (only shortly before its 1998 collapse). As LTCM undertook more complex, human-capital-dependent strategies such as risk arbitrage, firms such as BNP/Cooper-Neff Advisors leaned more heavily on information technology that leveraged codified knowledge to squeeze pennies from each of a huge volume of relatively low-risk trades.[31] As LTCM went down in 1998, BNP/Cooper-Neff made record profits.

Collectively, these forces, each linked to advances in information technology and theoretical knowledge and their displacement of human capital, conspired to force investment banks to put more financial capital into play. As financial capital becomes more central to investment banking, stability of the capital base takes on greater importance. Investment banks tend toward highly liquid balance sheets containing assets that are marked to market daily and often funded in the repurchase agreement (or Repo) market. (A repurchase agreement essentially is a loan secured by liquid securities and generally is a stable source of funding even in difficult market conditions.) But as capital demands grew and banks sought long-term, external capital commitments, their liquidity became a problem.

Contributors of external capital judge their risks from the nature of the balance sheet. But many investment banking functions are relatively opaque because they involve the preservation of strategic information for clients. Lack of transparency leads potential contributors of equity to fear that firms will seek funds at precisely those times when it sees equity as overvalued in the marketplace (the adverse selection problem). Lenders must be concerned that unforeseen risks will effectively lead to their exploitation for the benefit of equity holders (the moral hazard problem). A liquid balance sheet compounds both threats by making it easier for the bank to alter its risk profile (see Box 7-5).

A natural response, then, is to invest more heavily in risk management and to diversify operations to smooth cash flows. Like most other banks, during the 1980s and 1990s Goldman Sachs made a substantial commitment to risk management tools such as value at risk (VaR) and risk-adjusted return on capital (RAROC). Controlling risk taking internally took on greater importance as the firm moved toward a stronger bonus orientation for traders. Although the theory behind these tools is good, practice still has some way to go. Measurement is complicated, and it's easy to fall into the trap of rewarding only what is easily measured. Some would argue that this is precisely what led Bankers Trust down the path of sacrificing customer relationships for short-term trading gains in its dealings with Procter & Gamble and Gibson Greetings in 1993 and 1994.

This is where Goldman Sachs's interest in branching out to money management comes into play. The firm lagged substantially behind competitors such as Morgan Stanley Dean Witter and Merrill Lynch in this and other large-scale but stable sources of fee income such as retail brokerage and credit cards. In light of Goldman Sachs's emphasis on wholesale operations, the firm faced a substantial barrier to entry. One thing working in its favor was a substantial and wealthy private banking clientele that would complement investments in fund management. Thus far the firm has used this as well as its relationships with large corporations to great effect. By March 2001, the firm had about $300 billion of corporate funds under management and $200 billion to $300 billion from private banking clients. Goldman Sachs's goal is to double that over the next five years because as David Blood, co-head of the firm's asset management business, observed, the option is "to become extremely big or get out" of the business.[33] Money management is a highly codified, large-scale data-processing business. As such it requires a long-term commitment of capital to build or acquire infrastructure capable of achieving economies of scale.

Box 7-5   The Pecking Order Theory of Financing

Stewart Myers of MIT first argued that these information frictions imply a "pecking order" for raising funds.[32] External financing becomes a last resort, with equity at the bottom of the pecking order because investors will provide funds only on terms reflecting the risks associated with their informational disadvantage. The firm's first preference is for internally generated funds because they don't carry this risk premium. Other things being equal, opaque firms or firms with liquid balance sheets should then place more emphasis on generating a sufficiently large and stable internal cash flow to fund future investment.

A Currency for Acquisition

Why should Goldman Sachs acquire rather than build such assets? In chapter 6 we discussed at some length the difficulty of innovating within the complex web of expectations that binds relationship networks. Unfortunately, the best application of innovations may be within existing networks, given that relationships and reputations are built over time rather than acquired at arm's length. Among the Internet investment banks, OffRoad Capital appears particularly cognizant of this point.

Goldman Sachs's CEO, Henry Paulson, proved a man of his word as Goldman Sachs moved quickly to acquire and build the infrastructure to place the firm's mark on the global electronic marketplace. Goldman Sachs's first major acquisition after going public involved paying $531 million (in stock, options, and cash) for the Hull Group, a global market maker for equity derivatives based in Chicago. This deal is a prime example of the acquisition of a technology that is then plugged into the acquirer's broader network of existing relationships. As we'll see in chapter 8, the acquisition complemented smaller stakes taken in a variety of other electronic platforms, including those of Wit SoundView and OptiMark.

It's also eerily similar to earlier moves by commercial banks trying to gain a toehold in the OTC derivatives markets in the late 1980s and early 1990s. For example, perhaps the three most prominent derivatives operations of the 1980s, CRT, O'Connor and Associates, and Cooper Neff, were acquired by large commercial banks that sought to leverage the technology platforms developed by the derivatives firms by linking them to their large existing networks of corporate clients. In light of our thesis regarding the role of theoretical advances in driving the shift in emphasis from human to financial capital, the leading role played by derivatives shops is not surprising. Codification of this business, driven by advances in financial engineering, far outstrips that of most others.

In sum, Goldman Sachs's IPO reflected a shift in the relative importance of human capital and financial capital driven by advances in theory and information technology. This shift exposed the weakness of the partnership—risk sharing and financial capital formation—to the point that it ultimately outweighed any benefits of the partnership. Goldman Sachs probably held out longer than many of its peers as a result of its long-standing cultural commitment to client service. Even as the tide turned in deal making in the 1980s, Goldman Sachs remained a holdout by refusing to advise on hostile takeovers. Likewise, it was still possible for the senior partner (Weinberg) to express relief that Goldman Sachs lost in its bid to handle the RJR Nabisco LBO. Only with the passing of the baton to Friedman and Rubin and increasing pressure in the marketplace on spreads (both investment banking and trading) did Goldman Sachs place greater emphasis on capital-intensive businesses. In this regard, their strong client relationships, for better or worse, may have prevented them from moving down this path as quickly as firms such as Salomon Smith Barney or even Morgan Stanley.

The Passing of the Partnership: Was Anything Lost?

Is there anything special about the partnership per se in the development of human capital, or was it Goldman Sachs's implementation that made the difference? The answer to this question should lie in whether the public organization supports various elements of the firm's culture, compensation policy, and ownership structure discussed earlier. For example, as important as opacity and delayed rewards for outstanding performance may have been to Goldman Sachs's success, these features are not necessarily unique to private partnerships. Some degree of opacity is a feature of any form of team production. The large pay gap between middle managers and senior managers in many public organizations has incentive consequences similar to the delayed and uncertain reward of partnership. Incentives are further sharpened by a variety of strategies, ranging from bonus and equity compensation plans requiring vesting to option plans with relatively distant exercise dates. In fact, Goldman Sachs adopted a compensation scheme containing many of these fundamental building blocks. Likewise, public organizations constrain employee mobility with employment and noncompete contracts like those described in Goldman Sachs's IPO prospectus.

The real key is striking the right balance between mobility and freedom without undermining either performance incentives or incentives for talented people to join the firm in the first place. The recent flurry of job-hopping associated with acquisitions of Goldman competitors such as J.P. Morgan and Donaldson, Lufkin & Jenrette attests to the fact that this is easier said than done. By design or good luck Goldman Sachs appears to have been quite successful in striking the right balance during its partnership days, at least until the 1990s. But the difficulties then encountered suggest that perhaps the real key to maintaining Goldman Sachs's culture was the relatively small size of the firm prior to the mid-1980s. As the firm grew by leaps and bounds thereafter, the differences between public and private ownership probably had considerably less bearing on the firm's culture. Given the financial capital constraints imposed by the partnership, perhaps little was lost on net when the firm went public.

Back to the Future?

Goldman Sachs's public offering reflects the firm's commitment to joining the race for scale in the global financial services industry. If our analysis is correct, this race is another manifestation of recent advances in financial theory and information technology. Whereas human capital once dominated, many intermediary functions are more commodity-like. Commoditization of intermediary functions implies narrowing profit margins and a demand for financial capital to build the infrastructure required to achieve scale economies. In this world, the benefits of the small partnership, mostly associated with nurturing human capital, are diminished and financial capital constraints are increasingly binding.

One by-product of the race for scale in financial services is the bundling of human-capital-intensive functions with large-scale electronic distribution platforms on an unprecedented scale. More generally, we might think of this as a large-scale merging of content origination and distribution. The decade leading up to Goldman Sachs's IPO witnessed numerous conflicts between the two in the standoff between traditional relationship bankers or corporate finance specialists and the firm's various trading operations. If anything, the data-processing-intensive business of money management and the technology-intensive electronic platforms that Goldman Sachs has invested in so heavily recently represent an even bigger step from the firm's human-capital-intensive roots. Can these new financial behemoths manage the tension between the increasingly diverse businesses they bring together?

Or is the bundling of businesses more apparent than real? Bulge-bracket investment banks nominally command a wider array of resources than ever before. However, the level of turnover among human capitalists is reaching new heights. In the "good old days," key people commonly remained with one firm (often a partnership) for their entire career. Now the tension between human capital and financial capital leads to more frequent resorting of human assets with physical assets. Perhaps it is more useful, then, to think of the human capitalists as independent operators aligning themselves with the distribution platform that best serves their interests at the moment. In the words of Jeffrey Sechrest, who recently left the boutique firm Evercore Partners to become Merrill Lynch's vice chairman for investment banking, "I think the Merrill platform is an incredible platform, and one where I can use my client relationships and deal skills to take advantage of that platform."[34]

The same thinking, evidenced in the mobility of Frank Quattrone's team of technology bankers and in Geoff Boisi's taking command of J.P. Morgan Chase & Co.'s investment banking operations, is consistent with the property rights perspective on the firm (see chapter 6) to the extent that these dominant human capitalists really command the increasingly large physical assets of financial services firms. When their command is insufficient or the quality of the physical distribution platform declines relative to the human capital they bring to the table, they move on to greener pastures. All the while, they run their teams like the traditionally small partnerships that dotted the financial services landscape.

In sum, the industry is stumbling toward a new compact between financial and human capitalists. The new compact reflects the relative rise of financial capital, but not necessarily the dominance of financial capital that convergence to a relatively small number of behemoth public corporations might suggest. Rather, we contend that either formally or informally, the dealings between human and financial capitalists will be governed by loose affiliations not unlike the traditional syndicate, with the primary difference being the development of large-scale, branded distribution platforms. Teams of human capitalists, organized like the small partnerships of the past, will move fluidly from platform to platform in accordance with perceived opportunities and their command over physical assets. If so, the distribution platforms and their employees will look and be compensated in a manner similar to that of traditional commercial bankers, unless they develop exceptional brand recognition or otherwise dominate a market segment. The star human capitalists, though fewer in number, will be even more richly rewarded than in the recent past.

8

ONLINE STOCK
EXCHANGES

HAVING EXAMINED the new compact forming between human capitalists and financial capitalists, we turn to the turbulent but fascinating transformation underway within the members-only securities
exchanges where these same firms establish the boundaries and make
the rules. Here, too, we find tremendous upheaval both within securities exchanges and in their dealings with the outside world as nonmembers use the Internet to break their stranglehold on securities trading. Ironically, key members of the exchanges, primarily the dominant
investment banks, are instigating much of the upheaval. On the one
hand, we see acquisition of NYSE specialist firms placing more than
half of NYSE trading volume in the hands of only three firms. On
the other hand, some of the most acquisitive firms also stand behind
competing electronic trading venues and recent reform proposals that
would have the stock markets organized as a single electronic network.
How can an industry seemingly be consolidating and decentralizing at
the same time?

Our goal in this chapter is to win the battle between getting lost in
minutia and providing useful perspective on how the Internet undermines the physical and regulatory constraints that supported the traditional exchange model. This is a challenge because, more so than in
other areas, the devil is in the details of security market design. We

begin our balancing act by outlining the basic functions of intermediaries in financial exchanges. These functions are best understood if we think of the exchange as a kind of firm made up of its various members cooperatively engaged in the competitive production of securities prices. Once again we'll see that traditional practice bundled intermediary functions with the physical network, and that therefore human capital dominated the scene. For example, the NYSE specialist stood at the hub of an exclusive network of personal relationships with other exchange members through which most of the information that translated into prices moved about. This structure had both costs and benefits. On the downside, exchanges sometimes used their monopoly power to abuse customers and stifle innovation. On the upside, centralized markets provided intermediaries with necessary leverage, prevented fragmentation of the price discovery process, and narrowed the focus, and thus the cost, of regulatory attention.

To understand why the exchanges are changing and how and why the Internet is driving these changes, it is useful to recognize that stock exchanges are an exclusive domain. NYSE membership has remained constant at 1,366 since 1953, and the going price for admission was about $2 million as of November 13, 2000. Members include specialists, who provide liquidity for their assigned stocks, and brokers, who represent orders from the public at large. Exchange members generate valuable information by "discovering" the price of shares through their trading with one another. Outsiders receive just enough information to pique their interest in buying and selling shares via a member's representation.

The history of stock exchanges is sprinkled with accounts of the ingenuity of nonmembers in seeking direct access to information produced on the exchange floor. For many years, the stone walls of 18 Broad Street proved an imposing barrier. But since the advent of the telegraph and ticker tape, exchanges have fought a losing battle against information's desire to be free. The Internet poses a serious threat to the traditional exchange because it vastly lowers the cost of opening new trading venues and then aggregating the results of decentralized information production. Although advances in information technology threaten to fragment existing equity markets by erasing physical and national boundaries, the same advances support information aggregation. In the United States, national and regional exchanges have long been linked by the Intermarket Trading System (ITS), a communication network that Archipelago CEO Gerald Putnam neatly describes as the modern equivalent of two cans and a string. The Internet provides much greater capacity for aggregating the bits of information gleaned from decentralized price discovery. But as alternative trading venues pursue their own competing interests, we now face a far more severe problem of promoting cooperation in the sharing of information that once was the exclusive domain of a relatively small club of like-minded individuals.

Stepping back from the details to assess the broad impact of advances in information technology, we see the gathering force of decentralization standing out from the background. In the past, both the regulation and economics of exchanges led to a few key focal points for exchange. And in turn, a highly centralized exchange more nearly ensured that a single price prevailed. Now, much greater capacity for decentralized price discovery exists, which raises the threat that prices at any point in physical or virtual space will tell only a small part of the story. Timely and accurate information about company share prices, relative industry performance, and international exchange rates has significant bearing on how efficiently we allocate scarce resources across the economy. Therefore policymakers have a legitimate interest in balancing this common interest in efficient allocation of investment capital against the private interests of individual traders.

Later in this chapter, we use the insight gained from our discussion of mechanism design principles in chapter 4 to outline a hypothetical network structure and then use it to benchmark recent innovations in the marketplace. In contrast to the hub-and-spoke structure of traditional markets, we envision markets of the near future as being organized in a web of decentralized relationships not unlike the decentralized ecology of the Internet itself. Geographical constraints will be destroyed, and policymakers will find it increasingly difficult to promote the public interest in securities markets where they no longer have a captive audience. At various nodes throughout the network of exchange, intermediaries will continue down the recent path toward specialization in the services they provide. We might imagine some nodes, such as the trading desks of large investment banks, as providing the high level of human discretion that complex transactions require. Others will specialize in streamlined electronic execution of less sensitive transactions. The challenge for policymakers will be to encourage aggregation of information in this fragmented marketplace. But first, we return to the fundamentals of what exchanges are, the role played by member firms, and how they are being challenged by new technology.

The Functions of Securities Exchanges

Like other business organizations, securities exchanges offer products and services by means of a *production technology*. Simply put, securities exchanges are venues where market participants come together to produce liquidity and prices—the former by providing traders with a mechanism for price discovery (or price production) through various order placement strategies. An exchange's production technology includes both manpower and a vast array of communications and data-processing technologies, but it is also embodied in the standard operating procedures that flow from the rules and accepted practice: the choices made by the creators of the exchange regarding rules for access, interaction, and reporting.

Before taking up our discussion of the reorganization of securities exchanges, we need to at least develop some shorthand for referencing various exchange-design considerations. The following subsections provide succinct definitions for market liquidity, the various types of traders who participate in securities markets, and the meaning and mechanisms of price discovery, market transparency, and participant anonymity. A more detailed explanation of each concept, along with some concrete examples to reinforce the ideas, is provided in appendix B.

Liquidity

Market *liquidity* comprises *market width* (the bid-ask spread), *market depth* (the number of shares available at a quoted price), *market resilience* (how quickly the marketplace recovers from buy-sell imbalances), and *immediacy* (the speed of execution at a specific price). Liquidity is a function of the interplay between the trading public and the intermediaries that populate an exchange. On the New York Stock Exchange, for example, the specialist is bound by her affirmative obligation to immediately satisfy market orders in the absence of offsetting public orders on the limit-order book or within the community of floor brokers.[1]

Traders

Patient traders effectively *provide* liquidity to the exchange by their fixed bids, such as limit orders, enabling other traders to gauge demand to buy and sell at a stated price. *Impatient traders* effectively *consume* liquidity by placing market orders that demand immediate execution. Traders also are distinguished by their typical order size. Retail traders generally place smaller orders than institutional traders. Order size often is perceived as reflecting how well informed a trader is—other things being equal, well-informed traders place larger orders to more fully capture the benefits of their informational advantage.

Trading venues often position themselves to attract or exclude relatively large or small orders. For example, Bernard L. Madoff Investment Securities, the first prominent practitioner of "payment for order flow," paid several cents per share to brokers delivering orders of no more than 1,000 shares. In exchange, Madoff guaranteed execution at the best prices currently quoted on the NYSE. Of the 18 percent of trades in NYSE-listed stocks that took place off the exchange in 1999, about 12 percent were executed by dealers such as Madoff belonging to the National Association of Securities Dealers (NASD), many of whom offered rebates to attract these typically small orders. More recently, Knight/Trimark Group Inc., in which E*TRADE and Ameritrade have ownership stakes, established a dominant position in the market by executing the growing number of retail trades submitted through online brokerage firms.

Price Discovery

The various mechanisms for determining, or *discovering*, prices can be thought of as some form of auction. *Periodic auctions* have all traders in a given security participate simultaneously, and so they involve a trade-off between bringing together a larger proportion of the trading community and sacrificing new information that arrives between auctions. The *continuous auction* feature of most trading floors and continuously updated electronic limit-order books responds to the continuous arrival of information but sacrifices full participation at any point in time.

Market Transparency

Market transparency refers to the broad trading community's ability to observe quoted prices, market depth, and terms of recent transactions. Price discovery is improved by a clear picture of market demand. But too much transparency can lead to *unexpressed demand* as traders shy away from revealing their preferences to potential adversaries. Posting a price at which one is willing to buy or sell is like providing potential counterparties with an option. If someone likes your offer, they exercise the option to accept your terms; otherwise, they do not. But this places you at the mercy of those with better information. Thus, extreme transparency might yield a very clear rendering of very little information.

Anonymity

Absolute anonymity prevents identification of one's counterparty both before and after a trade is consummated. Market anonymity varies with the timing and precision of identification enabled by a market's trading and reporting rules. Well-informed traders benefit from anonymity at the expense of less well-informed traders. But recognizing this threat, uninformed traders (typically liquidity providers) will be put off by a high degree of anonymity.

With these five elements of exchange design in mind, consider the consequences of introducing a single new technology for transmitting information. The opening of the trans-Atlantic cable in 1866 vastly reduced communication time and thereby contributed to a 66 percent decline in the average price difference between the London and New York U.S. Treasury Bond markets. Likewise, domestic telegraph in the United States reduced average price differences between the New York and New Orleans foreign exchange markets and between the New York and Philadelphia equity markets by almost 50 percent. These two examples provide perspective on the potential effect of the Internet more than a century later.

The Traditional Exchange Model

Although a gross simplification, it's useful to think of traditional exchanges as having a hub-and-spoke structure. At the hub of trade stood human-capital-intensive membership organizations like the NYSE. Some members, such as the specialist, dealt exclusively within the boundaries of the membership. Others, such as floor brokers, provided an interface to the outside world. Some brokers operated as independent agents while others represented the interests of large member firms such as Goldman Sachs and Morgan Stanley. In either case, they provided the point of entry to the hub where the bulk of transactions were executed. Direct access to the hub was exclusive, but members at the interface provided broad indirect access. A variety of intermediaries, ranging from brokerage firms to mutual funds, formed the spokes intersecting with this interface. This characterization is simplistic in the sense that regional exchanges and the trading desks of the large brokerage firms provided for trade across or within spokes (an example of the latter being the "internalization" of order flow). But the bulk of trade found its way into the hub.

The layering of intermediation at the interface of the hub and along the spokes helped to balance the competing interests of traders dealing in strategic information. It is quite common, for example, for NYSE floor brokers to negotiate better terms with the specialist than their external clients could obtain by simply trading at currently quoted prices. But if the specialist providing "price improvement" learns that the broker has misrepresented a trade, the broker will not likely enjoy the same consideration in the future. In fact, violation of local norms is likely to have ramifications beyond the broker's relationship with the specialist in question. The trading floor is very much like a small town where everybody knows your name and your business. Norms for behavior thrive because violations become common knowledge and can be broadly sanctioned. Being branded an outcast is costly because brokers add value for outsiders only by gaining the trust of their peers. Thus, they will think twice before exploiting their peers on behalf of a client.

The complementary nature of network effects and regulatory self-interest reinforced the hub-and-spoke structure. People want to trade where other people are trading, and so liquidity attracts liquidity. This eased the problem of regulation because there were powerful incentives for self-regulation; where this was not enough, state regulators had only to attend to a relatively focused marketplace. In this environment, regulators were willing to have the likes of the NYSE operating as virtual monopolies.

Prices Are Property

Our earlier discussion of transparency focused on the trader's perspective, but the exchange also has a direct stake in its level of price transparency. Price discovery is costly. However, if prices are transparent to the world at large, there is little to prevent others from benefiting from the exchange's investment, much like the NASD dealers who pay for order flow in NYSE stocks. In other words, an exchange's level of transparency is the key determinant of its ability to preserve property rights over price information and thereby capture a fair return on the investment necessary to produce prices in the first place.[2]

The similarity of price information to intellectual property may go far in explaining why exchanges tend toward a membership organization. Maintaining an exclusive membership and requiring members to deal strictly with one another forced trade to a hub, but doing so limited access to intellectual assets over which property rights were quite weak. Maximizing members' expected net income from operation of an exchange would not absolutely rule out sharing of price information, since this almost certainly limits the exchange's ability to attract order flow, but excessive transparency undermines incentives to bear the costs of price production in the first place. Thus, from the perspective of the exchange membership, the optimal level of transparency will balance the need to attract order flow against the costs of free-riding.

Electronic Communication Networks

Electronic communication networks, or ECNs, are the most prominent challenge to existing exchanges. ECNs essentially layer the Internet over the existing communications and information linkages in the marketplace. They now handle about 40 percent of the trade in stocks listed by the National Association of Securities Dealers Automated Quotations (Nasdaq) system. In 1999, about 28 percent of trading (18 percent by volume) in NYSE-listed stocks took place off the exchange floor.

The distinguishing feature of an ECN is that it simply matches buyers and sellers in return for a commission. When an internal match does not exist, the order normally is sent to another ECN or placed in the Nasdaq system. In contrast, market makers such as NYSE specialists and Nasdaq dealers may use their own capital to complete a trade when a natural match does not exist. *May* is the operative word because the specialist, for example, is the counterparty to fewer than 30 percent of trades on the NYSE. The remainder are simply crossed against incoming orders or against offers to buy and sell in the specialist's limit-order book—the exchange's answer to the ECN. In fact, ECNs are perhaps best thought of as electronic limit-order books. In other words, ECNs provide a pure brokerage service, whereas most exchanges bundle brokerage with dealership services.

ECNs are regulated by Nasdaq's parent, the National Association of Securities Dealers, by virtue of their standing as NASD members.

There are more than 5,500 members of the NASD, which was chartered by Congress and the SEC in the 1930s to constitute a broad-based securities organization to accommodate firms that did not enjoy membership on the major or regional exchanges. In effect, ECNs have operated under traditional broker-dealer licenses as awarded by the NASD. But in 1999 a new SEC rule commonly known as Reg ATS (Alternative Trading System) enabled ECNs to apply for recognition as stock exchanges in and of themselves, and thereby to gain greater access to the information generated within the network of stock exchanges and presumably to trade in NYSE-listed stocks.

Prominent among the ECNs are established firms that specialize in institutional trading, such as Instinet (a subsidiary of Reuters) and POSIT (owned by Investment Technology Group, Inc.), and more recent entrants that provide access to retail traders, such as Archipelago, Island, and REDIBook. A distinguishing feature of the latter is the large number of exchange members with significant ownership stakes in the upstarts. REDIBook, for example, is wholly owned by Schwab; Fidelity; Donaldson, Lufkin & Jenrette; and Spear Leeds (a large NYSE specialist firm now wholly owned by Goldman Sachs). ECNs tend to be more anonymous, less transparent, and less exclusive than traditional exchanges.

If exchanges already provide trade-matching or pure brokerage capacity, why have ECNs been successful in forcing the unbundling of trade matching from dealership? There seems little question that trade matching is more efficiently carried out electronically. Why were the exchanges slow to adopt the new technology wholesale? One barrier that we've discussed throughout the book is the unwillingness of intermediaries to disturb the delicate balance of existing networks. In the present case, NYSE members were richly rewarded, at least in part, for nothing more than carrying out functions that now can be mechanized. Like it or not, simple information transmission, or pure brokerage, is being commoditized.

The timing of the recent gains among ECNs reflects a confluence of several forces. First, technological advances have sharply reduced the costs of information dissemination and increased the capacity for unbundling brokerage and dealership functions that previously depended largely on human capital. Thus they have cast a harsh light on the inefficiency of continued dependence on human capital in brokerage functions. Second, electronic trading is gaining traction as new markets proliferate worldwide. Network externalities make it difficult to oust an incumbent, and so electronic trading has taken off most rapidly where there is less entrenchment. But even where established venues are well entrenched, as the costs of establishing a virtual trading place decline, potential entrants are more willing to make the investment in luring traders from established venues.

Finally, an extensive investigation of the U.S. over-the-counter markets in 1996 revealed that Nasdaq dealers had conspired to virtually rule out trade on "odd eighths." Until recently, most U.S. stocks traded in increments of one-eighth of a dollar. A widely publicized academic article by William Christie and Paul Schultz documented the fact that Nasdaq stocks rarely traded at one-eighth, three-eighths, five-eighths, or seven-eighths increments.[3] This ensured greater profits for Nasdaq dealers (who effectively earn the bid-ask spread for their dealership services) by doubling the minimum spread from one-eighth of a dollar to one-fourth. The SEC responded by adopting rules that, among other things, made it much easier for ECNs to compete with Nasdaq dealers for order flow in OTC stocks. The net effect thus far has been to narrow spreads in Nasdaq stocks as ECNs have taken an increasingly larger share of the market.

Competition among Marketplaces

Centralization in securities markets minimized fragmentation of price discovery but blunted the forces of competition and innovation. In turn, intermediaries functioned as jacks of all trades but masters of none. The October 1987 market crash offers a striking example of how at times this system served no one particularly well. In spite of the growing role of institutional investors that began in the early 1960s, NYSE operations before 1987 still reflected an emphasis on the small-quantity trade execution for which the exchange historically was designed. With the development of portfolio insurance and other forms of program trading in the 1980s the markets regularly struggled to digest the large rapid-fire orders being placed by institutions. But it was only in the aftermath of the crash and the ensuing criticism that exchanges got serious about investing in the new technology required by an increasingly institutional clientele.

The "prices are property" argument offers some support for limited competition in securities markets. But the argument hinges on one party—the NYSE, for example—bearing the bulk of the costs of price discovery. Traditionally the marginal cost of aggregating liquidity and information was high relative to the marginal contributions of all but the largest investors. The argument is less compelling when individual investors have as much processing power on their desktops as the typical exchange once did. As the cost of coordinating distributed processing power declines similarly, decentralized price discovery will enable more individual investors to capture the marginal value of their contribution to price discovery. The Internet represents a giant step in lowering aggregation costs, and expanded capacity for metering (see chapter 5) means that individual contributions are now more easily measured and rewarded (see Box 8-1).

Tradescape's mechanism, described in Box 8-1, is clever, but it should be clear that they've only scratched the surface of what's now feasible. For example, why not condition both the commission and the payment for liquidity on investor characteristics and current market conditions? Surely, a limit order posted in times of distress is worth more than one posted during a stable market. Likewise, the company might reward consistent liquidity provision. Moreover, in the process of metering and rewarding investor contributions, Tradescape is building a treasure trove of information about investor preferences and behavior under a variety of market conditions that could be fed into fee determination. eSpeed, a global provider of electronic trading platforms for a wide range of financial instruments, provides a window into things to come. Among other things, the firm's December 9, 1999, S-1 filing with the SEC describes its proprietary Interactive Matching system as a rules-based mechanism that encourages participants to expose their orders in exchange for priority and commission rebates.

The Case for a Central Limit-Order Book

The primary question for market regulators remains whether competition will fragment prices. In the short run this seems a real concern as we struggle with sweeping together the information produced at alternative trading venues. But it is important to recognize that as the prices of central marketplaces become less informative, the prices at other venues may become more informative. The question then becomes whether the output from distributed processing can be efficiently aggregated so as to become more informative than the prices generated through highly centralized exchange.

Box 8-1   Getting Paid to Trade: Mom and Pop Market Makers?

Tradescape Corporation recently introduced a scheme to attract liquidity to its MarketXT ECN by paying investors to submit limit orders. Investors will still pay the standard commission of $7.95, but now will receive a penny per share for providing liquidity to those who demand immediate execution. In other words, posting a limit order to buy 1,000 shares earns a net payment of $2.05. In effect, MarketXT is sharing the fee it earns from investors who demand immediate execution. This fee ranges from 50 cents collected from broker-dealers to 1.5 cents collected from institutional investors. As the baby boom generation nears retirement, MarketXT appears to be an idea whose time has come. What better way to put idle minds and capital to work?

Former SEC Chairman Arthur Levitt has at times suggested an electronic central limit-order book that ensures price and time priority across competing venues as a solution to market fragmentation. Already, electronic limit-order books play a key role in major markets such as Paris and London. The rationale for a central limit-order book is strong (see Box 8-2).

There appears at least one way in which the electronic limit-order book could complement an existing dealer market. By definition, patient traders do not require the degree of immediacy offered by a dealer market. In the absence of an electronic limit-order book, however, they are forced to pay for this service whether or not they require it. Therefore patient traders at the margin refrain from trading, and the marketplace does not enjoy their contribution to liquidity. By offering a trading venue that does not require patient traders to pay for immediacy, an electronic limit-order book might increase the level of participation by patient traders in aggregate, particularly if patient traders have direct access to the order book. As long as the book is transparent and dealers can participate in the electronic limit-order book, the two trading venues should be well integrated. If so, despite the increased competition in the provision of liquidity services, dealers would receive support from patient traders in satisfying the demands of impatient or informed traders, or both. Dealers should welcome the competition if the introduction of an electronic limit-order book so increases the level

Box 8-2   The Electronic Limit-Order Book

In the September 1994, issue of the *Journal of Finance*, Lawrence Glosten develops a powerful argument for the superiority of the electronic limit-order book.[4] Glosten shows that among anonymous marketplaces an electronic limit-order book will provide as much liquidity as could be expected even under the most difficult circumstances. Moreover, he argues that the electronic limit-order book is the only trading mechanism that will not tend to engender additional competing exchanges. Glosten's argument turns on the observation that any potential competitor in the provision of liquidity could just as easily participate in the marketplace by submitting an order to the existing limit-order book. Therefore competition within an electronic limit-order book essentially mimics competition among exchanges.

The qualification "among anonymous marketplaces" is important. As technological advances further increase the ability of exchanges to unbundle the various elements of liquidity provision and price discovery and thereby compete in ever-narrower dimensions of the marketplace, several concerns arise. First, the previously mentioned potential for trading venues to free-ride on the price production efforts of one another might reduce aggregate investment in price production. If free-riders serve only the interests of the small traders who are least likely to maintain an informational advantage, the primary producers of price information will be further burdened with losses to informed traders as fewer uninformed traders become present to share in (or subsidize) their burden. In the extreme, this could lead to the collapse of price discovery.[5]

For example, on the NYSE the specialist takes the rough with the smooth. If an electronic limit-order book pegged to the specialist's quoted prices cannibalizes the specialist's "smooth" patient order flow, he is left with the (unsubsidized) rough. Consequently, the introduction of an electronic limit-order book might compromise the specialist's ability to enforce cooperation among different trader clienteles. Since the limit-order book itself is not likely to achieve the subtle benefits of cooperation ascribed to the relationship-intensive approach of human intermediaries, this benefit may be driven from the marketplace entirely and thereby compromise the exchange of strategic information. It is in

(continued)

> this spirit that Glosten suggests that it remains an open and
> important question as to whether "the securities industry can
> simultaneously enjoy the benefits of competition and liquidity that
> an open limit order book appears to provide with the information
> benefits that a floor may provide."

of patient trading that dealers are at least as well off with a smaller piece
of a larger (profit) pie.

Network Design Principles

Let's see if we can sum things up a bit before crashing onward. In
essence, we've argued that concentrated markets enabled intermediaries to spread the costs of price production across a large pool of uninformed liquidity providers without systematically overburdening any
individual or small group. When these liquidity providers had few options, each expected on occasion to be picked off by a better-informed
trader, or perhaps more often to just be matched against another liquidity provider with an offsetting position. But technological advances
are now enabling liquidity providers to opt out of the system and
thereby avoid the occasional loss to informed traders.

For example, by excluding all but trades under, say, 1,000 shares,
dealers who pay for order flow virtually exclude traders exploiting an
informational advantage or at least severely compromise their ability to
do so. Likewise, the ECN run by POSIT provides only periodic and
uncertain execution of large orders and provides for portfolio trades.[6]
Both serve a similar screening function for the institutional liquidity
traders. As liquidity providers flee to these safe havens, those left providing liquidity to informed traders face a greater burden that heightens their incentive to seek refuge as well. In short, there must be
capacity for fairly compensating liquidity providers to gain their voluntary participation in the difficult task of price discovery. But at the same
time, informed traders must retain an incentive to produce and reveal
information through their participation in the market.

Unfortunately, there aren't a lot of options at our disposal, and
there's ample complication here to create room for obfuscation—particularly for deeply entrenched exchanges seeking to fend off the chal-

lenges of technological innovators. So for the remainder of this section we'll attempt to outline some basic principles that should guide the design of a network market structure centered around a voluntary central order book.[7] The principles we outline are by no means comprehensive, nor will our outline do more than scratch the surface of some subtle design considerations. Rather, what we hope to do here is suggest where the skeletons are likely to be hidden in any such proposal. When we later examine the adoption process for the Nasdaq's recently approved SuperMontage proposal, we'll see that competitors indeed hauled many of these skeletons into the open and forced compromises as conditions for SEC approval.

A Design Goal

Perhaps the most promising goal if we are to both gain voluntary participation from liquidity providers and reward information production is to exploit the declining costs of participation, both direct and indirect, facing liquidity traders. The marginal direct costs of access, particularly to a wholly electronic environment, should be trivial in the near future. The popularity of online trading suggests an already powerful force at work. Moreover, by forcing the unbundling of intermediary services and therefore greater specialization, advances in information technology indirectly drive down participation costs as well. An electronic central limit-order book embodies these technological efficiencies and potentially can set off a virtuous circle whereby liquidity attracts liquidity. As liquidity trader participation increases, the costs of information production are spread more widely.

Voluntary Participation or Absolute Priority?

One way of controlling fragmentation is to establish a central order book that enforces price and time priority throughout the decentralized market structure. In other words, you can trade away from the central order book, but it has to be on better terms than what is on offer in the book. This is the essence of proposals floated by Arthur Levitt and others to address the threat of market fragmentation. But absolute price and time priority enforced through a central book is tantamount to mandatory participation in a single, integrated marketplace. The ECNs, even with their interest in greater access to existing networks that link exchanges, oppose such a heavy-handed approach because they view it as favoring entrenched market venues that likely will determine the priority rules.[8]

Strict priority also runs counter to the interests of both liquidity and information traders. The only way to enforce strict priority is to maintain absolute transparency throughout the marketplace—a feature even liquidity traders will not always find in their interest. Recall that a limit order, perhaps the most extreme commitment of liquidity, essentially requires the posting of an option. Although some traders may be willing to post such options indiscriminately in small quantity, it is unlikely that large-quantity liquidity providers will do so. This results in unexpressed demand, that is, the interests of some potential traders being suppressed.

Similarly, absolute priority violates the principle of choice in how broadly one's information is shared (the "participation constraint" in a mechanism design framework). An informed trader might be willing to negotiate a trade that immediately reveals his information within a relatively small circle but not to the market at large. Narrow dissemination of information might diminish price impact and thereby enable a greater return on investment in information. Submitting a large order directly to a central limit-order book is more likely to generate a flurry of activity resulting in more rapid embodiment of information in prices. This sounds like a good thing on the surface, but taken to an extreme can undermine the incentive to invest in information and thereby cause prices to be less revealing on the whole.[9]

Open Interface

Maintaining an open interface promotes competition and is an important first step toward attracting (rather than trying to force) liquidity to a central limit-order book. But calls for or claims of an open interface often are best interpreted as weasel words. By *open interface* we mean a capacity for any interested party to connect to the network on equal terms. This implies equal access to interface software and a common standard for connectivity (that is, all pipelines to the central platform are equal). This does not imply free access.

An open interface coupled with voluntary participation argues for absolute transparency at the level of the central order book. The rationale for this argument is that marginal costs of wider price dissemination are nil and that transparency of the central order book resolves potential conflicts of interest—recall the conflicts arising with internalization or payment for order flow. A transparent central order book provides even the least sophisticated retail trader with a benchmark for evaluating execution quality and so provides an alternative to heavy-handed proposals that would rule out internalization or payment for order flow. Again, the light touch is a good thing because payment for order flow and internalization provide intermediaries with additional flexibility as they seek to balance the many competing interests of their clients. The most obvious example is a rebate for order flow at times when information traders are placing a particularly high demand for liquidity on the marketplace at large. In other words, rebates per se aren't the problem. The problem is assuring sufficient transparency for investors to make well-informed decisions.

Access Pricing

Just as there are many dimensions to liquidity, so too there are many dimensions for pricing liquidity services. In terms of network access, two dimensions are key: bandwidth and whether participants consume or contribute liquidity. Disseminating information throughout an electronic network consumes bandwidth. Marginal cost pricing of bandwidth is complicated by a number of factors that we'll not address here, other than to suggest that network pricing should diminish the threat of defection by minimizing cross subsidies such as forcing some liquidity traders to bear an undue share of the costs of information production.[10] On the other hand, what may appear a cross subsidy—say, a lower access fee for those placing limit orders than for those trading against limit orders even though both consume similar bandwidth—might be appropriate for inducing widespread participation.

This example highlights an important difference between networks that simply disseminate information and those that promote sharing of strategic information. As an example of the former, in a telephone network the service provider and the customer are clearly distinguished. As such, we might expect customers to pay fees according to their demands on the scarce bandwidth they consume. But in networks such as securities markets, the distinction between service provider and customer is less clear. Keeping in mind the various illustrations of the prisoner's dilemma throughout this book, the hardware or bandwidth for communication alone may be worth little if the incentives to share information are weak. In securities markets, the pipeline effectively becomes wider as more people use it because greater participation enhances liquidity. In other words, although physical congestion increases as participation widens, the net effect might be to improve the transmission of information through the network. Another way of thinking about this is that wider participation provides for wider sharing of the costs of information production. And if the resource-allocation benefits of prices are largely a public good, there is good reason for the costs of information to be shared widely. This perspective not only suggests access fees that increase with a trader's demand for liquidity but also might argue for payment for order flow or liquidity provision at times when liquidity is particularly precious.

A Network Structure

Now let's compare the hub-and-spoke structure of the NYSE to an exchange structure that might emerge from these principles. The magnetism of the hub maintained by the NYSE depended in part on the long-standing requirement that NYSE member firms execute all trades in listed stocks on the exchange floor. In other words, the structure violated the voluntary participation principle. Likewise, only recently did the exchange open the national market system interface to ECNs, thereby assuring them price exposure on the Consolidated Quotation System.[11] Finally, as we saw at the outset of this chapter, NYSE access is filtered through member firms, and membership is highly exclusive and very costly.

Freed from these constraints, we envision the emergence of a network of competing trading venues, each of which could (but will not necessarily) serve as a portal to the broader network. Some venues will position themselves in terms of their degree of exclusivity and others perhaps by the human intervention they offer. The latter might include both institutional trading desks and exclusive trading floors like that of the NYSE. Alternatively, we might think of the Nasdaq dealer market as a less exclusive but still human-capital-intensive venue. ECNs offering the least human intervention might position themselves as specializing in institutional trading (like Instinet) or in retail trading and might offer varying degrees of transparency and anonymity. The level of variation among venues will reflect the range of investor preferences. The basic structure we've outlined provides for unbundling of the various intermediary services outlined earlier and thereby promotes innovation and specialization in trading mechanisms. In turn, these promote competition without ruling out beneficial cooperation between venues. Both the threat of fragmentation and collusion are balanced by the presence of the highly transparent benchmark set by the central order book.

Fragmentation is diminished in this setting because intermediaries at the perimeter of the network will voluntarily direct order flow (and its embedded information) either directly or indirectly to the central limit-order book as long as it offers a deep liquidity pool. For example, where discretion requires human intervention, intermediaries such as institutional trading desks often must carry risky inventory. But if the central limit-order book is highly liquid, they will lay off this risk and thereby ensure that information reflected in their local order flow finds its way to the center.

Similarly, electronic venues competing on the speed of execution often benefit from the ability to balance local order flow with trades executed at other venues—this is already common among ECNs. Again, information about local demand imbalances will find its way to the center if the central limit-order book provides the best source of backup liquidity. So even if the central limit-order book is not the direct point of entry for information, it will incorporate information indirectly if it provides more heavily intermediated venues with attractive terms for laying off risk or improving execution for their clients. Fragmentation remains a risk in a decentralized market without absolute priority rules when liquidity offered by a central coordinating mechanism is limited.

Robustness

One particularly desirable feature of a network structure is the likely achievement of a level of operational robustness beyond that of the traditional exchange. In the hub-and-spoke model, if systems failed or were overwhelmed by market circumstances, the information network collapsed. Again, the October 1987 crash offers a case in point. Parity relationships between the Standard & Poor's (S&P) 500 index and futures contracts exploded as trade in both the centralized stock and futures markets ground to a halt. In a decentralized network, if one venue goes down, others can pick up the load. Even if the central limit-order book in our model goes down, communication and trade around the perimeter is not ruled out. Aggregation of information and perhaps even trade will be compromised in the short run, but less dramatically than in a highly centralized mechanism.

Robustness also is served by the proliferation of experiments in intermediation and exchange that is likely to occur in a decentralized market structure. For example, until quite recently, any innovation in the trade of NYSE stocks had to occur within the NYSE because exchange Rule 390 required member firms to carry out all trade on the exchange. The NYSE's control over ITS almost surely had a similar dampening effect on innovation by nonmember firms who could trade NYSE stocks off the exchange.

Who Owns the Central Order Book?

We've made a case for a network structure potentially broadening participation, promoting both competition and innovation, and being more robust in the face of operational failure. But the same ingredients that generate these benefits undermine incentives for maintaining a central limit-order book. The analogue in the hub-and-spoke model was maintained by the exchange at the hub and was subsidized in part by the exchange's monopoly power. Now we need to think about how the public good generated by the central mechanism can be sustained when investors have many options for trading while free-riding on the coordination function of the central order book.

Note that the central order book in our network model is analogous to the backbone of the Internet. In the early days of the Internet, the U.S. government subsidized the backbone. As a practical matter, this made sense because the government was the primary user—it internalized most of the benefits. As private benefits became more apparent, private ownership of the backbone increased. Now the primary Internet backbone providers are Cable & Wireless, Sprint, MCI WorldCom, GTE, and AT&T.[12]

The benefits of coordination associated with a backbone-like central order book are primarily a public good. And in contrast to the experience of the Internet, the relative balance between public and private interests in securities prices will not change substantially over time. Thus, there is a strong argument for public investment in the infrastructure necessary for aggregating information in securities markets. In the past, the investment was real but perhaps not apparent. As government regulatory bodies permitted exchanges to operate as near monopolies, at times perhaps even undermining competition, they effectively provided for a wealth transfer from the public at large to the providers of exchange services.

The costs to a potential sponsor of a central mechanism will be primarily in software development and maintenance. But a successful sponsor must also be of sufficiently high repute that its imprimatur would be valued in the marketplace. Again, this favors a government body, or more likely a collection of government bodies, that can credibly claim to represent the public interest.

Perhaps the primary concern that might be raised against such a dominant role for a government body is that it would undermine innovation. But keep in mind that the primary function of the governing body will be to sponsor the central coordinating mechanism, which is nothing more than a set of rules or incentives embodied in computer code. These could be developed and modified through the same kind of participatory process currently maintained between exchanges and their regulators.

Ideally the central coordinating mechanism is not the source of innovation but rather a device for aggregating the benefits of decentralized experimentation without crowding them out. This structure also provides a natural mechanism for more coordinated injections of liquidity when market forces alone cannot meet demands in the marketplace. Just as the Federal Reserve System (the Fed) and other central banks use monetary policy to influence liquidity in the economy at large, so the governing body could use the central coordinating mechanism to directly inject liquidity by stepping in as the buyer and seller of last resort. This already occurs on an informal basis when, for example, the banks, backed by the Fed, provide liquidity for specialist firms to carry them through difficult markets. The structure we're suggesting would simply provide a formal mechanism for resolving temporary liquidity shocks and would have the added benefit of being open to inspection.

If participation is voluntary but deep liquidity is central to the success of the mechanism, one might question how a central limit-order book would attract liquidity. In the presence of deeply entrenched venues such as the NYSE, payment for order flow in the form of access fees that fall below competitive levels might be necessary. This would draw criticism as it displaced order flow from existing venues, but the goal would be to achieve a level of participation or liquidity that existing venues do not provide. The long-term aim would be to have liquidity attracted on terms more reflective of costs sustained by the network.

Aside from this transfer of market share from existing venues to other private sources of liquidity, there would seem little reason for complaint from market participants except on the grounds that such a device could be used in a coercive fashion. For example, once in place, the leverage associated with a voluntary central limit-order book might enable the governing body to more easily impose absolute price and time priority throughout the network of trading venues. But even if this threat is substantial, if the primary cost of establishing a coordinating mechanism is software development, then the competing threat that another credible governmental body might step in and offer an alternative mechanism should provide a substantial counterbalance. The key to this counterbalance having force is the relative ease of plugging an alternative central order book into the existing network. In turn, this depends on a high level of standardization in network connectivity or, more likely in the short run, flexible portals to the network.[13] Both are supported by the open-interface principle outlined earlier.

Alternatively, the central coordinating mechanism could be sponsored by a collection of the most active members of the network, much like Nasdaq's recently approved SuperMontage system. The advantage of this approach is that a deep liquidity pool already exists. The disadvantage is the threat, perceived or real, that the backbone will favor some participants over others. Obviously, this assumes that an alternative government sponsor is invulnerable to one or more participants gaining the upper hand by seeking political favor. Many would view this assumption as wishful thinking, but clearly it varies from country to country in its applicability. As the markets struggle through the ongoing technological revolution, traditional exchanges retain considerable leverage and can be expected to continue steering reorganization to serve their interests over those of potential entrants. The SuperMontage approval process sheds light on this dynamic (see Box 8-3).

The existing exchanges have deep interest in protecting their dominant positions if not their traditional technology. We can surely expect more proposals like SuperMontage as restructuring and consolidation begin to cut across existing exchanges and even national boundaries.

Exchange Regulation

In existing markets, rules for engagement are established and enforced by a few central bodies, primarily the exchanges acting as self-regulatory organizations and their government overseers. But a consid-

Box 8-3 The SuperMontage Debate

On October 1, 1999, the National Association of Securities Dealers, through its wholly owned subsidiary, the Nasdaq Stock Market, requested approval from the SEC for a set of modifications to its trading platform referred to as the SuperMontage proposal.[14] After numerous amendments, the proposal was approved on January 19, 2001.

Although SuperMontage represented a giant step forward in transparency and integration of ECNs into the existing network for trading OTC stocks, the proposal initially drew severe criticism for alleged anti-competitive features. Chief among these were the concerns of ECN operators that rather than providing them with greater access to the network, SuperMontage would actually have the effect of favoring Nasdaq dealers by making unfair comparisons between their quotes and dealer quotes. The approval of SuperMontage came only after the NASD agreed to become an independent self-regulatory organization and Nasdaq agreed to substantial revisions that in large part provide investors with greater choice in the venue to which their orders are directed for execution.

In its final form, SuperMontage captures many of the features of the network model outlined in this chapter. Among other things, it aggregates and displays quotes for each market maker or ECN dealing in an OTC-traded stock, much as a central limit-order book would. It also enables traders to decide whether to reveal their identity and control the transparency of their orders. The approved version of SuperMontage provides for investors to direct orders to the ECN or market maker of their choice or to obtain automatic execution by way of a menu of price, size, and time priority algorithms at the best bid or offer in the system. It thus satisfies the voluntary participation principle outlined earlier while providing a high degree of transparency, and in the view of the SEC provides a "balance between encouraging liquidity, accommodating the preferences of market participants, and maintaining time priority." Access to the system requires only membership in the NASD, a relatively open and low-cost membership by comparison with membership in the NYSE.

erable body of research suggests that norms for behavior are more likely to evolve and be successfully enforced within smaller, local networks where people deal repeatedly with one another.[15] Exchange floors have long provided this benefit, but within a relatively narrow segment of the market and sometimes in instances where the value added is minimal. For example, the S&P 500 futures contract probably suffers little from the kinds of informational frictions most likely to warrant human intervention and yet trade is still dominated by an exclusive trading pit.

Decentralization of trade provides opportunity for a wider variety of exclusive arrangements to flourish where demand conditions suggest they are most likely to add value. But for this to happen, regulators must allow experimentation within broad guidelines. As Elinor Ostrom points out, "externally imposed rules tend to crowd out" the evolution of norms for cooperative behavior.[16] This threat is of particular concern when supervisory resources are limited, because in the absence of aggressive monitoring and enforcement of externally imposed rules, there are no norms to fall back on for guiding behavior.

In practical terms, what this means is that less well-developed economies intent on developing liquid securities markets in a world where alternative venues are readily established would do well to focus their attention and limited resources on establishing or linking with an electronic platform that can provide a transparent benchmark for alternative trading venues. This approach to market development economizes on regulatory resources by permitting regulators to focus on promoting efficiency in a transparent benchmark such as a central order book. Investors who prefer the services provided by alternative venues can then benchmark their execution with some degree of confidence even in the absence of direct regulation of the alternative venue. The indirect regulation of alternative venues has the added benefit of promoting the development of local norms or rules for behavior. Once again, Ostrom speaks to this issue with her observation that in circumstances where public goods are at stake "[a]mong long-enduring self-governed regimes, smaller scale organizations tend to be nested in ever-larger organizations."[17]

The Boundaries of Regulation

Note that we've said nothing about national boundaries on securities exchange. This is not an oversight. Rather, we think that such boundaries as still exist will continue to diminish as the Internet weakens a regulatory body's grasp over local exchange. Regulators who impose rules perceived as undermining the interests of market participants will increasingly see demand for their regulatory services diminished as trade migrates to virtual spaces that offer a more desirable bundle of regulatory services. This does not imply that the regulatory function will be diminished. Rather, we expect to see more competition among regulators, with the likely outcome of rapid extinction or irrelevance of ineffective regimes.

The Road to Reform

At the outset of this chapter we asked how an industry can seemingly be consolidating and decentralizing simultaneously. We examined the technological forces behind decentralization in some detail. We conclude the chapter by arguing that consolidation is a precondition for the reforms that ultimately will leave us with more decentralized securities markets.

For this purpose, there is perhaps no more instructive firm than our continuing standard for the investment banking industry. Since going public, Goldman Sachs has acted with a vengeance on Henry Paulson's observation, quoted at the beginning of chapter 7, that the firm expects the market to converge to a world of predominately electronic trading platforms. Prior to going public, it tested the waters by taking ownership stakes in a variety of electronic trading platforms, including Wit SoundView and the ECN Archipelago. Following the firm's acquisition of the Hull Group in 1999, Goldman Sachs, along with Merrill Lynch and Morgan Stanley, became a vocal proponent of reform proposals for strengthening linkages between trading venues with a central order book that would pit exchanges more directly in competition with ECNs. And shortly after their CEOs were nominated for the NYSE's board, Goldman Sachs and Merrill Lynch announced that they were building Primex, an electronic trading system.

After submitting a white paper on market reform to the SEC in early 2000, Goldman Sachs, in an apparent reversal, then acquired one of the dominant specialist firms on the NYSE, with major trading operations in Nasdaq, by paying $6.5 billion for Spear, Leeds & Kellogg. As we wrote this chapter, Goldman Sachs had just announced an agreement to acquire for $250 million another NYSE specialist firm,

Benjamin Jacobson & Sons. As other large banks follow suit, some old-line exchange members must feel as though the traditional organizations are being gutted from within.

As counterintuitive as it may first appear, we believe that Goldman Sachs is following a natural strategy of putting aside deeply entrenched interests in the status quo to ensure that when new technology displaces human-capital-intensive methods of price discovery and liquidity provision it retains its dominant status in the marketplace. As membership organizations, the NYSE and, to an even greater extent, Nasdaq represent a wide variety of interests. Presumably all members are interested in maximizing profits from their ventures, but not all members face the same path for doing so. Until fairly recently, the membership of these organizations stuck together to defend the traditional exchange model from interlopers. However, as it has become increasingly apparent that electronic platforms will take a more prominent role in the future, member interests are diverging.

The smaller specialists and dealer firms have an interest in sustaining the status quo for as long as possible as they milk what remains from their human-capital-intensive market-making technology. When the time comes for replacing the existing technology, there will be little room at the table for these firms because they are neither rich in the financial capital that would make them players in the new regime nor will their existing technology add much marginal value going forward. The Goldman Sachses of the world had a common interest in milking the old technology for a time, but the music is about to stop and the scramble for dominance will be won by those that have substantial investments in technology in place. The problem is that the votes of the smaller firms carry more or less equal weight with those of the larger member firms, and so they have considerable power to block moves that would damage their interests but promote the interests of the membership at large.

The obvious solution to this problem is demutualization—a tack taken with some early success by the Australian Stock Exchange, which now maintains a frontrunner position in the adoption of new technology. With the agreement to separate the NASD's self-regulatory function from Nasdaq in place, Nasdaq has plans to pursue a public offering in 2002. But even an agreement to demutualize can be blocked, as evidenced by the NYSE dropping plans announced in July 1999 to go public.

Thus, the consolidation effort being carried out by the dominant players can be interpreted as an alternative means of buying out the technological have-nots. The have-nots will likely suffer rapid erosion of the traditionally rich rewards of exchange membership in any event. But the longer the technologically savvy firms wait, the greater is the likelihood of their dominance being challenged, if not by the ECNs then by large non-U.S. exchanges and exchange consortiums that, by virtue of their less deeply entrenched exchange mechanisms, have already adopted modern trading platforms. Only time will tell.

9

CONCLUSION

We BEGAN THIS book with a simple idea: Sharing information multiplies its value but also makes one vulnerable because information cannot be taken back from those who would use it for exploitative purposes. Thus the nonrival nature of information begs for widespread dissemination, while strategic considerations demand hoarding. After a whirlwind tour of the financial markets and a healthy dose of academic theory and evidence, we hope you're persuaded that financial intermediaries make their living balancing this tension.

Likewise, we've tried to emphasize that recent advances in information technology are causing changes in the execution of this intermediary function but do not foreshadow its decline. In fact, in the short run, we predict rising demand for the intermediaries' services. One thing that is changing profoundly with recent technological advances is the nature of property rights over information. Fundamentally, financial intermediaries, and infomediaries in general, thrive where property rights are ambiguous or difficult to enforce. Information as a form of property has always presented special problems, but intermediaries, as well as a host of other institutions, evolve to address these problems. Technological shocks upset the delicate balance and set off a reordering of property rights and of the institutions and intermediaries responsible for their enforcement.

Our final goal was to suggest that we're in the midst of such a re-ordering and that the long experience of financial intermediaries in dealing with conflicts arising in the exchange of information can help us understand recent events in the financial markets and other parts of the economy where information exchange is taking on a more central role. In the remainder of this chapter we offer some observations aimed at driving home this point.

Marshaling Human Capital

Any casual follower of the business press has to be struck by the ongoing reordering of claims over human capital. It seems that we daily read of the latest high-profile employee defection and the employer's attempts to cope. For example, in 1999 three money managers who left State Street Global Advisors for Deutsche Bank were sued for violating their contracts in an attempt to foil the defection; ultimately the three were prohibited from soliciting clients or former colleagues through February 2001.[1] Similar events arise with increasing frequency in the economy at large, particularly in tight labor markets surrounding hot technologies like fiber optics. As firms bid more aggressively for one another's talent, noncompete clauses that effectively remove key people from the workforce for a period of time are more frequently invoked.[2]

In Silicon Valley, it seems all in a day's work. In fact, many organizations encourage the pattern by rewarding current employees who identify potential recruits and by providing highly visible online listings of opportunities aimed at their competitors' employees. In the valleys of Wall Street, until quite recently it was common for prominent bankers to spend their entire careers with one firm. Likewise with law firms and consulting firms. Although embedded in a larger pattern of employee mobility in the United States, this clearly is no longer the case.

University of California at Berkeley professor of regional planning Annalee Saxenian suggests that mobility and fraternization between organizations provides cross-fertilization of ideas and thus regional advantage.[3] John Seely Brown and Paul Duguid see this from an ecological perspective in which "[f]rom the point of view of an individual firm, knowledge that leaks to another is lost. From the perspective of the ecology as a whole, however, it is much more productively used."[4] Individual firms still maintain an interest in protecting home-grown knowledge, however, so we're in the midst of unprecedented experimentation in the design and enforcement of employment and compensation contracts.

As transaction costs associated with many arm's-length transactions continue their sharp decline, the viability of an organization depends on its capacity for codifying or otherwise capturing the best practices, reputation, and relationships nurtured within it. (If it is possible to write unambiguous contracts, there's little need for the artifice of the firm.) Failure to do so means that more often than not you'll end up on the losing side of the balance identified by Brown and Duguid. Organizations that become repositories for these intangible assets set off a virtuous circle that attracts ever more talented people and persuades them to stay.

Remember Oliver Hart's observation that "control over nonhuman assets leads to control over human assets," but not in a manipulative sense. If you push things too far, you're likely to lose, or not attract in the first place, the human capital that over time sustains the organization. From this perspective, aggressive employment contracts that limit employee mobility in a heavy-handed fashion are more indicative of a problem than of a solution. If you have to force people to stay, it simply means that the assets that stick to the organization are not a very strong magnet for talented people. Although such contracts have their place during periods of transition—say, in the wake of Goldman Sachs's IPO or Chase's acquisition of J.P. Morgan—their long-term effect is to attract lower-quality employees. You'll end up with more control over less valuable assets.

Organizations have further responsibility for fostering contracts, both implicit and explicit, that ensure the preservation of their intangible assets through mentoring and the like. The longevity of prominent names within the financial community suggests that financial and other professional firms have been relatively successful in preserving codified human capital in the face of technological change. In part, this reflects less dramatic advances in the technology of financial intermediation and other professional services than, say, the technology of transportation. However, firms like IBM have weathered technological advances every bit as fundamental as those faced by the railroading concerns that dominated the economy at the turn of the twentieth century.

A key to success, then, is encouraging individuals to contribute to a common pool of intellectual capital. We learned from our examination of investment banking syndicates, however, that contributions to common asset pools, and teamwork generally, are undermined by the threat of free-riding. We suggested that both the traditional syndicate and recent adaptations in the debt markets diminish this problem by helping to ensure that shirking carries its own punishment in the new syndicate. In the traditional setting, the ability to easily dissolve existing relationships and to make visible individual failings were key elements of success. But the former was costly because it required frequent, and otherwise wasteful, recontracting. Here again, the creation of a codified asset, the physical distribution platform, from which shirkers could be excluded, coupled with a high degree of transparency in their contributions to that asset, provided the control mechanism suggested by Hart.

Encouraging knowledge workers to simultaneously contribute to proprietary and nonproprietary knowledge pools or to gain external visibility can serve a similar function. Management consulting firms that encourage consultants to publish books, or law firms that encourage certain attorneys to gain an individual high profile, use this mechanism. Obviously, external visibility and nonproprietary knowledge production create outside opportunities for key employees. But these outside opportunities also provide heightened incentives for investment in human capital. Successful organizations maintain a healthy balance in this tension.

The perspective of the investment banking syndicate might also help us to understand the variety of cooperative efforts among human-capital-intensive firms, ranging from mergers to partnering arrangements to loose affiliations like the networks of professional practice envisioned by Brown and Duguid. In settings that are not human capital intensive, an ability to precisely measure the quality of individual contributions to team production provides more latitude for arm's-length transactions. For example, personal computer assembly and distribution operations such as Dell and Gateway are able to outsource fabrication of processors and other components to multiple suppliers because quality assessment is straightforward. Outsourcing thus heightens competition and incentives for innovation in component design and fabrication.

Where contributions to team production depend more heavily on human capital developed and maintained through day-to-day effort that is relatively difficult to measure, we should expect weaker formal affiliations but with a more select group of contributors. If we consider the online debt platforms maintained through alliances among bulge-bracket banks such as Goldman Sachs, Morgan Stanley, Merrill Lynch, and the like, we see distinct and highly competitive organizations selectively cooperating with one another. Work teams within professional services firms commonly organize in a similar fashion. From this perspective, we are not surprised by the rise of similarly fluid team affiliations across professional firms, sometimes referred to as *network organizations* for their emphasis on work process over structure and their capacity for continuous reshaping.[5]

Finally, our examination of the Internet investment banks suggests that pioneers of new technology for existing industries would do well to undertake a careful assessment of the intangible assets bound up in the traditional organizations they plan to challenge. Intangible assets such as reputation, client and customer networks, and best practices are difficult if not impossible to replicate in the short run. In industries where intangibles are carefully nurtured within a large cross section of firms, such as aggressively branded retail chains, the value of a new distribution technology is perhaps best captured through licensing agreements that enable widespread adoption. On the other hand, if there are a few dominant incumbents, an alliance or partnership around the new technology will be more effective. Only in the case where incumbents are generally poor in intangibles can a pioneer expect to go it alone to great effect.

From this perspective, we might have predicted that the business-to-consumer dot-coms would provide for one of the largest concentrated wealth transfers in history with their ad campaigns centered on Super Bowl 2000. We'll leave for future research the task of measuring the relative gains of owners and players, advertising agencies, and ABC. But surely the National Football League, the advertising industry, and ABC owe their current financial health in no small part to the dot-com bubble.

Regulatory Policy

Antitrust policy always has suffered its share of internal conflicts. We want to encourage business organizations to excel, and one measure of a successful competitor is its ability to dominate the competition. But in business winning has a cumulative effect. Unlike sports, where each game is an independent event and the scoreboard is reset at the conclusion, successful companies such as Microsoft carry the point (profit) differential from their latest conquest into the next competition. If this head start is marshaled wisely, it can ultimately prove insurmountable. Most professional sports leagues maintain a semblance of balance and fan interest by giving weaker competitors first choice from among new talent. We might think of antitrust policy as the solution to this problem in the business world.

When property rights over productive assets are weak, as is the case in many human-capital-intensive industries, the problem is amplified. Incentives to invest in human capital are undermined by the threat of expropriation before a fair return on investment is realized. Our analysis of the financial markets suggests that in the absence of formal legal protections, financial firms used a variety of organizational strategies, at both the firm and industry level, to great effect in this cause.

We think you'll see more of this in the economy at large as information exchange plays a more central role in production. In many instances, the organizational response to weak property rights straddles the line between competitive and anticompetitive behavior. This is not surprising in light of the problem at hand and the fact that technological shocks often shift the line. Policy makers must accept this tension and do their best to maintain a clear understanding of the competing interests they serve and a clear distinction between acceptable and unacceptable behavior given the balance they seek.

Microsoft's recent battle with the U.S. Department of Justice provides a useful case in point. On the one hand, Microsoft has been a successful but hard-nosed competitor. The firm established a worldwide standard for computer operating systems that saves untold time and resources that otherwise would have been devoted to resolving problems of incompatibility. They've also consistently lowered the price (on a quality-adjusted basis) of their products and services. On the other hand, they've consistently crushed competitors who would upset the status quo and thereby potentially ruled out innovations that would improve upon the Gatesian world in which we live. But on yet another hand (and you thought economists only have two hands!), Microsoft's willingness to invest in the first place in a business where competitors can mimic creative ideas and consumers can copy the embodiment of these ideas at will is in large part dependent on the small but real odds of winning such a lottery. Microsoft's competitors are hoping for the same.

In essence, antitrust policy aims to determine the "right" reward for the winner of this lottery both through its efforts to set initial conditions for competition and through its power to redistribute winnings after the outcome is determined. The problem is that we have no precise formula to guide the use of either of these policy instruments. We're probably going to see more rather than less instances like that posed by Microsoft, so we had better get used to it.

Perhaps getting used to it will be the best remedy for what has been a tumultuous affair. By this we mean that demonizing the likes of Bill Gates is not particularly productive. Rather, we need to recognize that the landscape is changing and thus requires rebalancing of the rules of engagement. There is no right or wrong answer. Where we draw the line ultimately is a collective reflection of the relative values we place on innovation and on public and private interests. Politicizing the debate tends to blur the consequences of the choices we make and often makes for a blurred line that creates undue and costly confusion among the players. It took us over half a century to remedy a largely political decision to separate commercial from investment banking. Do we really want to set a precedent for separating the production of operating systems from application software?

To that end, we believe that considerable caution is warranted in the ongoing review of the new online debt-market platforms outlined in chapter 6 as well as in analogous efforts to link content production with distribution online in the broader media industry. The recent approval of the AOL/Time Warner merger indicates that regulators are at least implicitly tuned into the enormous benefits of scale in distribution created by the Internet and the simultaneous fragility of control of content production. In the case of the debt market, if we felt that Goldman Sachs, for example, controlled the human capital that contributed to the power of its online distribution platform, we might fear the threat of the sort of anticompetitive behavior that stifled InterVest and other potential competitors in the past. In fact, we believe that the physical separation of distribution from content production actually increases the power of individual or small teams of human capitalists and therefore weakens the control over content exercised by owners of large-scale distribution platforms.

The real question for policymakers is whether content providers are sufficiently powerful that they could break away from an existing distribution platform to rally behind a potential entrant. If so, even if there is little immediate competition, the threat held out by content producers can force more nearly competitive behavior in distribution. A good example of this is found in the world of stock exchanges, where a few key institutional investors so dominate trade that if they were to boycott, say, Nasdaq and coordinate around a new trading platform, they'd immediately achieve the critical volume necessary to sustain a liquid marketplace. The replication of the trading platform itself is relatively straightforward. Can the same be said of the entertainment industry? As things stand, cable connections are not easily replicated. However, as alternative pipelines into the home become technically feasible at low cost, perhaps it will be possible.

Who Owns Information?

Finally, the hot debate surrounding ownership of personal information in a world where e-commerce ventures are launched with a central focus on their capacity for gathering and massaging personal information from their customers has many parallels with the history of financial markets. In fact, Richard Grasso, CEO of the NYSE, recently claimed that the exchange's primary competitive threat is not other exchanges or ECNs but rather the likes of eBay that have mastered data mining.[6] The parallels stem in large part from common tensions at the foundations of intellectual property and privacy law. With intellectual property, there is no natural right to control over an idea. Likewise, there is no natural right to privacy. Societies strike a balance between private and public interests in both. Advances in information technology routinely upset the balance.

We are in the midst of a profound technological shock. Although we're not qualified to suggest how the balance in law defining property rights or rights to privacy will be restored, we have offered some thoughts from the economist's point of view on the design of institutions for balancing the many competing interests. At the core of this book stands the idea that financial intermediaries, and similar institutions generally, evolve to complement the rule of law. When the rule of law is ambiguous, intermediaries step in to grapple with information's desire to be free.

An Incentive-Compatible Mechanism

THIS APPENDIX develops an incentive-compatible mechanism for promoting trade between two parties when one might be at a considerable informational disadvantage vis-à-vis the other. Chapter 2 noted that the threat of adverse selection under these circumstances can be a barrier to and perhaps even rule out trade. Here we show how a very simple set of rules overseen by a trusted intermediary might resolve the problem. To make things concrete, we cast the discussion in terms of an institutional money manager seeking to sell a large block of stock and a potential counterparty who cannot judge the money manager's motivation for undertaking the trade.

Roughly speaking, we can think of the trading strategy of an institutional money manager as being either passive or strategic. An example of the former might be a manager of an indexed stock portfolio whose interest in selling a stock is driven by portfolio rebalancing considerations and who has no particular need for immediate execution. For the purpose at hand, think of a strategic manager as one who sells in the belief that the stock is overvalued. Now suppose that the potential counterparty to a large institutional sell order is passive and believes that the seller is just as likely to be passive as strategic. The potential counterparty might respond to this uncertainty in one of three ways. Since he does not require immediate execution, he might refuse the offer to trade and wait out the potential arrival of new information.

Alternatively, the counterparty might follow the cautious strategy of buying only some fraction of the shares offered and thereby satisfying only some fraction of his (passive) demand for shares. Finally, the counterparty might satisfy his entire demand for shares by agreeing to purchase the entire block of shares offered by the seller. We refer to this as the *cooperative* response.

Suppose that the gains from trade in each case can be quantified according to table A-1. When the counterparty refuses to trade, there are no gains from trade. When the counterparty cooperates by purchasing all shares offered for sale, the total gains from trade are $500 regardless of the seller's motives. If it turns out that the seller was passive, the counterparty's share of the total gain is $300. The counterparty's larger share of gains from trade when the seller is passive implies that the counterparty benefits more from immediate rebalancing when both are passive. On the other hand, if the seller is strategic, trading is costly to the counterparty: The $300 loss from trade reflects the unnecessary immediate purchase of shares at the inflated price recognized by the strategic seller. The expected private gains are simply each party's equally weighted average of the two possible outcomes. Thus, the counterparty is no better off in this case (in expectation) than had he refused to trade. In contrast, although the cautious response reduces the counterparty's gain from trading with a passive seller from $300 to $200, it nets the counterparty an expected gain of $50 by reducing his exposure in the event that the seller is strategic. Unfortunately, the cautious response also diminishes total expected gains from trade by $200.[1]

Because the counterparty determines whether a trade is completed, we can hope for no more than his responding cautiously. In fact, it's not hard to imagine circumstances in which a small positive expected gain

Table A-1
Results of Various Counterparty Responses to Trade (in Dollars)

	Cooperative		Cautious		Refuse Trade	
	Seller result	Buyer result	Seller result	Buyer result	Seller result	Buyer result
Seller						
Passive	200	300	100	200	0	0
Strategic	800	–300	400	–100	0	0
Expected private gain	500	0	250	50	0	0
Total expected gain	500		300		0	

from trade will be insufficient to offset transaction costs and the counterparty's aversion to the risk of actually encountering a strategic trader. At best, therefore, total gains from trade are positive but fall well short of the total benefits associated with a less cautious response from the counterparty. This means that a passive seller has an interest in communicating to the counterparty that his interest in selling is not strategically motivated. Unfortunately, a simple claim to this effect, even if it can be transmitted to all potential counterparties, is not credible because the seller is always better off making this claim regardless of his true motivation. A strategic seller who can persuade the counterparty that he is passive gains $800 as opposed to the $400 gain from trading with a cautious counterparty. Thus any unsubstantiated claim of passivity should be treated as cheap talk by the counterparty.

Now suppose that a trusted intermediary sponsored the following mechanism:

- If the seller claims to be passive, draw randomly from a distribution that calls for advising the potential buyer to be cooperative 75 percent of the time and cautious 25 percent of the time.

- If the seller claims to be strategic, draw randomly from a distribution that calls for advising the potential buyer to be cooperative 25 percent of the time, cautious 50 percent of the time, and refuse to trade 25 percent of the time.

Although the rules are explicit, the outcome given the seller's representation of his motives is not deterministic. But if the intermediary follows this program and the seller is honest and the buyer obedient, the total *expected* gains from trade increase to $362.50,[2] which is less than the maximum possible gain from trade of $500, but more than the $300 feasible gain in the intermediary's absence.[3] Will the seller be honest and the buyer obedient? Well, doing so increases both the seller's expected gain from trade (from $250 to $287.50) and the potential buyer's expected gain from trade (from $50 to $75). Moreover, although the potential buyer can infer that the seller is motivated by strategic considerations when the mediator advises against trade, this will not cause the potential buyer to violate the recommendation—it is still in his best interest not to trade. Assigning even a small positive probability to advising no trade when the seller claims to be passive will close even this insight into the seller's motivation at little cost to either party. In short, the mechanism is incentive compatible.

THE FUNCTIONS OF
SECURITIES EXCHANGES

L IKE OTHER BUSINESS ORGANIZATIONS, securities exchanges offer products and services by means of a *production technology*.[1] Simply put, securities exchanges are venues where market participants come together to produce liquidity and prices—the latter by providing traders with a mechanism for price discovery through their order placement strategies. The production technology of an exchange includes both manpower and a vast array of communications and data-processing technologies, but it is also embodied in the choices made by the developers of the exchange regarding rules of access, interaction, and reporting.

Liquidity

Liquidity has multiple dimensions. Four commonly cited dimensions are market width, market depth, market resilience, and the immediacy with which a trade can be executed.[2] The *market width*, or *bid-ask spread*, is the difference between the quoted price at which shares can be sold and the quoted price at which shares can be bought. *Market depth* is the number of shares that can be bought or sold at the existing quotes. Focusing on the spread and depth alone, it becomes clear why the bid-ask spread is not a comprehensive measure of the cost of liquidity. For example, two markets with equal spreads but different depths at the inside quotes will offer a different average execution price to a trader who places an order slightly larger than the number of shares available at the inside quote of the shallowest market.

Market resilience refers to how quickly the marketplace recovers from large order-flow imbalances. Whether a large trade reflects the arrival of new information into the marketplace or is simply an information-free trade for portfolio rebalancing purposes, it will create volatility as market participants restructure their risk profiles and the marketplace searches for a new equilibrium price. In more resilient markets, any temporary volatility associated with risk shifting dissipates rapidly, and permanent price revisions associated with the arrival of new information occur quickly and with minimal residual volatility.

Immediacy refers to the speed with which a trade of a given size can be executed at a given cost. Immediacy can arise naturally or by design. The NYSE offers an example of the latter by virtue of the specialist's affirmative obligation to immediately satisfy market order demands in the absence of offsetting orders on the limit-order book or within the community of floor brokers.[3] However, there are also noteworthy examples of markets, such as the S&P 500 index futures market, that offer a high level of immediacy in the absence of such affirmative obligations simply because traders are active.

Types of Traders

Because different traders value each element of liquidity differently, an exchange's business strategy is embodied in how it bundles various liquidity services to meet the demands of its target clientele. Broadly speaking, traders vary along three dimensions. *Patient traders*, such as those who place limit orders, effectively provide liquidity to others at a given price and up to a given quantity. *Impatient traders* consume liquidity by placing market orders that demand immediate execution. Recognizing that the several elements of market liquidity interact with one another, we think of patient orders for larger quantities and prices less distant from the midpoint of the prevailing best quotes as providing more liquidity. Likewise, impatient orders for larger quantities consume more liquidity. In a well-functioning marketplace, traders provide liquidity when it is dear and consume it when it is plentiful.[4]

Traders also differ in the amount of private information they bring to a trade. Considering the resources they devote to firm and industry analysis and the economies of scale under which they operate, we think of institutional investors generally as better informed than retail investors. Having said this, there are a variety of passive management strategies favored by institutional investors, such as mimicking the S&P 500, that clearly are not information intensive.

Finally, traders differ in the size of the orders they place and thereby in the amount of liquidity they provide or consume, with retail traders generally placing smaller orders than institutional traders. Order size influences both how trades are carried out within venues and how venues compete with one another. As an example of the former, traders placing orders in excess of 10,000 shares in NYSE-listed stocks (block traders) often seek price improvement through negotiations off the floor before having their orders brought to the floor for execution. Even orders sent directly to the floor frequently benefit from negotiations that lead to execution at prices better than current quoted prices. In contrast, the NYSE recently unveiled a plan for an Internet-based electronic trading system that would execute orders of 1,000 shares or less in a few seconds at the best quoted price in the marketplace for traders willing to forgo the possibility of price improvement.

Using these three dimensions, we can categorize most types of traders commonly encountered in securities markets. For instance, passive investors such as index funds are typically uninformed, trade in large quantity, and are mostly patient. Active investors can be either informed (stock pickers or block traders) or uninformed (program traders or arbitrageurs), with their level of patience depending on how long-lived the opportunity they perceive is. Successful arbitrage usually is dependent on small and fleeting price discrepancies between markets and therefore is a relatively impatient and large-quantity trading strategy. Likewise, those trading on the basis of information that will soon be publicly revealed, such as a favorable earnings announcement, will be impatient consumers of liquidity. In contrast, fundamental analysts can provide liquidity by patiently establishing a position with the expectation that their unique insight will be appreciated only over a relatively long time horizon.

Price Discovery

Any exchange's price discovery mechanism essentially is a form of auction. *Periodic auctions*, which compel all traders in a given security to participate simultaneously, are efficient devices for price discovery at a given point in time. But periodic auctions involve a trade-off. Concentrating trade at discrete points in time brings together a larger proportion of the trading community and therefore more nearly ensures that the auction price is based on the collective opinion of the security's value. However, discrete auctions sacrifice rapid dissemination of information that arrives in the interval between auctions. The *continuous auction* feature of most trading floors and continuously updated electronic limit-order books respond to this concern.

This dichotomy suggests that traders will prefer different means of price discovery depending on the rate and mode of information arrival. Other things being equal, the more rapid and public the arrival of information related to a security, the more naturally that security will lend itself to trade in a continuous auction setting. Where information arrives less frequently or is only revealed through the actions of traders, a periodic auction is perhaps more appropriate.

Price discovery can be influenced by the degree to which the market for a security is fragmented. Fragmentation occurs when trade in a single security can occur at multiple venues on terms that are not reflective of aggregate conditions in the broader marketplace. Market fragmentation reduces the efficiency of price discovery by limiting the ability of market participants to perceive the full scope of market conditions at any point in time: Prices are set on the basis of only part of the order flow.

Clearly, fragmentation is related to both the state of information technology and the level of transparency adopted by competing trading venues. For example, the opening of the trans-Atlantic cable in 1866 vastly reduced communication time and thereby contributed to a 66 percent decline in the average price difference between the London and New York U.S. Treasury Bond markets. Likewise, domestic telegraph in the United States reduced average price differences between the New York and New Orleans foreign exchange markets and between the New York and Philadelphia equity markets by almost 50 percent. Recent technological advances have similarly reduced fragmentation, although with diminishing impact on the margin: The consolidated NYSE tape introduced in 1975 cut the average price difference between the New York and Midwest Stock Exchanges only by about 6.5 percent.[5] As we noted in the introduction to chapter 8, the Internet provides great capacity for aggregating information from competing venues, but also encourages fragmentation by lowering the direct costs of establishing a new venue. The net effect on stock prices will be determined by the ability of independent venues to block aggregation and their incentives to do so.

Market Transparency

Price discovery, even in fully integrated markets, is influenced by decisions regarding the level of market transparency. It is common to think of transparency as a good thing, but too much of a good thing in this case can lead to unexpressed demand. Posting a price at which one is willing to buy or sell is like providing potential counterparties with an option. If someone likes your offer, he exercises the option to accept your terms; otherwise, he does not. But this places you at the mercy of those with better information. Price discovery is served by the clear picture of demand conditions yielded by a high level of transparency. But if transparency also means that clear expressions of demand raise the threat of being made a sucker, then extreme transparency might yield a very clear rendering of very little information.

Thus exchanges often maintain a capacity for submitting hidden limit orders (Paris Bourse) or all-or-none orders (NYSE) that limit the exposure or transparency of a demand expression. Where the stakes are particularly high (or the option value is great), a trader will engage a broker to test the waters for a transaction prior to formal submission by revealing interest to a select clientele. The long-term relationships developed on exchange floors and within dealer communities serve this purpose and so promote price discovery by increasing the flow of otherwise unexpressed demand information.[6]

Anonymity

Finally, the production technology of an exchange embodies the level of anonymity afforded market participants. A marketplace can be simultaneously transparent in the trade-history sense and anonymous in the sense that market participants learn neither the source of an offer to trade nor the identities of counterparties to consummated trades. When some traders are better informed than others, the anonymity of a marketplace can have important and differential implications for various trader clienteles. Other things being equal, well-informed traders benefit from anonymity at the expense of less well-informed traders. However, in the extreme the threat of exploitation by informed traders drives uninformed traders from the marketplace and therefore deprives informed traders of profit opportunities and prevents market prices from reflecting their information.

In this setting, some cooperation on the part of informed traders *as a group* may serve both their interests as a group and the interests of the broader marketplace. Unfortunately, it may not be in the private interest of any *single* informed trader to cooperate. In this situation it may be in the interest of market participants to endow a third party, like the metaphorical traffic cop of chapter 1, with the power to enforce cooperation. Here again, the long-standing relationships among traders on the floor of the NYSE or among dealers in the Nasdaq network can serve to balance individual interests against those of the group. In some instances, these relationships, by providing the foundation for suppressing anonymity and enforcing cooperative behavior, can make both informed and uninformed traders better off.[7] Of course, we can imagine rules, perhaps a special auction format, designed for a similar purpose. But in the extreme where information has great strategic value, there remains a role for the human intermediary's capacity for discretion.

NOTES

Chapter 1

1. Paul Romer, "Roundtable on the Soft Revolution," *Journal of Applied Corporate Finance* 11, no. 2 (1998): 12.
2. "A Survey of Technology in Finance," *The Economist*, 26 October 1996, 4–22.
3. "Chase's Beacon of Hope," *The Economist*, 27 May 2000.
4. Carliss Y. Baldwin and Kim B. Clark, "Managing in an Age of Modularity," *Harvard Business Review*, October 1997, 84–93.
5. Roger Lowenstein, "Milken's Junk-Bond Legacy Still Stirs Debate," *The Wall Street Journal*, 5 September 1996, C1.

Chapter 2

1. Gary Gorton's *Journal of Political Economy* article provides a fascinating account of the impact of distance on bank notes. See "Reputation Formation in Early Bank Note Markets," *Journal of Political Economy* 104, no. 2 (1996): 346–397.
2. Robert C. Merton and Zvi Bodie, "A Conceptual Framework for Analyzing the Financial Environment," in *The Global Financial System: A Functional Perspective*, Dwight B. Crane, Zvi Bodie, Kenneth A. Froot, Scott P. Mason, Robert C. Merton, Andre F. Perold, et al. (Boston, MA: Harvard Business School Press, 1995). See also Robert C. Merton, "The Financial System and Economic Performance," *Journal of Financial Services Research* 4, (1990): 263–300.
3. "Finance: Trick or Treat?" *The Economist*, 23 October 1999.
4. The experience of the former Soviet Union countries has shed much light on the importance of a legal system that recognizes and protects contracts and property rights as a precondition for developing a market economy. Mancur Olsen, in his posthumously published book entitled *Power and Prosperity: Outgrowing Communist and Capitalist Dictatorships* (New York: Basic Books, 1999), offers deep insight on this point.

5. Olsen, *Power and Prosperity: Outgrowing Communist and Capital Dictatorships* (New York: Basic Books, 1999).

6. Brad DeLong provides an interesting development of this argument in "Did J.P. Morgan's Men Add Value? An Economist's Perspective on Financial Capitalism," 12 August 1995, <http://econ161.berkeley.edu/pdf_files/Morgan_Temin.pdf> (accessed 24 November 1999).

7. Peter Tufano, "Financial Innovation and First-Mover Advantage," *Journal of Financial Economics*, 25 (1989): 213–40.

8. Carl Shapiro and Hal Varian, *Information Rules: A Strategic Guide to the Network Economy* (Boston: Harvard Business School Press, 1999).

9. Brad DeLong, "Speculative Microeconomics for Tomorrow's Economy," <http://econ161.berkeley.edu/> (accessed 22 November 1999).

Chapter 3

1. See Edward J. Kane, "Technological and Regulatory Forces in the Developing Fusion of Financial-Services Competition," *Journal of Finance* 39 (1984): 759–772, and Merton Miller, "Financial Innovation: The Last Twenty Years and the Next," *Journal of Financial and Quantitative Analysis* 21 (1986): 459–471.

2. For further background, see Vincent P. Carosso, *Investment Banking in America: A History* (Cambridge, MA: Harvard University Press, 1970); Charles W. Calomiris and Carlos D. Ramirez, "The Role of Financial Relationships in the History of American Corporate Finance," *Journal of Applied Corporate Finance* 9 (1996): 52–73; and Robert G. Eccles and Dwight B. Crane, *Doing Deals: Investment Banks at Work* (Boston: Harvard Business School Press, 1988).

3. Calomiris and Ramirez, "Role of Financial Relationships," 52–73.

4. Ron Chernow, *The Death of the Banker* (New York: Vintage Books, 1997), xiii.

5. The critical reader will ask, "Why now?" If there has always been some "optimal" mix of volatile and nonvolatile business lines, what has changed? One important change in the industry has been a weakening in client/bank relationships. Historically, firms maintained a relationship with one or a few banks and dealt with them in a relatively noncompetitive fashion. The beginning of the end of these relationships usually is marked by Morgan Stanley's 1979 refusal of IBM's request to include Salomon Brothers as a co-manager for IBM's $1 billion debt offering. But why did these banking relationships weaken? Economists view relationships as a means of economizing on the costs of producing information about and monitoring the client. Firms that put transactions out for bid bear the cost of multiple banks getting up to speed. One possibility that is consistent with the broader argument made in this book is that these costs have been diminished by advances in information technology. If so, banks should move away from businesses where spreads are under pressure to those where they are not. We argue, for example, that securities underwriting lends itself to codification, which, in turn, increases competition and narrows historically wide spreads. Conversely, the (perceived) talents of money managers remain uncodified, and so spreads remain wide.

6. Klein offers a first-hand account of Wit's early days in "WallStreet.com," *Wired*, February 1998, <http://www.wired.com/wired/archive/6.02/wallstreet_pr.html> (accessed 10 August 2000).

7. Investors who sell their allocations within sixty days are excluded from future offerings. These so-called penalty bids have become a common feature of the

primary equity markets. See William J. Wilhelm Jr., "Secondary Market Stabilization of IPOs," *Journal of Applied Corporate Finance* 10 (1999): 78–85, for a detailed account.

8. *Tombstone* refers to the traditional format of announcements of securities offerings printed in the financial press. The issuing firm's name appears at the head of the announcement, followed by some particulars of the offering in smaller print. At the bottom of the announcement, members of the underwriting syndicate are listed, with the leader or leaders appearing in the upper left-hand corner of the list in larger type. Banks devote considerable energy to moving up and to the left in the membership list because the list is perceived as reflecting, in part, their relative standing within the industry.

9. William Hambrecht, interview by William J. Wilhelm Jr., tape recording, San Francisco, CA, 14 January 2000.

10. Ibid.

11. Andover.Net merged with VA Linux Systems, Inc. on February 3, 2000.

12. "Underwriting Tables," *Investment Dealers' Digest*, 28 February 2000, 17.

13. For example, about 55 percent of the IPOs completed during the first half of 1999 were managed by Goldman Sachs, Morgan Stanley Dean Witter, or Merrill Lynch.

14. Much of the description here of the practice of bookbuilding is drawn from Lawrence M. Benveniste and William J. Wilhelm Jr., "Initial Public Offerings: Going by the Book," *Journal of Applied Corporate Finance* 10 (1997): 98–108.

15. In fact, the SEC recently has undertaken a large-scale investigation of IPO allocation practices. See Susan Pulliam, Randall Smith, and Charles Gasparino, "Heard on the Street: SEC Intensifies Inquiry into Commissions for Hot IPOs," *The Wall Street Journal*, 13 December 2000, C1.

16. Quoted by Ian Springsteel in "The Rush Is On!" *Investment Dealers' Digest*, 14 February 2000, 16–21.

17. Steven Wallman was a member of OffRoad's first board of directors and in 1998 founded FOLIOfn, an online investment management concern that recently entered a strategic alliance with OffRoad. See the description of key management personnel and the related discussion that follows.

18. Stephen Pelletier, interview by William J. Wilhelm Jr., tape recording, San Francisco, CA, 13 January 2000.

19. Ibid.

20. See <http://www.offroadcapital.com/about/index.html>.

21. Ibid.

22. OffRoad recently fired more than half its staff. Co-chief executives John Forlines and David Weir left the firm as it began a retrenchment, with Stephen Pelletier returning to the CEO position, and a separation of its corporate finance and software units (*Bloomberg News*, 16 May, 2001).

Chapter 4

1. John Seely Brown and Paul Duguid, *The Social Life of Information* (Boston: Harvard Business School Press, 2000), 17.

2. Robert Axelrod, *The Evolution of Cooperation* (New York: Basic Books, 1984), 73–87.

3. The importance of designating a party with the power to exclude others should not be underestimated. Certainly, the membership might rise up collectively to

exclude a misbehaving party. But collective behavior is notoriously difficult to coordinate and often falls prey to divide-and-conquer strategies. One need look no further than OPEC for an example of how difficult it is for a collective to co-ordinate on what is clearly the group's dominant strategy.

4. Roger Myerson, "Mechanism Design," in *The New Palgrave: A Dictionary of Economics*, eds. John Eatwell, Murray Milgate, and Peter Newman (London: Macmillan Press, 1987), 191–206.

5. Ibid.

6. This example is designed to capture the essence of arguments first developed by Lawrence M. Benveniste, Paul A. Spindt, and William J. Wilhelm Jr. For the technical details, see Benveniste and Spindt, "How Investment Bankers Determine the Offer Price and Allocation of New Issues," *Journal of Financial Economics* 24 (1989): 343–361, and Benveniste and Wilhelm, "A Comparative Analysis of IPO Proceeds Under Alternative Regulatory Environments," *Journal of Financial Economics* 28 (1990): 173–207.

7. Kevin Rock, "Why New Issues Are Underpriced," *Journal of Financial Economics* 15 (1986): 187–212.

8. At the break-even price, retail investors do not care whether institutional investors are optimistic or pessimistic. In other words, the dollar value of their allocation in either case is the same. Algebraically, this can be represented by finding the offer price, P, that solves

$$700,000(\$10 - P)[700,000/(1,000,000 + 700,000)] = 700,000(P - \$8)$$

The left-hand side of the equality is the dollar value of the expected allocation to retail investors given that shares will be rationed on a pro rata basis among both retail and institutional investors. (The effect of rationing is reflected in the bracketed term.) The right-hand side reflects the case in which institutional investors perceive the deal as overpriced and the entire retail demand of 700,000 shares is satisfied. Setting $P = \$8.58$ satisfies the equality.

9. This is true unless the institutional investors believe that the bank will make up the losses expected from the present deal in more profitable transactions in the future. See Benveniste and Spindt, "How Investment Bankers Determine the Offer Price," 343–361.

10. Kathleen Weiss Hanley and William J. Wilhelm Jr. provide evidence from a small U.S sample. See Hanley and Wilhelm, "Evidence on the Strategic Allocation of Initial Public Offerings," *Journal of Financial Economics* 37 (1995): 239–257. Alexander P. Ljungqvist and Wilhelm J. Wilhelm Jr. ("IPO Allocations: Discriminatory or Discretionary?" working paper, 2001, available at <http://www2.bc.edu/~wilhelmw>) show that the same pattern appears worldwide.

11. See Francesca Cornelli and David Goldreich, "Bookbuilding and Strategic Allocation," *Journal of Finance* (forthcoming), and Ljungqvist and Wilhelm, "IPO Allocations."

12. Kathleen Weiss Hanley first documented this "partial adjustment" phenomenon among U.S. IPOs brought to market in the 1980s. See Hanley, "The Underpricing of Initial Public Offerings and the Partial Adjustment Phenomenon," *Journal of Financial Economics* 34, no. 2 (1993): 231–250. The pattern holds across time and countries in which bookbuilding methods are used. See Alexander P. Ljungqvist, Tim Jenkinson, and William J. Wilhelm Jr., "Global Integration in

Primary Equity Markets: The Role of U.S. Banks and U.S. Investors," CEPR Discussion Paper No. 2484, April 2001 (available at <http://www2.bc.edu/ ~wilhelmw>).

13. Axelrod in *The Evolution of Competition* provides a fascinating account of a computer "tournament" in which cooperative strategies demonstrated a greater capacity for survival than more aggressive strategies in a repeated prisoner's dilemma game.

14. Lawrence M. Benveniste, Walid Y. Busaba, and William J. Wilhelm Jr., "Price Stabilization as a Bonding Mechanism in New Equity Issues," *Journal of Financial Economics* 42, no. 2 (1996): 223–255.

15. See Lawrence M. Benveniste, Sina M. Erdal, and William J. Wilhelm Jr., "Who Benefits from Secondary Market Price Stabilization of IPOs?" *Journal of Banking and Finance* 22 (1998): 741–767.

16. Carosso, *Investment Banking in America*, 11.

17. We develop an example in appendix A to illustrate this potentially counterintuitive point.

18. In the example in appendix A, if the seller could enter a binding contract to share his gains from a strategic trade with the counterparty, he should willingly sacrifice up to $500 of the $800 gain. At this point, he would be indifferent between the expected gain of $250 [(200 + 300)/2] and the expected gain from doing nothing to address the counterparty's incentive to proceed cautiously.

19. The characterization of reputation as a substitute for contracts received early attention from Eugene Fama in his discussion of how external labor market perception of a manager's performance (the manager's reputation) disciplines managers of firms characterized by diffuse risk bearing. See Eugene Fama, "Agency Problems and the Theory of the Firm," *Journal of Political Economy* 88 (1980): 288–307. Bengt Holmstrom studies the limits to the use of reputation in this capacity. In particular, he points out that the pursuit of reputation in the absence of complete contracts can lead to an inefficient supply of labor—either too much, as some would argue occurs with junior members of professional services firms, or too little depending on one's initial status. See Holmstrom, "Managerial Incentive Problems—A Dynamic Perspective," in *Vetenskap Och Foretagsledning: Studier I Ekonomi Och Ledarskap Tillagnade* (*Lars Wahlbeck: Essays in Economics and Management in Honour of Lars Wahlbeck*) (Helsingfors: Svenska handelshogskolan, 1982).

Recall that in financial markets, intermediaries make a variety of contingent commitments to make cash payments in the future. The obvious way to make such commitments credible is to set aside sufficient cash to guarantee that future obligations can always be satisfied—in other words, to establish a performance bond. This is precisely the role that maintaining a (costly) reserve of financial capital plays for financial intermediaries. However, an intermediary that has established a reputation for satisfying its obligations can maintain a smaller reserve and still make credible commitments—a good reputation can substitute for costly capital. See Arnoud Boot, Stuart Greenbaum, and Anjan Thakor, "Reputation and Discretion in Financial Contracting," *American Economic Review* 83 (1993): 1165–1183.

20. An insightful discussion of sales strategies and client relationships on Wall Street can be found in Robert G. Eccles and Dwight B. Crane, *Doing Deals: Investment Banks at Work* (Boston: Harvard Business School Press, 1988).

21. Eccles and Crane characterize the relationship manager as an agent for the CEO whose success depends in large part on the relationship manager being both "part of—yet outside—the organization" (*Doing Deals*, 87). The relationship manager mediates the private interests of product specialists within the organization and *between* the organization and its clients. The latter role arises because clients recognize the potentially adversarial nature of their dealings with the organization.

Chapter 5

1. Michael Polanyi, *The Tacit Dimension* (Garden City, NY: Doubleday, 1966). In his often prescient book *The Coming of Post-Industrial Society* (New York: Basic Books, 1973), Daniel Bell identified the growing capacity for codifying theoretical knowledge as an "axial principle" reshaping modern society.
2. The vocabulary developed in this section builds on a classification structure used by Patrick H. Sullivan in *Profiting from Intellectual Capital: Extracting Value from Innovation* (New York: John Wiley & Sons, 1998), 3–41.
3. This obviously is a simplistic characterization of the transformation of information into knowledge and sidesteps an enormous literature in the philosophy of science focused on the distinction between the two. John Seely Brown and Paul Duguid provide a concise overview of the latter in *The Social Life of Information* (Boston: Harvard Business School Press, 2000), 117–146. Max Boisot provides a detailed analysis of the codification of information and its organizational consequences in *Knowledge Assets: Securing Competitive Advantage in the Information Economy* (New York: Oxford University Press, 1998).
4. This topic is explored by John A. Kay in *Foundations of Corporate Success* (Oxford University Press, 1993), including a discussion of the consequences of Drexel's failure to codify a significant element of the human capital in Milken's team.
5. See Josh Lerner, "Where Does State Street Lead? A First Look at Finance Patents, 1971–2000," working paper 01-005, Harvard Business School, Boston, 2000 and working paper 7918, National Bureau of Economic Research, 2000.
6. U.S. Patent and Trademark Office special report, March 2000, <http://www.uspto.gov/web/offices/ac/ido/oeip/taf/apat.pdf> (accessed 15 September 2000).
7. Charles Gasparino and Rebecca Buckman, "Horning In: Facing Internet Threat, Merrill to Offer Trading Online for Low Fees," *The Wall Street Journal*, 1 June 1999, A1.
8. See Janet Cooper Alexander, "The Value of Bad News in Securities Class Actions," *UCLA Law Review* (1994): 41, for a detailed discussion of the liability associated with violations of Section 11 of the Securities Act of 1933 or Section 10(b) and Rule 10b-5 of the Securities Exchange Act of 1934.
9. As the SEC considers whether to open road shows to individual investors, the Securities Industry Association, which more nearly represents the interests of the established banks, persists in its opposition, claiming that "firms would dummy down their presentations" to avoid saying something "that's too sophisticated for an individual investor to understand." See "SEC Exploring Ways to Open IPO Roadshows to Small Investors," *Bloomberg News*, 7 September 2000, <http://quote.bloomberg.com/newsarchive/?refer=newsad>.
10. John Seely Brown and Paul Duguid, "Balancing Act: How to Capture Knowledge without Killing It," *Harvard Business Review*, May–June 2000, 73–80.
11. Having made this sweeping statement, it is ironic that one of us just spent over an hour in an unsuccessful search through the Dow Jones News Retrieval

archives for a vaguely recollected article that provided a more detailed account of McKinsey's internal database than was available at the firm's Web site.

12. Brown and Duguid, "Balancing Act," 74.

13. See William Vickrey, "Counterspeculation, Auctions, and Competitive Sealed Tenders," *Journal of Finance* 16, no. 1 (1961): 8–37. An *English auction* is the familiar mechanism whereby the last remaining bidder is allocated at his bid price the indivisible item being sold. When Vickrey and most economists refer to a *Dutch auction*, they have in mind an auction in which the offer price initially is set at a high level and then lowered until a price is reached at which a bidder is willing to buy the item. An important difference between the English and Dutch auctions is the ability of bidders to observe one another's bidding strategy in the former but not the latter. *Sealed-bid auctions* require bidders to simultaneously submit bids, and so again individual bidding strategy is unobservable. A *first-price auction* allocates the item to the highest bidder at her bid price, whereas the *second-price auction* allocates the item to the highest bidder but at the next best bid price. Strategic equivalence implies not only revenue equivalence but also that a bidder would bid the same regardless of the rules of the two auctions under consideration.

14. See John McMillan, "Selling Spectrum Rights," *Journal of Economic Perspectives* 8, no. 3 (1994): 145–162.

15. "The Heyday of the Auction," *The Economist*, 24 July 1999, 67–68.

16. Note that the definitions provided in this section suggest that references within the financial community to Dutch auctions more nearly correspond with the economist's definition of a second-price auction. WR Hambrecht's OpenIPO is similar to a sealed-bid, second-price auction in the sense that bidders only know their own bids and that the clearing price at which all shares are sold is lower than that of the highest bidders.

17. Bruno Biais and Anne Marie Faugeron-Crouzet, "IPO Auctions: English, Dutch, . . . French and Internet," *Journal of Financial Intermediation* (forthcoming).

18. For a detailed analysis of the complications in auctioning divisible goods or shares, see Robert Wilson, "Auctions of Shares," *Quarterly Journal of Economics* 93 (1979): 675–689.

19. *Standard & Poor's Emerging & Special Situation* (New York: The McGraw-Hill Companies, Inc. 2000).

20. Richard J. Peterson, *PR Newswire*, 29 December 2000.

21. Richard J. Peterson, *PR Newswire*, 29 December 2000. See also Hoover's Online at <http://www.hoovers.com/hoov/ads/sprintPopup.html> (accessed 1 June 2001).

22. Lawrence Lessig, *Code and Other Laws of Cyberspace* (New York: Basic Books, 2000), 132.

23. Mark Stefik, *The Internet Edge* (Cambridge, MA: The MIT Press, 1999), 85. Also see Brown and Duguid, *Social Life of Information*, 248.

24. Tom Bethell, *The Noblest Triumph: Property and Prosperity through the Ages* (New York: St. Martin's Griffin, 1999), 265.

25. For a detailed analysis of markets dominated by star performers, see Sherwin Rosen, "The Economics of Superstars," *American Economic Review* 17, no. 5 (1981): 845–858.

26. For additional detail, see *The Mutual Fund Fact Book*, published annually by the Investment Company Institute, Washington, D.C. or <http://www.ici.org/pdf/

01fb_ch1.pdf> (accessed 1 June 2001). Also, see "Money Managers: Profile and Statistics" in *Pension and Investments*, May 1, 2001, <http://www.pionline.com/moneyman/> (accessed 1 June 2001).

27. Existing theory assumes a level of rationality among market participants to which well-established findings from research in psychology pose a serious challenge. Ongoing research in this area might provide a clearer understanding of relative asset prices, but more important, could shed light on what determines the absolute level of asset prices. By this we mean that existing theory can tell us quite a lot about how a stock and an option on that stock should be priced relative to one another, but it provides relatively little insight into the level of the stock price or the stock market generally.

28. Robert G. Eccles and Dwight B. Crane, *Doing Deals: Investment Banks at Work* (Boston: Harvard Business School Press, 1988).

29. Paul M. Scherer and Joseph B. White, "Deals and Deal Makers: Ford Makes Some Offer Some May Refuse," *The Wall Street Journal*, 12 July 2000, C1.

30. Claiming that production costs are declining and competition increasing might strike some readers as wishful thinking in light of the generous compensation of many Wall Street bankers. But keep in mind that this movement has taken place against a background of unusual economic and financial market growth. However, for the first time in many years, the Wall Street banks are struggling to attract talent from top M.B.A. programs as recent graduates join the Internet gold rush. More substantial support will rest in whether spreads or profit margins are narrowing within the commoditized segments of the industry, leading banks to shift their resources to new, more profitable lines of business.

31. See Lerner, "Where Does State Street Lead?"

32. "The Knowledge Monopolies: The Patent Wars," *The Economist*, 8 April 2000, 76.

33. "The Knowledge Monopolies," 75.

Chapter 6

1. Kevin Werbach, "Syndication: The Emerging Model for Business in the Internet Era," *Harvard Business Review*, May–June 2000, 85–93.

2. For more information on the topic of investment bank syndication, see William J. Wilhelm Jr., "The Internet and Financial Market Structure," *Oxford Review of Economic Policy* (forthcoming).

3. If the reader can bear with us for a moment, we'll come back with a bit more support for these assertions later in this chapter and in the case study of Goldman Sachs in chapter 7.

4. Barry E. Supple, "A Business Elite: German-Jewish Financiers in Nineteenth Century New York," *Business History Review* 31 (1957): 143–178, and Vincent P. Carosso, *Investment Banking in America: A History* (Cambridge, MA: Harvard University Press, 1970), especially chapter 4.

5. Adolf A. Berle and Gardiner C. Means, *The Modern Corporation and Private Property* (New York: Macmillan, 1932).

6. Ronald H. Coase, "The Nature of the Firm," *Economica* 4 (1937): 386–405.

7. Michael Jensen and William Meckling, "Theory of the Firm: Managerial Behavior, Agency Costs and Ownership Structure," *Journal of Financial Economics* 3 (1976): 305–360.

8. See Oliver Hart, *Firms, Contracts and Financial Structure* (Oxford University Press, 1995), especially Part I, chapters 1 to 4, for a comprehensive review of this "property rights approach" to the theory of the firm. See also, Sanford J. Grossman and Oliver Hart, "The Costs and Benefits of Ownership: A Theory of Vertical and Lateral Integration," *The Journal of Political Economy* 94 (1986): 1691–1719; and Oliver Hart and John Moore, "Property Rights and the Nature of the Firm," *The Journal of Political Economy* 98 (1990): 1119–1158.

9. Hart, *Firms*, 58.

10. A recent article by Raguram Rajan and Luigi Zingales generalizes the Grossman, Hart, and Moore perspective by recognizing that *access to* (but not necessarily ownership of) critical resources provides opportunity for specializing one's human capital to the resource. This newly specialized human capital itself becomes a critical resource that provides its owner with bargaining power because it too can be withdrawn. Had the owner of the newly specialized human capital owned the existing critical resource, she might not have chosen to create the new critical resource. Thus access to critical resources can sometimes provide better incentives for investment in new critical resources than will direct ownership of critical resources. See Rajan and Zingales, "Power in a Theory of the Firm," *Quarterly Journal of Economics* 113, (1998): 387–432.

11. The perspective on the syndicate in this section is developed formally by Pegaret Pichler and William J. Wilhelm Jr. in "A Theory of the Syndicate: Form Follows Function," *Journal of Finance* (forthcoming). Alternative theories of the syndicate's function interpret it as a risk-sharing device—risks that one bank cannot absorb are comfortably spread across a group of banks. But these theories shed little light on the seemingly inefficient practice of dissolving syndicates upon completion of a transaction only to reform similar if not identical teams for future transactions. Moreover, the process of building a book for securities offerings, coupled with deals being priced just hours before trading begins, substantially diminishes the syndicate's risk of paying more for securities than market conditions will support. Add the fact that risks borne by bulge-bracket banks are now spread widely through public ownership, and the risk-sharing rationale for underwriting syndicates appears quite fragile.

12. Robert G. Eccles and Dwight B. Crane, *Doing Deals: Investment Banks at Work* (Boston: Harvard Business School Press, 1988), 147–162.

13. Alec Petro, personal conversation with authors, 14 February, 2001.

14. See Alexander P. Ljungqvist, Tim Jenkinson, and William J. Wilhelm Jr., "Global Integration in Primary Equity Markets: The Role of U.S. Banks and U.S. Investors," CEPR Discussion Paper No. 2484, April 2001 (available at <http://www2bc.edu/wilhelmw>).

15. Information provided by Alexander P. Ljungqvist of New York University.

16. James M. Utterback, *Mastering the Dynamics of Innovation* (Boston: Harvard Business School Press, 1996), xxvii. This work and Jeremy Stein, "Waves of Creative Destruction: Firm-Specific Learning-by-Doing and the Dynamics of Innovation," *Review of Economic Studies* 64 (1997): 265–288 explain how successful entrants produce a "shakeup" externality by opening the door to other technologically strong entrants. Lawrence M. Benveniste, Walid Y. Busaba, and William J. Wilhelm Jr. suggest that the relative dominance of the primary equity markets by a few investment banks can further strengthen the hand of an entrant seeking to alter the technological foundations of an industry. See Benveniste,

Busaba, and Wilhelm, "Information Externalities and the Role of Underwriters in Primary Equity Markets," *Journal of Financial Intermediation* (forthcoming), available at <http://www2bc.edu/wilhelmw>.

17. Both quotations are drawn from Ian Springsteel, "The Rush Is On!" *Investment Dealers' Digest*, 14 February 2000, 16–21.

18. William Hambrecht, interview by William J. Wilhelm Jr., tape recording, San Francisco, CA, 14 January 2000.

19. The U.S. Department of Justice recently has launched an investigation "looking at the competitive effects of certain joint ventures in the online bond-trading industry and in online foreign exchange." See Randall Smith and Gregory Zuckerman, "Web Bond-Trade Systems Draw Regulators' Scrutiny," *The Wall Street Journal*, 1 December 2000, C22.

20. The development of theories explaining the path of financial innovation is a growth industry in the recent academic literature. Key contributions that inform the discussion in this section include Frank Allen and Douglas Gale, *Financial Innovation and Risk Sharing* (Cambridge, MA: MIT Press, 1994); Robert C. Merton, "On the Applications of the Continuous-Time Theory of Finance to Financial Intermediation and Insurance," *Geneva Papers on Risk and Insurance* 14, (1989): 225–261; and Stephen Ross, "Institutional Markets, Financial Marketing, and Financial Innovation," *Journal of Finance* 44 (1989): 541–556. A recent paper by Bharat Anand and Alexander Galetovic formalizes the competitive effects of the industry's dependence on human capital. See Anand and Galetovic, "Information, Nonexcludability, and Financial Market Structure," *Journal of Business* 73 (2000): 357–402.

Chapter 7

1. Niall Ferguson, *The World's Banker: The History of the House of Rothschild* (London: Weidenfeld & Nicolson, 1998), 296. This work provides a detailed account of the Rothschilds' early attempts to broaden the span of their network beyond the capacity of immediate family members. Interestingly, the group of paid agents that the Rothschilds and others relied upon often were drawn from extended families as well.

2. Ferguson, *World's Banker*, 284.

3. Barry E. Supple, "A Business Elite: German-Jewish Financiers in Nineteenth-Century New York," *Business History Review* 31 (1957): 143–178.

4. Supple notes a similar pattern among the early New England bankers of British origin.

5. Supple, "A Business Elite," 176.

6. In "The Role of Financial Relationships in the History of American Corporate Finance," [*Journal of Applied Corporate Finance* 9 (1996): 52–73], Charles W. Calomiris and Carlos D. Ramirez argue that the separation of commercial and investment banking also weakened the network of relationships that underpinned the securities markets, thereby contributing to a decline in activity not reversed until the 1960s.

7. Vincent P. Carosso, *Investment Banking in America: A History* (Cambridge, MA: Harvard University Press, 1970), 507, citing the U.S. House of Representatives Report of Special Study of Securities Markets of the Securities and Exchange Commission, 1963.

8. Ron Chernow, *The House of Morgan* (New York: Touchstone, 1990), 470. However, to say that the NYSE limited members' options misses the point. The

NYSE is nothing more than its member firms. Collectively, they establish best practices for the membership.

9. Lisa Endlich, *Goldman Sachs: The Culture of Success* (New York: Alfred A. Knopf, 1999), 15.

10. Vincent P. Carosso, *The Morgans: Private International Bankers, 1854–1913* (Cambridge, MA: Harvard University Press, 1987).

11. Michael C. Jensen and William H. Meckling, "Specific and General Knowledge, and Organizational Structure," *Journal of Applied Corporate Finance* 8, no. 2 (1995): 4–18. Originally published in *Contract Economics*, eds. Lars Werin and Hans Wijkander (Oxford: Blackwell Publishers, 1992), 251–274.

12. Jensen and Meckling, "Specific and General Knowledge," 10.

13. Oliver E. Williamson, "Organization Form, Residual Claimants, and Corporate Control," *Journal of Law and Economics*, no. 26 (1983): 351–366.

14. Endlich, *Goldman Sachs*, 21.

15. See Robert G. Eccles and Dwight B. Crane, *Doing Deals: Investment Banks at Work* (Boston: Harvard Business School Press, 1988), especially chapter 7, 147–162.

16. Of course this does not rule out the defection of an entire team of bankers, but that is more difficult to coordinate than an individual defection.

17. See Raghuram Rajan and Luigi Zingales, "The Firm as a Dedicated Hierarchy: A Theory of Origin and Growth of Firms," working paper, University of Chicago, 1998. Available at <http://gsblgz.uchicago.edu>.

18. Endlich, *Goldman Sachs*, 136.

19. Endlich, 20.

20. Endlich, 15.

21. Endlich, 188, 232.

22. Gilbert E. Kaplan, "Gus Levy Answers 132 Questions about His Firm, His Business—and Himself," *Institutional Investor*, November 1973, 33–41.

23. Endlich, *Goldman Sachs*, 134–135.

24. One innovative feature of BroadPark was a master loan agreement signed by syndicate members that enabled rapid commitment of funds relative to structures that called for syndicate members to sign separate loan agreements with borrowers. In essence, the structure economized on paperwork and negotiations by codifying the relationship among syndicate members. For further details, see "Another Diver in the Buy-Out Pool. Why Tokyo Should Go Higher," *The Economist*, 15 April 1989, 82.

25. Endlich, *Goldman Sachs*, 187.

26. Endlich, 183.

27. Endlich, 11, 255, and 260.

28. This breakdown is based on firm estimates of $891 million paid out in cash, $295 million in face value of subordinated debt, and 47,270,551 shares (about 10 percent of the total shares outstanding) valued at the offer price of $53 per share.

29. *The Economist*, "The Moonies Come to Market," 20 June 1998.

30. Endlich, *Goldman Sachs*, 131.

31. For a description of BNP/CooperNeff's trading philosophy, see Greg Ip, "By the Numbers: Trading Vast Volumes, Stock Firm Consults Only Its 'Black Box'," *The Wall Street Journal*, 16 December 1997, A1.

32. Stewart Meyers, "The Determinants of Corporate Borrowing," *Journal of Financial Economics* V (1977): 147–175. Also see Stewart Myers and Raghuram

Rajan, "The Paradox of Liquidity," Quarterly Journal of Economics 113, no. 3 (1998): 733–771 for a recent extension that highlights the threat to lenders when the borrower's assets are too liquid.

33. Quoted by Charles Pretzlik and Simon Targett in "Goldman Targets Managed Assets: US Bank Aims to Build Dollars 1,000bn Investment Business," *The Financial Times*, 5 March 2001.

34. Quoted by Steven Lipin in "Deals & Deal Makers: Merrill Lynch Is Expected to Announce Hiring of Evercore's Respected Seechrest," *The Wall Street Journal*, 18 October 2000, C23.

Chapter 8

1. A *market order* calls for immediate execution at the current best bid or offer in the marketplace. A *limit order* is an offer to buy or sell at a price away from the best bid or offer. Traditionally, exchange specialists kept these orders in the limit-order book and executed trades against the book as prices moved such that a limit order became the best bid or offer.

2. In "Prices Are Property: The Organization of Financial Exchanges from a Transaction Cost Perspective" *Journal of Law and Economics* 34 (1991): 591–644 Harold Mulherin, Jeffry Netter, and James Overdahl provide a fascinating historical account of the give-and-take between U.S. exchange members and outsiders presided over by the courts and reflected in evolutionary change in the organizational structure of exchanges. The current minimum standards of transparency overseen by the SEC require significant market centers to make public their best prices and the quantity for which these prices hold. The consolidation of this information yields a national best bid and best offer (NBBO) for each security, which is disseminated to broker-dealers and information vendors. For further details, see SEC Release No. 34-42450, 23 February 2000.

3. William G. Christie and Paul H. Schultz, "Why Do Nasdaq Market Makers Avoid Odd-Eighth Quotes?" *Journal of Finance* 49 (1994): 1813–1840.

4. Lawrence R. Glosten, "Is the Electronic Open Limit-Order Book Inevitable?" *Journal of Finance*, 49 (1994): 1127–1161.

5. Lawrence R. Glosten uses this insight as a rationale for endowing market makers with some degree of monopoly power. See Glosten, "Insider Trading, Liquidity and the Role of the Monopolist Specialist," *Journal of Business* 62, no. 2 (1989): 211–235.

6. A *portfolio trade* involves the submission of an order to buy or sell an entire portfolio of stocks simultaneously. Although it is quite plausible that an institution will have developed private information regarding one or a few stocks, the likelihood that private information extends to an entire portfolio declines rapidly as the portfolio increases in size.

7. This section draws on a more detailed analysis by Alan Morrison and William J. Wilhelm Jr., "Design Principles for Online Securities Exchange," working paper, University of Oxford, 2000.

8. See Matthew Andresen (president of the Island ECN), "Don't Clobber ECNs," *The Wall Street Journal*, 27 March 2000, A48.

9. The notion that markets benefit from some degree of informational inefficiency is known as the Grossman-Stiglitz paradox. See Sanford Grossman and Joseph Stiglitz, "On the Impossibility of Informationally Efficient Markets," *American*

Economic Review 70 (1980): 393–408. Because the guidance of resource allocation by securities prices is a relatively discrete process, some delay in the embodiment of information in prices should not cause much harm in the long run. Intel's stock price at any particular point in time is not likely to bear heavily on the decision of whether to invest billions in a new chip fabrication plant. On the other hand, a long-term trend in either direction will have an impact, and if there is sufficient return on the investment in information that would drive such a trend, the information will surely find its way into prices in due time.

10. An accessible but rigorous outline of the problems in network pricing is provided in Gerald Faulhaber, "Pricing the Net: What Economists Do," 1995. The article can be downloaded from Hal Varian's Web site: <http://www.sims.berkeley.edu/resources/infoecon/> (accessed 16 March 2001). For a detailed development of problems arising in network pricing see Robert B. Wilson, *Nonlinear Pricing* (Oxford University Press, 1993), and Jean-Jacques Laffont and Jean Tirole, *Competition in Telecommunications* (Cambridge, MA: MIT Press) 2001.

11. See Greg Ip, "NYSE Trading Widens via Link to Archipelago," *The Wall Street Journal*, 8 August 2000, C17.

12. For an analysis of competition in the backbone market, see Jacques Cremer, Patrick Rey, and Jean Tirole, "Connectivity in the Commercial Internet," working paper, University of Toulouse, 1999.

13. See Angus Richards (deputy managing director for market operations of the Australian Stock Exchange), "Models for Cross-Border Securities Trading and Settlement," Australian Stock Exchange, January 2000, for a discussion of connectivity problems arising in cross-border trading and proposals for designing interoperable systems.

14. For details, see Securities and Exchange Commission, Release No. 34-43863, File No. SR-NASD-99-53, 19 January 2001.

15. For a review of the literature, see Elinor Ostrom, "Collective Action and the Evolution of Social Norms," *Journal of Economic Perspectives* 14 (2000): 137–158.

16. Ostrom, 147.

17. Ostrom, 153.

Chapter 9

1. "Deutsche Bank Exec Barred from Soliciting State Street Clients," *Bloomberg News*, 27 October 1999, <http://quote.bloomberg.com/newsarchive/?refer=newsad>.

2. Scot Thurm, "No-Exit Strategies: Their Outlook Bright, Fiber-Optics Firms Put Job Hoppers on Notice," *The Wall Street Journal*, 6 February 2001, A1.

3. Annalee Saxenian, *Regional Advantage: Culture and Competition in Silicon Valley and Route 128* (Cambridge, MA: Harvard University Press, 1996.)

4. John Seely Brown and Paul Duguid, *The Social Life of Information* (Boston: Harvard Business School Press, 2000), 165.

5. See Nitin Nohria and Robert G. Eccles, eds., *Networks and Organizations: Structure, Form and Action* (Boston: Harvard Business School Press, 1992), 1–22.

6. Richard Grasso, "The Battle for Efficient Markets," *The Economist*, 17 June 2000, 70. It's also noteworthy that the NYSE recently requested that the SEC allow it to withdraw from the Consolidated Tape Association and Consolidated

Quote system, the stock market cooperatives that provide price and trade information to data vendors and brokerage firms, in the interest of further protecting its stake in the information generated by the exchange.

Appendix A

1. The use of "unfortunately" suggests that total expected gains from trade, as opposed to the expected gains from trade for one or the other party, is the appropriate measure of market performance. Even if we set aside the possibility of side payments between the two parties, the objective of maximizing total expected gains can be rationalized in the (likely) event that the two parties expect at various times to be on both sides of similar transactions.
2. The expected total gain when the seller is passive is $0.75(500) + 0.25(300) = 450$. The expected total gain when the seller is strategic is $0.25(500) + 0.5(300) = 275$. Since the seller is equally likely to be either passive or strategic, the expected total gain from trade is the equally weighted average of the two, or $362.50.
3. This strategy was chosen for simplicity, not because it represents the best possible set of rules.

Appendix B

1. This appendix draws liberally from Alexander P. Ljungqvist and William J. Wilhelm Jr., "Tradepoint," Oxford Economic Research Associates Ltd., 30 June 1998.
2. For further development of this taxonomy, see Lawrence E. Harris, "Liquidity, Trading Rules, and Electronic Systems," *Monograph Series in Finance and Economics*, 1990–1994, New York University Salomon Center.
3. A *market order* calls for immediate execution at the current best bid or offer in the marketplace. A *limit order* is an offer to buy or sell at a price away from the best bid or offer. Traditionally, exchange specialists kept these orders in the limit-order book and executed trades against the book as prices moved such that a limit order became the best bid or offer.
4. Bruno Biais, Pierre Hillion, and Chester Spatt, "An Empirical Analysis of the Limit Order Book and the Order Flow in the Paris Bourse," *Journal of Finance* 50 (1995): 155–169, provide evidence of such behavior in the Paris Bourse's electronic limit-order book (CAC).
5. Kenneth Garbade and William Silber, "Technology, Communication and the Performance of Financial Markets: 1840–1975," *Journal of Finance* 33 (1978): 819–832.
6. Lawrence M. Benveniste, Alan J. Marcus, and William J. Wilhelm Jr., "What's Special about the Specialist?" *Journal of Financial Economics* 32 (1992): 61–86.
7. Ibid.

INDEX

About the Authors

William J. Wilhelm Jr. is a Professor of Management Studies at the Saïd Business School and a Professorial Fellow of St. Edmund Hall, University of Oxford. He earned a B.A. in finance and an M.A. in economics from Wichita State University. Professor Wilhelm then studied for a Ph.D. in business administration at Louisiana State University.

Joseph D. Downing is a partner in General Finance, LLC, a Boston, Massachusetts–based investment banking firm. Mr. Downing holds an A.B. degree, cum laude, in government from Harvard College. He earned his M.B.A., with a concentration in finance, from New York University and holds an M.S. degree in finance from Boston College.